Relating Rape and Murder

Relating Rape and Murder

Narratives of Sex, Death and Gender

Jane Monckton Smith

Senior Lecturer, Department of Natural and Social Sciences,
University of Gloucestershire, UK

First published 2010 by
PALGRAVE MACMILLAN

Palgrave Macmillan in the UK is an imprint of Macmillan Publishers Limited,
registered in England, company number 785998, of Houndmills, Basingstoke,
Hampshire RG21 6XS.

Palgrave Macmillan in the US is a division of St Martin's Press LLC,
175 Fifth Avenue, New York, NY 10010.

Palgrave Macmillan is the global academic imprint of the above companies
and has companies and representatives throughout the world.

Palgrave® and Macmillan® are registered trademarks in the United States,
the United Kingdom, Europe and other countries.

ISBN 978–0–230–24202–9   hardback

This book is printed on paper suitable for recycling and made from fully
managed and sustained forest sources. Logging, pulping and manufacturing
processes are expected to conform to the environmental regulations of the
country of origin.

A catalogue record for this book is available from the British Library.

A catalog record for this book is available from the Library of Congress.

Printed and bound in Great Britain by
CPI Antony Rowe, Chippenham and Eastbourne

This book is dedicated to the memory of Camilla Petersen

Contents

Foreword

I have known the author for some time. Our paths have crossed at criminology conferences which she first attended as a mature student. She showed the familiar diffidence and lack of confidence of someone who had come later to higher education. But there was also perhaps an underlying recognition – which had to be carefully moulded and encouraged – that her past working experience could produce something special in the criminological arena. This book is an important outcome in that process and will, hopefully, be the first of a series where Jane continues to produce refreshing insights on familiar issues and problems.

Academic books that have a *prima facie* interest for a reader will, after being read, produce the reaction that either it is just 'more of the same' or, more unusually, be identified as doing something more. For me, this book does something more than expected. I have written on homicide (Soothill *et al.*, 1999) and on rape (Soothill, 1991) but also with a particular focus on media representations of sex crime (Soothill and Walby, 1991) and homicide (Peelo *et al.*, 2004; Peelo and Soothill, in press). In the present volume Jane Monckton-Smith has powerfully demonstrated how the analytically distinct crimes of homicide and rape are dangerously linked. In short, she argues that 'there is a relationship constructed in sexual murder discourse between the offences of rape and murder which allows them to share meaning' (p. 000). The implications of sexualizing violent acts in the way that are discussed in this text are enormous. It has implications for the way that human fears are constructed but also, at a more practical level, of how police investigations are conducted.

It is not my task to rehearse all the arguments but I do want to emphasize the importance of the project. First, however, the modesty of the author precludes her stressing the scale of the work undertaken. The evidence is drawn from narratives produced in police investigations, press reporting and entertainment media. Each type of source could have produced a volume of its own. The topics are similarly rich and diverse. A chapter on the 'Jack the Ripper Narrative' is matched by 'Police Narratives' on very contemporary crimes. In fact, there are a series of chapters which, as the author notes, can be read separately – they have their own integrity. Readers are likely to return to the book and read again a chapter for a particular task in hand. However, in the first instance, readers would be wise to accept the challenge of reading the text in its entirety, for it is the impact of the cumulative evidence that makes the message so convincing.

I think most readers will eventually identify with at least one of two versions of the message. Certainly, after reading the book it would seem unlikely that the message will fail to convince at some level. The strong version is that the routine linking of homicide and rape has become so insidious and pervasive – with the police and the media colluding in the misrepresentations – that the dangers are already manifest and that change will be impossible to achieve. However, a blander interpretation is that the inappropriate linking of homicide and rape is simply a tendency that may on occasion happen. With this interpretation the dangers of the tendency are not fully recognized and the difficulties of challenging such misrepresentations would not be thought to be great.

My own position moves towards the strong version but with some modifications. I think current police practice and contemporary media frenzies about crime have, indeed, both fed into the development of the linking of homicide and rape exactly in the ways that the present author describes. Sadly, however, the dangers of this routine conflation have not yet been fully understood and articulated although this book begins to do so. Indeed, the main merit of this book is that it identifies the potential importance of the message. The question of whether much can be done about it reminds – at a time when the UN's climate summit in Copenhagen is of topical interest – that there are some issues which have to be confronted. In fact, this book lays down the gauntlet in stressing that some of the ways we talk about homicide and rape, in effect, make matters worse. This is the important challenge which needs to be confronted.

Keith Soothill
Emeritus Professor of Social Research

Acknowledgements

This book is passionate and leans towards the polemic but it would be difficult to write about such emotionally charged issues without partiality. My passion has sometimes consumed my energies and it would be true to say that I have had to prioritise and compromise, and not always to the benefit of my family; that is my husband Keith, and my three children Rhiannon, Ffion and Kieran. I would therefore like to take this opportunity to thank them for their unquestioning support; it is a treasured gift that I hope to always reciprocate. Keith, I owe you special thanks, both for your willingness to endlessly engage with my reflections, and your extraordinary ability to critically consider thorny gender issues with aplomb.

Special thanks to my mother Maeve for the long, long chats on tricky subjects which were always an oasis of wisdom and fun; also my father David who shared experience, knowledge and crime scene equipment! Not always the typical conversations for family gatherings but all the more memorable and cherished for that.

Dr Paul Mason, I thank for his excellent guidance and support over many years, and especially his collaboration in Chapter 5. Professor Keith Soothill, who is the most generous of academics, has played a bigger role in my journey into the academy than he realises and is someone to whom I am truly grateful. Dr Carol Davis is another who is probably unaware that her patient listening and advice had a profound impact on my own confidence. To all these people I give heartfelt thanks.

Acknowledgement too is given to certain police officers from the Serious Crime Team who generously gave of their time; especially one officer who coordinated my access. It became clear whilst speaking with them that they are deeply affected by the job they do. They were all passionate and caring and consummately professional. It is easy to confuse critical analysis with simple criticism and the police services suffer much of both. I would therefore like to make it clear that it was abundantly evident to me that all these officers were clearly dedicated to achieving justice, appreciably compassionate and greatly skilled. Many, many thanks for your time and insights.

Finally, thanks to *The Times*, the *Sun*, the *Guardian* and the *BBC* for such uncomplicated permissions.

I could not end these acknowledgements without including the women in this book whose stories have been with me on a daily basis: Hannah Foster, Margaret Muller, Vicky Fletcher, Camilla Petersen, Louise Beech, Marsha MacDonnell, Mary Anne Nicholls, Annie Chapman, Elizabeth Stride, Catherine Eddowes, Mary Jane Kelly, Jane Longhurst, Milly Dowler, Sally Anne Bowman, Rachel Nickell and Samantha and Jazmine Bissett. These women and girls were real, vibrant human beings who impacted the lives of their loved ones and the people around them.

1
Relating Rape and Murder

Introduction

The catalyst for writing this book was partly a personal and mundane experience of my own. Alone in my home one night I felt distinctly vulnerable and afraid and as a woman alone it probably wouldn't surprise anyone to hear that this anxiety was related to fear of rape or sexual assault. It was only after intellectualizing this fear and thinking of the repercussions for my children that I recognized I was less afraid of a sexual assault than I was of not surviving it. However, the seemingly commonsense association of the crime of rape with the crime of murder that I made did not occur as an isolated and irrational thought for the terms are routinely collocated in popular discourse and roll off the tongue together in a disturbingly familiar way. Such is the power of this relationship that in some contexts rape and murder are even conflated and able to act as analogies for each other. This conflation is exemplified in cases defined as serial/sexual murder like, for example, the crimes of Jack the Ripper and Peter Sutcliffe, the Yorkshire Ripper; both of whom are characterized as sexual offenders and sometimes rapists even though this was not part of their *modus operandi*. In this context rape is far more than its legal definition; it is acting as a metaphor, powerfully suggesting an essential sexual dimension to this fatal violence and infusing it with heterosexual symbolism. Joanna Bourke says that rape is a form of ritualized social performance which has been bestowed with meaning (2007:6) and it is no coincidence that the defining characteristics of a rape are closely associated with the performance of heterosexuality and embody religious/patriarchal ideas of the destruction of the feminine. It is this dimension to the meaning made of rape which allows it to act as a metaphor for the worst of human destruction and suffering. Bourke illustrates this point by citing the routine use of such common phrases as 'the Rape of Nanking' or 'the Rape of the Planet' (2007:6) reminding us that rape signifies a particularly destructive and wanton violence. In this respect it is a multi-faceted concept heavy with the burden of simultaneously representing extreme truths of heterosexuality, the deepest of human suffering, death on a grand scale, mutilation, stabbing, torture and deviant homicidal practices. It must also, lest we forget, define and frame our response to forced or coerced sexual penetration in a criminal justice setting.

Even though rape can and does cause terrible suffering to victims, it should not be considered worse or even equal to, a physical and brutal loss of life. However, women often do perceive the seriousness of rape as exceeding that of murder (Ferraro 1995); the symbolic power distorting the perception of what it actually is. We should not need to represent rape by extremes; it is an essentially and uniquely intimate violence which Bourke suggests is a 'confrontation with the aggressor's entire body – teeth, nails, belly. Assailants insist on kissing...massaging, masturbating...and so on' (2007:418). Rape requires no cosy connection with death and mutilation to be considered one of the most serious violent offences.

The problem of rape

It is well established now that violence against women is a pressing social problem. In the UK there is a focused political response which recognizes that cultural and societal attitudes play a significant role in sanitizing and legitimizing such violence. The move from a largely tertiary 'after the event' strategy to reduce its prevalence, is being combined with a more primary and preventative framework. It is suggested that educating children in schools is a particularly effective method to combat or change prevailing beliefs about violence against women; though Bruce George MP argues that this strategy was recommended to government some thirty years ago but was not implemented (*Hansard* 2010:163). Given that in 2009/10 it is reported in the press that there are fears of an increase in incidents of domestic abuse as a result of the prevailing economic difficulties (Gentleman 2009), focus on the problems is crucial.

Rape is part of the wider problem of male violence against women but the meanings attached to it exemplify and amplify the power of prevailing cultural beliefs and attitudes towards women. The case of taxi driver John Worboys, convicted of nineteen counts of rape in 2009, brought into focus, yet again, the reach of societal and institutional prejudice against female victims of sexual violence. An IPCC (Independent Police Complaints Commission) enquiry resulted in five Metropolitan Police officers facing sanctions for behaviour which fell well short of expected standards. It was clear that some of the victims were not believed and some were allegedly openly scorned (Laville 2010). This type of allegation is reminiscent of the behaviour of police investigators in the now infamous Thames Valley fly on the wall documentary *Police* (broadcast 18.01.82 BFI 2005) which first brought these types of issues to wide public attention and instigated the formation of all female rape investigation teams and more sympathetic services for victims. MP Fiona MacTaggart said of the findings:

> I was depressed by the Independent Police Complaints Commission report into Warboys, because it showed that still there persists, even among specialist police officers, insufficient sensitivity to the experience of the victim of rape and an insufficient determination to treat rape as a major violent crime that must be investigated (*Hansard* 2010:180)

The Cross Government Action Plan on Sexual Violence and Abuse explicitly states that sexual violence 'is a consequence and cause of gender inequality' and that 'women are more worried about rape than any other crime' (CGAP 2007:5). Such is the concern about the prevalence of, and problems with rape, that Baroness Stern reported in 2010 on a major inquiry into the treatment of rape victims, public confidence in the criminal justice response to rape and attrition rates. Attrition in cases of rape is still extremely high and has been the subject of sustained research interest (Bourke 2007, Kelly *et al.* 2005, Lees 2002, Myhill and Allen 2002, Gregory and Lees 1999, Howe 1998, Estrich 1987). The Fawcett Society claims that a rape is reported to the police every 34 minutes in the UK, but of those rapes reported only 6.5 per cent will attract a conviction (*Hansard* 2010). This figure reflects convictions as a percentage of rapes reported, not those charged. Vera Baird reports that of those rapes where the alleged offender is charged by the CPS, 59 per cent will receive a conviction (*Hansard* 2010, Stern 2010) suggesting that most problems are at the very start of a victim's involvement with the criminal justice system. This is not a problem peculiar to the UK, it is a worldwide issue. Across Europe Kelly and Regan found similar low conviction rates, for example; of the 468 rapes reported in Finland in 1997 only 46 resulted in a conviction; of the 1,962 reported in Sweden only 115 achieved a conviction; of the 424 reported in Norway only 35 achieved a conviction. In the USA similar problems are documented suggesting that on average a sexual assault is reported every two minutes (DoJ 2007) with a conviction rate of just 12 per cent (Kelly *et al.* 2005). In Australia it is reported that 100,000 women were sexually assaulted within a twelve-month period (ABS 1996) but conviction and attrition issues are similar to the UK and USA. South Africa has one of the highest rates of sexual violence against women in the world but it is estimated that only 1 in 36 is reported (SAPS 2005) and only around 16 per cent of those reported attracted a conviction (Soul City 1999). The Stern Review which reported in March 2010 specifically raises the idea that focusing on attrition and conviction rates which indicate a failing Criminal Justice System is counter-productive and may lead to a defeatist attitude in women stopping them from reporting assaults. Stern suggests that the conviction rate has taken over the debate and the focus should be switched to victim care and services. The Haven's Wake up to Rape Survey (2010) suggests also that a lack of trust in the criminal justice and police response is stopping women from reporting assaults. The routine focus on conviction rates may also displace discussion of sexual violence which occurs in other contexts.

In countries where wars are being fought rape is a systematic weapon against the women of the country, for example, the mass rapes that occurred in Yugoslavia, and the 'comfort women' of World War II (May 2005:96). According to Ruth Seifert many of the 200,000 women raped in the Bangladesh Liberation War in 1971 remain in slum camps set up for them when they were subsequently rejected by their husbands and families (1999:147). Seifert argues that there is a perverse and cruel logic to the mass rape of women in war, but in peacetime in evolved and sophisticated cultural economies why is rape so prevalent and difficult to prosecute? Political and academic discussions of rape have acknowledged a conceptual shift in perceptions of the rapist; that is that the typical rapist is a serial offender (*Hansard* 2010:188) and not a man confused by victim 'signals' who finds himself innocently accused of a heinous crime. This conceptual shift, it is argued, needs to be shared by the wider public, juries and criminal justice personnel if conviction rates are to be increased and should also be shared by victims; prompting them to confidently pursue complaints of rape out of social conscience and the need to protect potential future victims. This position suggests that Kelly *et al.*'s (2005) findings, that there is a skewed perception of what constitutes rape within the criminal justice system and wider society, still holds true.

It is worth discussing Kelly's findings briefly for they are crucial in comprehending why rape is difficult to prosecute, and also how the rape and murder of women can share meaning. A key problem they highlight is that there is a skewed public and criminal justice perception of what constitutes a 'real rape'. There is still a belief that a 'real rape' occurs in a public place, committed by a stranger to the victim and involves aggravating violence and use of a weapon; a perception that is described as more akin to an aggravated rape assault (Kelly *et al.* 2005, Young 1998). This perception however, is setting the standard for what 'rape' is and reflects what Kelly *et al.* (2005) refer to as the 'rape template'. This template which forms part of the skewed perception affects how rape is understood by everyone, even the victims themselves. The British Crime Survey found, for example, that 'less than half of women who experienced an assault that met the legal definition of rape defined it as such themselves' (Kelly *et al.* 2005:33) with most women perceiving that a rape should include physical injury, and in the case of rape by an intimate that the level of violence should be comparable to the brutality commonly associated with the 'real rape' template (Kelly *et al.* 2005:34). It is interesting to note then that the constituent characteristics of the template which describe what is perceived to be a 'real' rape are identical to those which popularly describe a sexual murder and it is this similarity that reveals the fundamental problems with rape and homicide against women experienced in the UK and in North America, and which resonate with practically every hetero/patriarchal society across the world. Rape is still popularly perceived as a sexually motivated offence related to biological sexual need in males. Similarly, many homicides of women are perceived as sexually motivated or precipitated by natural biological sexual jealousies in men, and this evolutionary biological discourse can act as mitigation for men and infer culpability in women.

The problem of murder

Rates of homicide perpetrated by men against women are also high, but largely will be in cases where victim and offender are known to each other (Coleman 2009, Coleman and Osborne 2010). Until recently the fairly stable figure of two women per week killed by their intimate partners and former partners held (Richards 2006). However, Solicitor General Vera Baird reports that this figure has dropped to one woman per week (*Hansard* 2010) and this is as a result of sustained political, academic and third sector research and action. It should be noted that although the number of homicide victims recorded in 2008/09 have fallen overall, a substantial drop in female intimate partner homicide is not reflected in the latest Home Office statistics; as of 2008/09 the proportion of females killed by their intimate partner shows a rise from 50 per cent to 69 per cent (Coleman and Osborne 2010) and the headline figure quoted in the Commons of one woman per week, is rounded down from the actual figure of about 1.9 women killed per week, so may be a little misleading. Again Intimate Partner Homicide, like rape is a not a problem peculiar to the UK; in the USA three women are killed by their intimate partners every day (BJS 2005) and in South Africa where the female murder rate is the world's highest, a woman is killed every six hours by an intimate partner but less than 40 per cent will achieve a murder conviction (Matthews *et al.* 2004).

The way we respond to and understand the killing of women by men is the subject of much criticism (Burton 2008, Mason and Monckton-Smith 2008, Seuffert 2002, Websdale 1999, Lees 1997, Tatar 1995, Caputi 1987) with the implication being that certain types of homicide of women, particularly where the latter and the male offender have shared a sexual relationship, are perceived as more tolerable or excusable, attracting lesser charges and discounted sentences (Dawson 2003). It is also argued that homicides of women by intimate partners will often result in manslaughter rather than murder convictions with men claiming sexual infidelity by the woman as a legitimate provocation (Burton 2008, Websdale 1999, Lees 1997) and this is the subject of political concern; though a move by Equalities Minister Harriet Harman to stop sexual infidelity being used as a partial defence in murder charges was defeated in the House of Lords in October 2009. Harman's attempt to stop men using this excuse was called 'obnoxious' by a retired Judge and Law Lord (Slack 2009).

Burton found that despite convictions for murder rather than manslaughter in some cases being more common, the length of sentences revealed judicial bias. She notes that sentencing for men convicted of killing allegedly unfaithful women were comparable to sentences for women convicted of killing violent and abusive men. Burton argues that based on her observations it is plausible to argue that 'the courts regard a history of domestic violence as, roughly, as provocative as seeing your girlfriend flirt with someone' (2008:86) which reveals serious inequalities for women at a cultural/societal as well as institutional level.

There is a powerful perception despite the relative prevalence of intimate partner homicide that women are in most danger from strangers. However, in 2007/08 only 28 women were murdered by strangers in the

UK, out of the 208 deaths of women recorded as homicide (Coleman 2009) and only 23 in 2008/09 (Coleman and Osborne 2010) and this is a trend reflected across the world. Women are in far more danger from people they know and in the domestic sphere, but there are powerful discourses in circulation which encourage women to protect themselves from 'stranger danger' and seek safety in the specious security of the home. This notwithstanding, it is also true that stranger sexual/serial killers as popularly defined, do target women and other feminized or violable groups. Women are represented as the natural 'prey' of predatory killers and often, murders of women will be assessed using a conservative political morality which implicates the victim in her own death; in much the same way that a rape victim's behaviour is routinely scrutinized for contributory negligence. This is not unrelated to the practice of gendering and sexualizing all violence against women (Mason and Monckton-Smith 2008, Howe 1998, Lees 1997, Soothill and Walby 1991) which is prevalent in media, police and cultural narratives and is the focus for this book.

Both the rape and the murder of women by men then are argued to attract an inadequate response in both criminal justice and cultural terms. It is crucially important therefore that the way we make meaning of violence towards women and the forums which may perpetuate, reinforce or disseminate those powerful discourses are the subject of scrutiny especially given the policy decision to educate children in schools that current cultural beliefs and practices are not acceptable (*Hansard* 2010). The messages from media and criminal justice which undermine that education focus on the sexual symbolism attached to rape and homicide against women. It appears these images and messages are more powerful than the legally defining characteristics of certain violent acts. This homogenizes violence against women, reducing diverse forms to one sexual rather than gendered problem, and creating relationships between violent acts which are illegitimate and problematic.

One key forum where a relationship between the violence of rape and murder is constructed, reinforced and disseminated is that of crime narratives and in this context I mean the stories told of individual crime events by the media and within the criminal justice system. A crime narrative will present a coherent and plausible version of what happened and why, and it is here we reveal what motivations we as a culture find plausible for explaining violence against women. I specifically argue that rape and murder share meaning in these narratives and have even become conflated in some contexts. It is stories of serial/sexual murder that exemplify the relationship between rape and murder, and in particular, stories like those told of Jack the Ripper and his crimes. It is important to explore exactly what it is about this type of killing that allows the perpetrators to be characterized as sexual offenders or rapists, for this reconstructs the victim and the offender and I will argue that this has serious repercussions.

Sex crime? Sex killer?

Jack the Ripper is perhaps the most notorious example of what is defined as a serial/sex killer and he has been variously described as the 'archetypal rapist' (Frayling 1986) and a killer who committed what seemed like 'the ultimate rape' (Marriner 1992); yet there is no evidence to suggest that any attempts to rape the victims were made, neither did the killer ejaculate over the bodies; the mutilation and disembowelment of his victims is merely analogized as rape. This violence was mutilation and strangulation, not any legally defined form of sexual assault but this is an aspect to these crimes that is given little, if any attention. Of course the sexual dimension to this kind of offending should not be simplistically equated with a conventional sexual assault or rape; neither should it be assumed that the killer's physical sexual functioning would be stable and certain. Expert definitions of what constitutes the sexual dimension to this kind of offending present a far more complex interpretation of the offender's psychology. However, there is a lack of clarity in expert definitions of what constitutes sexual motivation in a sexual homicide which can lead to a very broad conception of what can be considered sexual and very little agreement on where the parameters should lie (Schlesinger 2003). Howe captures this problem succinctly in stating 'try defining sex crime and the concept slips away from you' (1998:1). She claims that many so-called sex crimes could be more meaningfully understood as 'sexed' crimes given that the gender of the victim and offender is significant in creating meaning. Crimes of violence where the offender is male and the victim female are often represented in the press as being sexually motivated based on these characteristics alone revealing the importance of hetero/sexuality in interpreting gendered violence as sexual. Howe (1998) suggests that a sexual assault followed by a murder is often, because of this, automatically labelled a 'sex crime' and questions the chain of reasoning which makes this a convention in press reporting. It will also be shown that there need be no evidence of sexual assault prior to a gendered stranger murder for the crime to be labelled as sexual and often a female victim and male offender is sufficient.

In some expert definitions of sex killing, explicit sexual contact is required, yet in others sexual motivation can be embodied in an internal feeling of arousal with no sexual act involved (Schlesinger 2003). In the dominant FBI definitions of what constitutes 'sexual homicide' it is stated that the motivation is based on fantasy, though Ressler *et al.* (1992:33) are clear that the offender is 'devoted to violent, sexualized thoughts and fantasies' which indicates the significance of violence and its expressive rather than instrumental nature in these crimes. However, they also suggest that the sexual nature of a homicide is not always obvious, as sexual evidence may be absent from the crime scene (1992:1). Milligen argues that 'of the multiplicity of definitions of serial murder the FBI's (is) the most vague and simplistic' (2006:125) relying on exaggerated occurrences of sex killing and tailoring the definition to fit its systems and agenda. This broad interpretation of what is sexual and lack of agreement on characteristics, means that almost any gendered violence could conceivably be construed or interpreted as sexual. In many forums this dimension to the offending is often imagined through the concept of rape which can create what Foucault describes as 'the psychologically intelligible link between the offence and the offender' (1994:188). This linkage distils the crimes to a deviant form of heterosexual practice but often fails to interrogate the social conditions which may produce such violence, focusing instead on individual offender psychopathology. Sexual explanations for rape, especially when linked to homicide, have immense rhetorical impact and are perceived as particularly plausible. So that even with its ambiguous heterosexual symbolism, its broad and at times inappropriate application and its lack of analytical precision, the vague concept of sex appears to bring clarity to the problem of knowing the motivations of those who come to be defined as sex killers. The sex defines the crimes, the victims and also the criminal. If we see rape, or acts that we can interpret as symbolic of rape, where we should see violence, mutilation or murder, this re/constructs the offending, the offender and the victim; the offence becomes a sex crime, the offender becomes a sex offender and the victim is no longer 'human' but female. Often, when stories of rape and/or murder are told in the media and in prosecution or defence case files in the form of the crime narrative, sexual motivations are dominant.

Crime narratives

Clarity, plausibility and intelligibility are of crucial importance when constructing the story of a crime and crime narratives organize the events, characteristics and characters to form a believable story with a logical chronology so that we may begin to understand what happened and why. This is what makes the crime narrative so important, it is far more than merely a story, the way in which a crime story is constructed will reveal what we as a culture or society find to be plausible motivations and acceptable or excusable behaviours. If we find the concept of sex, imagined through the concept of rape, a plausible and routine explanation for murder or mutilation of women by men then we should at the very least interrogate why this is so, and what the repercussions might be.

The 'literature of criminality' (Foucault 1994:192) is vast and largely split into two key categories, the popular and the academic (Klein 2006, Rafter 2007). There is a predomination in the popular criminality literature of stories of sensational and salacious crimes. We should not distance academic criminology from these forums or subject areas merely in order to avoid the more voyeuristic or obtuse aspects of popular criminological material or because, as Rafter notes, it 'does not pretend to empirical accuracy or theoretical validity' (2007:415). This may result in too little resistance to the knowledge produced in such widely disseminated discourses and narratives. With this in mind I deliberately focus on those forums which widely disseminate stories of what are defined as sexual murders, to explore how the concept of rape is embedded in the narratives. One of the key practices which widely circulate authoritative versions of crime stories to a broad audience is institutional narrative construction; the formal story telling processes of powerful institutions that act to clarify and explain the crimes and the motivations of the offender. It is the institutional response that is the focus for the analysis drawing from Foucauldian ideas of discourse and discursive formations as a forum for constructing meaning. From this perspective the relationship between rape and murder is legitimated in and through discourse, specifically the dominant discourse of sexual murder. To explore the structure and content of these narratives, data was drawn from three of the most powerful institutional sites where crime narratives are routinely and formally produced and which also form part of a discursive formation and they are: law enforcement, news media and entertainment media. In law enforcement and news media this is a formal process; for journalists the process is to report on the crime and package it as a story for news consumers (Carter 1998); for law enforcement the narrative will direct investigative strategies and form the basis for the prosecution case file (Innes 2002). In entertainment media, narratives may be less constrained by attention to the so-called facts of the case, but will nonetheless attempt to produce a plausible story of a crime for the consumer. Journalists, film directors and police officers are not expert in knowing the complexities of sex killer psychology, but the power of these institutions in constructing meaning should not be underestimated, especially when they may appear to concur. Neither should the importance of their almost sole access to forums which disseminate knowledge about the offence and the offender to the public be overlooked (De Lint 2003).

Discourse

In its very simplest terms discourse, in a Foucauldian sense, is a framework for a way of talking, a way of acting and a way of knowing about something. Though different discourses are produced over time and place in response to prevailing cultural, political, institutional or other societal influences, they are not characterized by Foucault as having any sort of linear progression and are not a site for a cumulative building of objective knowledge. Foucault (1972) said that nothing has any meaning outside of discourse; that although events occur and objects have a material existence, it is discourse which gives those events and objects meaning. Discourse then should be understood as a 'system which structures the way we perceive reality' (Mills 2003:55) and will tell us what is normal and natural, and what is acceptable and appropriate (Carabine 2001). However, in the process of giving meaning to something it becomes reconstructed in response to what we believe we know about it, and what we believe we know changes over different periods and in different contexts. Foucault suggests then that we should consider discourse as a violence we do to things or a practice we impose upon them (1972:229). The concepts of rape and murder from this perspective only exist meaningfully in the discourses about them and may have numerous and diverse meanings within different discourses. However, some are more powerful than others and have dominance, which gives more authority to the 'knowledge' and 'truths' they produce indicating that no particular discourse has any inherent authority or universal claims to truth. Crucially, Foucault (1972) also described certain procedures which work to constrain what can be considered truth and may inhibit resistance to the knowledge produced in dominant discourses; one of these procedures which amply illustrate his point is in the distinction made between those who are authorized to speak and those who are not. Consequently, discourses are structured by institutions which can authorize the truthfulness of statements;

statements authorized as true may then have the status of knowledge. Conversely those who utter statements not authorized as true, or statements which resist the knowledge produced in dominant discourses can appear to be incomprehensible to others (Mills 2003) devaluing their statements and making it difficult for them to be taken seriously. It is not easy, for example, to suggest that the sex in a sex killing should not be given primacy in knowing what happened and why; it is a resistance to dominant perceptions and appears almost anti-intuitive.

Discourse then is not abstract it is a practice and it produces that of which it speaks. In this respect discourse produces what we come to know as the sex killer or the serial killer, or even the rape victim. They become discursive objects composed from knowledge constructed in, and legitimated through, discourses of sexual murder and/or rape and as such we know something about them and can also become them. They are a species to be recognized and described within a knowledge system authorized in medical, criminological, psychological and law enforcement discourse. It is important then that those who are authorized to speak, those institutional sites that produce the knowledge we have about rape and murder are examined to establish how and where the 'knowledge' and 'truths' they produce may give meaning to the violence and conflate the offences of rape and murder. Hickey (2001) and Jenkins (1994) identify three institutional sites which produce what is referred to as disinformation in relation to sexual murder and it is broadly these three sites that are the focus in this book; law enforcement, news media and entertainment media.

Organization of the book

There are some points about the arguments and the manner in which they are made which require clarification: I situate the research within a postmodern and feminist framework with the explicit purpose of effectively resisting a dominant sexual discursive formation, an exercise which at times requires some polemicism. My arguments are intentionally provocative and the evidence I present is calculated to stimulate contemplation of the issues. Professor Soothill, in the foreword, suggests that I throw down the gauntlet which is a fitting appraisal of my intentions.

It is specifically the problems associated with the linking of rape of women with murder of women that are interrogated in this book. Of necessity, given the vast amount of data generated in exploring discursive formations, some of the complex issues and arguments are summarized. There are also aspects to fatal and sexual violence which I do not address; violence by men or women against children, violence against and between homosexual men and women, and what is called male rape; these types of violence are also the subject of an inadequate response in the criminal justice system, as well as skewed perceptions of the offences and offenders (Abdullah-Khan 2008, Graham 2006, Renzetti 1999, Kitzinger 2004). They require specific attention to do justice to the issues raised; this book is focused solely on the specific problems associated with sexual and fatal violence against women by adult males. I think however, that it is important to note that male sexual victimization in hetero/patriarchal culture suffers from similar problems to that of the sexual victimization of women in that the problems are underpinned by the same belief systems. Male sexual victimization appears almost paradoxical as it undermines dominant constructions of masculinity and notions of what it is to be a man. Thus this type of violence is largely unacknowledged and Graham argues that 'men do not appear to worry about personal corporeal safety to the extent that women do, and particularly do not see themselves as vulnerable to sexual assault.' (2006:188). Men are in fact statistically more likely to be victims of a violent assault by a stranger than women (Brookman 2005) but, and this is a central theme in this book, they are not continually reminded of their vulnerability or routinely identified as violable as part of their gendered social identity in the way that women are (Graham 2006, Stanko 1996). I have also not explicitly addressed matters of class, race or ethnicity which may exacerbate many of the generic issues I will discuss. Neither have I explicitly addressed the increased levels of sexual and other violence experienced by migrant women with uncertain or irregular status. Often they have been trafficked from countries with strong hetero/patriarchal cultures into countries where they have no status or support systems but it is the case that all the issues I will be raising are relevant to all women irrespective of how their identities are delineated.

In summary this book is about relating rape and murder in both senses of the term; that is the way rape and murder are linked and related and also how stories of rape and murder are related or told in the context of crime narratives and two key arguments are presented:

First, that there is a relationship constructed in sexual murder discourse between the offences of rape and murder which allows them to share meaning and often sees the *perception* of them collocated in crime narratives. In the context of sexual murder discourse rape has a sexual meaning as do violent acts especially those that are potentially fatal like, for example, stabbing or mutilation. It is argued that it is this shared meaning which allows the concepts of rape and murder to act as analogies for each other as if they were qualitatively related.

Secondly, it is argued that there are insidious and pervasive effects to perceptually linking rape with murder in this way; one of the most powerful being that it reverses the proposition that we should see rape as a form of violence; instead we have a powerful framework for interpreting and representing violence against women as a form of rape. This can have the effect of sexualizing violent acts and feminizing female victimization which has its own repercussions.

What is heterosexual in the context of these arguments is far more than merely an attraction to the opposite sex; it is a set of practices, customs, language and relationships authorized as normal and natural by many powerful institutional sites. For this reason when I refer to this set of practices it is as *hetero/sex* or *hetero/sexuality*. I make no argument that sexual attraction itself between males and females is a constructed practice, merely the manner in which the attraction is translated into a social practice. I would also like to make clear my reason for using the term victim rather than survivor when referring to those who have experienced rape. I am aware that the term survivor is more often preferred and that it is a term which is more powerful than victim. However, given the arguments that I make in this book and my problematizing of the relationship which is constructed between rape and murder, use of the term survivor may appear in this particular context, inconsistent with my arguments.

The book is organized into seven chapters which explore narratives of rape and murder produced across different institutional sites and the way they operate within a highly sexual discourse. Chapter 1, this chapter, introduces the idea that the concepts of rape and murder are routinely collocated in crime narratives and even conflated within the dominant discourse of sexual murder; Foucauldian ideas of discourse are discussed to place the wider analysis in its theoretical context. Chapters 2 and 3 present a selected and brief genealogy of rape discourse with a focus also on rape trauma, identifying two key and competing discursive perspectives. First, what I refer to as the biological/historical and secondly, the feminist perspectives. Drawing from many areas including art, history, religion, literature and biology, the ways in which biological/historical discourses have given meaning to, and rationalized, the idea of rape and rape trauma over different historical periods is discussed. The feminist perspective, which is not to be understood as a homogenized and unified single perspective, is presented as the only real resistance to the historical/cultural approach and is discussed in relation to this resistance as a powerful and alternative set of discourses. These two chapters represent a selected overview only to illustrate the historical legacy of certain powerful discourses and the resistance to them by feminism. They are not designed to provide a comprehensive summary of discourse in this area. The focus for these chapters is predominantly rape and sexual violence rather than murder as it is argued that it is the meaning made of sexual violence that is creating the meaning made of fatal violence against women.

In Chapter 4 the crimes of Jack the Ripper are discussed in the context that they are a widely disseminated, widely known and very influential example of a conflating of the concepts of rape, mutilation and murder. Via an examination of the narratives produced in Jack the Ripper film this chapter explores how the concept of rape and the alleged sexual dimensions to the offending are embedded in those narratives. In Chapter 5 the narratives produced by news media to rationalize and explain the murder and/or rape of women are the focus. Drawing from case studies, including the murder of Hannah Foster by Maninder Pal Singh Kohli in March 2003 and the murder of Camilla Petersen by Richard Kemp in July 2002 and selected others, the analysis again focuses on how speculated sexual elements to the offending are rationalized and placed in the story or narrative produced by journalists. News media is a powerful medium for circulating crime narratives and, as Howe notes, claims to tell the truth and holds 'a virtual monopoly on information about crime' (1998:2). These narratives are widely disseminated and form part of a discursive formation of sexual murder showing, it will be argued, remarkable consistency of approach with little or no resistance across publications to the discursive truths they re-produce.

Chapter 6 discusses police narrative construction in investigating and prosecuting cases of sexual murder. The narrative formally constructed by the police firstly, forms the basis for investigative strategies in the early stages of an investigation and secondly, the basis for the story of the crime presented in the prosecution case file. The data is drawn from interviews with five homicide investigators from a major crime team of a county service, ranging from Constable to Superintendent and of both genders. There is general discussion of violence against women and then focus on two modern cases of male on female homicide, those being the murders of Hannah Foster and Camilla Petersen which are also discussed in Chapter 5. Both these murders had definite sexual dimensions, and the way that the sexual component was rationalized and placed in the story of the crime by the officers themselves is a focus. There is an extra dimension offered in this chapter and that is the perspective of Lonni Petersen, the mother of Camilla Petersen. Her feelings about the way the story of Camilla's murder was formally told by the police are the focus and present a voice rarely heard in such discussions.

Finally, Chapter 7 draws from all the data and presents a discussion structured around the relationship between rape and murder and the primacy given to the concept of sex in rationalizing so-called sex killings and rape. It is argued in conclusion that the concept of 'sex' is too vague as an analytical tool and too broadly applied to give clarity to motivation of offenders, it is also too powerful in its symbolism to allow unambiguous assessment of offences, offenders or victims. So, instead of understanding rape as a form of violence, due to the primacy given to the concept of 'sex' in interpreting and rationalising offences and offender motivation, we have a powerful framework for interpreting and representing violence against women as a form of rape. This has the effect of feminizing female victimization and female victims, which may be implicated in exacerbating many of the problems identified in responding to violence against women. Some of these problems are explicitly addressed; in particular; the high rate of attrition in reported cases of rape (Kelly *et al.* 2005); the suggestion that intimate partner homicide is devalued in comparison to other categories of homicide (Lees 1997); the suggestion that women's reported levels of fear of crime are higher than men's and are related to fear of sexual assault (Scott 2003, CGAP 2007); and that fear of rape or sexual assault may be correlated with a fear for life. The book can be negotiated as a whole progressing through the chapters sequentially which will progressively support the main arguments; alternatively, each chapter can be read as an independent discussion.

2
Biological/Historical Sexual Violence Discourse

Introduction

It would be impossible to talk about sexual violence without first contemplating the issue of human sexuality. Sex and sexuality are important organizing concepts in modern life and are said to be powerful behavioural drivers. There is a strong theoretical strand that considers human sexuality a dynamic process vulnerable to environmental and experiential influence; an equally powerful set of discourses exist which represent human sexuality as fixed, stable and genetically encoded as heterosexual. We can make sense of who we are with reference to our sexuality and Mottier describes a world 'populated by people who define themselves as gay, lesbian, straight, bisexual, bi-curious, exhibitionists...' and so on (2008:1). Foucault identified what he perceived as an immense apparatus for producing truths around the concept of sex and claimed that the historically dominant framework which constructed heterosexuality as normal demonized certain sexual practices, like, for example, sodomy, by representing them as 'against nature' (1998:101). Conversely, heterosexual sexual practices and conventions were and are represented as natural, normal and biologically inscribed. Heterosexuality in this respect is more than merely an attraction to the opposite sex; as noted it is a set of practices, customs, language and relationships authorized as normal and natural by many powerful institutional sites. The way heterosexuality is practised today is argued to have grown out of religious discourses and patriarchal belief systems which quite strictly define gender roles. In this sense it is perfectly practised in the conjugal family unit, an institution sanctified by all three religious exemplars of patriarchy; Christianity, Judaism and Islam (Shlain 1999). Broughton and Rogers even characterize the family as reflecting God's own template for human social existence:

> The Victorians inherited a highly moralized understanding of the family as a microcosm of God's kingdom, and a concomitant reverence and deference toward the position of head of household as representing God's authority within the family. (2007:16)

This religious conception of the natural order of things is underwritten in both natural and social scientific discourses which are not always completely divorced from the influence of religious dogma. As a direct consequence of the legitimating of the family as both natural and sacred, the legally and religiously inscribed micro power relations operating within it enjoy much protection from scrutiny or interference. It was not until 1991, for example, that it was recognized in law that a husband could rape his wife, partly due to the historical legacy which constructed rape as a crime against the property of men, and partly because it is considered that tacit agreement to sexual intercourse is given in the marriage ceremony with a corresponding duty for women to be always sexually available to their husbands. The rationalization for this duty being that heterosexual men in particular have a biological *need* for sex which must be satisfied or the need will grow to dangerous levels which threaten his health and wellbeing and may compel him to secure sexual contact even through force (Hite 2005, Polaschek and Ward 2002). In many respects this approach characterizes rape as an extreme but fundamentally normal heterosexual practice which, whilst condemned, is also sometimes excused precisely because it has such strong links to masculine heterosexual practices which are perceived as normal and natural (Bourke 2007, Lees 1997, Box 1992, Brownmiller 1975).

It is from these beliefs that most of the so called rape myths which are established as inhibiting the successful prosecution of rape offences emanate (Kelly *et al.* 2005, Gregory and Lees 1999). Broadly these rape myths include but are not confined to: women lie about rape; only certain types of women get raped; women encourage rape in their manner of dress and so on; rape is sexual; you can recognize a rapist by the way he looks; women fantasize about rape; rape is impulsive and spontaneous; rape is about passion; a person who has been raped will be hysterical. In this chapter the concepts of rape and rape trauma (as they have been represented and characterized across several different sites) will be explored beginning with a look at some of the theories which are based on the biological model and which underpin the notion of hetero/sexuality as primal.

The biological model

Biological theories have pervaded issues of human sexuality tracing the proclivity of men to rape to ancient times (Potts and Short 1999). Claims that rape is an instinctive behaviour with an evolutionary inheritance remain popularly dominant and were largely unchallenged up until the 1980s (Mottier 2009). Bourke, like many of the challengers, argues that 'sexual aggression is not innate to masculine identity' (2007:436) and recent discoveries in the area of genetic inheritance would appear to suggest that 'human genes evolve much more quickly than anyone imagined' (Begley 2009:4) having a far more flexible and responsive role which undermines the idea that we have a direct behavioural link with our prehistoric ancestors. It wasn't until the late nineteenth and early twentieth century that sexuality became the focus for structured scientific study (Seidman 2007). It was at this time that the emerging discipline of sexology, a field which draws from natural scientific methodologies to study human sexual behaviour, produced what was considered the first extensive scientific study of human sexuality. The authors, Kinsey *et al*, stated that there was a need to obtain 'data about sex which would represent an accumulation of scientific fact completely divorced from questions of moral value and social custom' (1975:3). Among the principal protagonists were Havelock Ellis, Richard von Krafft-Ebing, Magnus Hirschfield, Alfred Kinsey and Iwan Bloch, all of whom positioned sexuality at the very core of experiential consciousness, defining what it means to be human with a concomitant assumption that sexual instinct is naturally heterosexual (Seidman 2007:3). Their adherence to biological scientific discourses, Seidman suggests, stamped their theories with the 'imprimatur of science' (2007:3) which helped to shape modern sexual culture. Certainly this is evidenced in the cultural preoccupation with claiming a heterosexual essence to all our daily behaviours, underwritten popularly, not in social scientific theories of culture, but in evolutionary biological orthodoxy. The biological model regards human sexuality as fundamentally a natural drive or instinct to reproduce and this approach claims an objective and observable nature to sexuality. This is determined by evolutionary genetic inheritance and hormonal influence, and in the context of sexual violence implies that male behavior is destined to be sexually aggressive (Hite 2007). There are numerous arguments which suggest that far from being an immutable part

, raping behaviour may be more an immutable part of the construct what is masculine heterosexual behaviour in modern ...ro/patriarchal societies.

The basis for one of the most recent and controversial arguments which gives rape an evolutionary inheritance is that of Thornhill and Palmer's (2000) application of Darwin's theory of natural selection to raping behaviour. They argue that raping behaviour evolved through a process of natural selection, an argument which is premised upon an assumption that males and females have differing, if not oppositional, mating strategies. Thornhill and Palmer occupy conventional ground in suggesting that men seek to copulate with as many females as possible whilst women are more selective. They depart with more modern convention when they suggest that raping behaviour is written onto male behaviour at the level of the gene. This raises the very problematic idea that raping behaviour is to some extent reproductively superior to non-raping behaviour. Thornhill and Palmer also speculate that a host of responses associated with rape, like, for example, male sexual jealousy and male paranoia about the truthfulness of rape accusations, have an evolutionary inheritance (2000:87). Their suggestion is that female psychological anguish or rape trauma exists to encourage women to resist rape (2000:86). This contains the implicit suggestion that women would not necessarily resist 'rape' without the adaptation which reminds them that there may be reproductive costs to the activity. This is an ambiguous assertion for Thornhill and Palmer appear to be describing a passive promiscuity and calling it rape to support their theories. By this I mean that they appear to be arguing that there is an evolutionary adaptation which encourages women to be aggressively more selective and resist all uninvited sexual interest. There is a degree of difference between uninvited but passively accepted, and unavoidable, sexual intercourse. There has been an historical resistance to acknowledge women as active agents in the mating game and especially as naturally promiscuous. It is now suggested that even Darwin failed to recognize female promiscuity and the idea of sperm competition in the fight to perpetuate the species, due in part to the prevailing and powerful Victorian beliefs about human female sexuality and his own daughter's censoring presence (Birkhead 2009). Thornhill and Palmer rely on their assumptions of female monogamy to situate their speculations about the aftermath of rape in a particular psychological frame and not as a more 'human' response to a violent physical assault. They discuss those rapes where there is little evidence of overt physical violence and injury to the victim as exemplifying those that may be correlated with intense psychological anguish. However, female victims in both models of rape, that is overtly and non-overtly violent, are considered to be more concerned about their sexual and reproductive integrity than their physical and reproductive health. They go as far as to say that the less violence used the more trauma the woman will experience, for the greater the violence the more support for claims of rape to a paranoid partner who might otherwise suspect her of infidelity. They suggest that this information would be of particular use to counselors who should be alerted to the theory that 'mated' females with no injuries will experience more intense psychological anguish (2000:93), whereas Rape Crisis (1999) argue that the amount of violence used is not a yardstick for measuring the level of trauma at all. Thornhill and Palmer fail to consider that any rape assault is multi dimensional and pay only lip service to the fact that it is a violent and intimate *physical* assault irrespective of whether grievous violence is necessary to complete intercourse. Their myopic focus on rape as an attack on reproductive or sexual integrity misses any more inherent *human* trauma that could result from any violent physical assault. The fear or trauma of rape in their discussion is not associated with the fears or traumas that men are likely to experience. The fear and trauma is feminized and distanced from men and as Bourke (2007) suggests, this type of approach may limit the ability of males to empathize with the victim. Begley takes issue with evolutionary psychology as a whole and especially Thornhill and Palmer's thesis which she claims is 'well within the bounds of evolutionary psychology' (2009:1). She argues that the thesis does not stand up to scientific scrutiny and cites the calculations of anthropologist Kim Hill, a former colleague of Thornhill, which suggest the benefits of raping behaviour are outweighed by the costs, and that a strategy of rape does not suggest evolutionary fitness for the male. Evolutionary biologist Pigliucci refutes the idea that behaviour is pre-conditioned in the way Thornhill and Palmer suggest and says:

> If the environment, including the social environment, is instead dynamic rather than static – which all evidence suggests – then the only kind of mind that makes humans evolutionarily fit is one that is flexible and responsive, able to figure out a way to make trade-offs, survive, thrive and reproduce in whatever social and physical environment it finds itself in. (cited in Begley 2009:2)

In a bizarre piece of anecdotal evidence presented to support their theory Thornhill and Palmer tell of a woman raped by an orangutan who, it is claimed, suffered no great stigmatization or trauma from the event. They argue that because she was not assaulted by a human male, there could be no negative repercussions for her reproductive integrity. It is further suggested that the male partner of the woman suffered no great trauma either, there being no paternity threat and no particular of the assault to create paranoia or sexual jealousy. They quote from Wrangham and Peterson's (1996) publication:

> Fortunately, the victim was neither seriously injured nor stigmatized. Her friends remained tolerant and supportive. Her husband reasoned that since the rapist was not human, the rape should not provoke shame or rage. (cited in Thornhill and Palmer 2000:87)

Galdikas, the researcher who was using the orangutan in question for research purposes quoted the husband of the victim as saying 'Why should my wife or I be concerned? It was not a man.' (1995:294). The female victim is represented as having no concerns whatever for her own physical welfare, but *is* apparently concerned that she remain 'uncontaminated' by a man other than her husband. Her husband similarly displays no concern about his wife's experience. It simply cannot be unproblematically assumed that women have no 'human' anxieties about threats to their bodies for this implies that they lack full human capacity. These assertions are contradictory to most feminist and social science positions which would at least perceive the woman as a full human subject. Thornhill and Palmer openly question the validity of social science research and in particular the arguments put forward by Feminism on the subject of rape and they state:

> Not only is the bulk of the social science literature of rape clearly indifferent to scientific standards; many of the studies exhibit overt hostility toward scientific approaches, and specifically to biological approaches. The message of these studies is clearly political rather than scientific. (2000:148)

They describe feminists as those 'whose research has been guided more by ideologically driven social arguments than by science' (2000:123) and they vilify them for failing to embrace Darwinian notions of natural selection. This kind of conflict exemplifies the tensions between different discourses, though it is also fair to say that Thornhill and Palmer's thesis is not universally accepted even within their own discipline; it is after all merely an extrapolation; to disagree with it is not to reject natural selection as a theory, but to question the interpretive habits of the authors. Elaine Morgan's (1972) slightly irreverent female centred examination of natural selection is very critical of mainstream androcentric interpretations and aptly illustrates where some of the frictions lie. Morgan gives an alternative account of human evolution taking account of the fact that women are human too, an element which she claims is often ignored. She points out that in all their postulations on the reasons for humans being the way they are, women are ignored by evolutionary theorists except as the 'sexual interest' for the male. She argues that according to popular anthropologists like Desmond Morris, every evolvement in the female has been to sexually excite the male and that the anthropological concentration on 'man' has led them to ignore the female except when it comes to sex:

> Of course, she (woman) was no more the first ancestor than he was – but she was no *less* the first ancestor, either. She was there all along, contributing half the genes to each succeeding generation. Most of the books forget about her for most of the time. They drag her onstage rather suddenly for the chapter on Sex and Reproduction, and then say: "All right, love, you can go now," while they get on with the real meaty stuff about the mighty hunter.... (1972:9–10)

Morgan's assessment reveals just how androcentric some interpretations of Darwinian Theory are and merely by re-framing evolutionary theories to equally or significantly include the female she reconstructs human evolution using a natural science biological discourse. It is not that feminism or social science reject the arguments of natural selection, there is however, a critical position taken with the way some of the evolvements are, or have been, interpreted to the detriment or disregard of women. Feminist theorizing has a significant presence in all disciplines and it is misleading to argue that the feminist perspective is independent of, and in contradiction to, all other knowledge; it is a counter discourse or an alternative interpretation. Darwin's theory of evolution is itself a counter discourse, a direct challenge to much accepted historical knowledge and became a rival authority to entrenched religious discourses. However, at the time that Darwin's ideas were made public, science and religion were more bedfellows than combatants and Denton notes that:

> As far as Darwin's contemporaries were concerned, few felt anything of the conflict between science and religion which is so characteristic of twentieth century thought. The conflict between science and

religion only erupted later in the nineteenth century when it became generally acknowledged that discoveries in geology and biology were incompatible with a literal genesis. (1986:20)

This suggests that there was not the intellectual divide between science and religion that is so characteristic of contemporary debates. In fact religion and science in this time complemented and supported each other, and as Betty Friedan (1992) notes, especially where questions of gender and human sexuality were concerned. Jeanette King (2005) points out that Darwinian Theory, far from undermining religious discourses of gender, complemented and reinforced them, in direct contrast to its adversarial stance on the origins of man. She states that Fiona Erskine, in her critique of Darwin, presented 'persuasive arguments to suggest that from 1859, *The Origin of Species* provided a mechanism for converting culturally entrenched ideas of female inferiority into permanent, biologically determined, sexual hierarchy' (2005:38). According to King (2005) science, religion and medicine all provided powerful authority for the idea that women are naturally submissive, weak and inferior to men; thus providing definitive answers to the question 'What is a woman?' which has significant repercussions especially with respect to their sexuality. The belief that women are examples of 'less evolved' human subjects who live their lives through their bodies rather than their minds (as men are understood to do) creates a society where women's sexuality and sexual behaviour are monitored and regulated (King 2005) even by women themselves (Lees 1997). However, even though some of the religious arguments for a naturally submissive weaker and inferior female were supported by biological discourses of the time, more modern interpretations of evolutionary science accept that these discourses lack scientific merit. Richard Dawkins (2006), one of the most vociferous critics of religious discourse, insists that religion is uniquely privileged in being able to deflect challenges to its authority without providing any proof for its claims. But the power and authority which historical religious discourses enjoy, when apparently supported by some biological scientific discourses, leaves a formidable legacy; religious discourse is an anchor of patriarchy which is the framework within which entire cultures operate.

The meaning of rape in historical and religious discourse

It is very difficult to establish anything definitive about history and rape and Roy Porter says that 'ingrained misogynistic caricaturing has always allowed men to trivialize rape and render it titillating to the pornographic imagination. These stereotypes in turn infect the way men have written its history' (1986:216). He also argues that rape cannot be explained away as the 'individual psychopathology of perverts' or the biological urge to reproduce, further suggesting that patriarchal attitudes appear to be implicit in the way the offence of rape was criminalized as primarily a crime of theft against men.

Mottier notes that even in pre-Christian society seduction of married women was written as more serious than rape because 'a secret liaison meant that a man could not be sure of the lineage of his children, whereas in the case of rape any offspring could be identified and killed' (2008:13). Women were understood as the property of their fathers and then their husbands and a means of establishing property rights (Bourne and Derry 2005). This historical position, which has a powerful legacy in modern Western culture, and an immediate relevance in many more religiously fundamentalist environments, cannot be meaningfully separated from religious belief. It is argued that the residual legacy is a presumption of male sovereignty. John Greenway MP stated in a commons debate on violence against women that women's lack of status is tied to religious culture and that:

> Eventually, we will have to recognize that women need a status independent of their spouse. I accept that these are challenging concepts, but I believe that we must take primarily a human rights approach to change. That is the key to political action and the vehicle to overcoming cultural and religious barriers' (*Hansard* 2010:170)

There is clear acknowledgement that even now female equality is a challenging concept due to religious and cultural beliefs. Nearly all monotheistic organized religions and other quasi religious belief systems like Hinduism are founded upon the primacy of the male. Women across the world currently live and die with ancient ritual beliefs which denigrate and kill them. Some religious leaders and apologists now attempt to distance themselves from the more barbaric practices which truly torture women, but this does not mean that those practices have disappeared or that the beliefs which support the practices are meaningfully challenged. For example, in India the traditional Hindu practice of *Sati* has been outlawed (this is the expectation that a woman will 'commit suicide' on the death of her husband). However, the practice is still legitimated by what Benson and Stangroom call the 'ritual humiliation' (2009:13) of women after their husbands die. Such is the horror of these religious practices that Benson and Stangroom ask the question 'Does God hate women?' and document horrific and sickening violence all in the name of religion occurring now across the world; killings in the name of religious honour where brothers hack their sisters to death with axes; or grown men rape their nine-year-old brides; or doctors refuse abortion even where such refusal kills the woman; or women are beaten to death by groups of men for writing poetry. One might seriously question the veracity of religious teaching and belief in the face of such maltreatment especially as it always appears to condone violence, torture or death of women in particular. Even the more liberal religious apologists routinely sanitize these practices with the claim that they are sound beliefs practiced corruptly; the beliefs themselves are not considered corrupt. Benson and Stangroom say:

> What would otherwise look like stark bullying is very often made respectable and holy by a putative religious law or aphorism or scriptural quotation...Religion dresses up power in robes and mitres; it disguises *force majeure* as the will of God. This makes everyone feel better. (2009:10–11)

Even in the apparently humane Western cultures religious beliefs justify sexual violence against women and the sexual control of women. We witness the legacy of these beliefs and their application daily in our courtrooms where the rape and/or murder of women is downgraded in comparison to other violent offending. Benson and Stangroom say that we all perform a self deception when we appeal to the goodness of God and that the *God loves everyone equally* mantra appears to be a cruel hoax. However, equally powerfully written into religious discourse is the notion of martyrdom which can lend victimization a noble function; it can dampen revolt and encourage pacifism giving the lived experience of oppression of women some meaning. The discursive belief that women should defer to men to keep the natural order of things leaves the real oppressor unchallenged, whilst defending God's apparent ambivalence towards the suffering of women and girls.

As noted, historically rape was a crime written in law and culture as an assault against the property of a man, usually the victim's father or husband. Because of this there is little historical discussion or documentation of rape trauma as women were not the legally wronged individuals in a rape. When we see modern assessments and criticism of historical representations of rape in Art, for example, writers will warn that we must put the assault in its historical context and not back project our own more modern perceptions of rape trauma onto those female subjects, the victims of rape. Often there are considered political and legal rationalizations for the aftermath of rape which sometimes tell us that women didn't suffer then, in the same way as women do today. The major cause of any trauma is posited as 'dishonour' or loss of social status, but this should not be confused with lack of trauma. If we look at one of the earliest depictions of rape, found in Deuteronomy, the repercussions of the 'dishonour' of rape were not insignificant and could be forced betrothal to the rapist or even death:

> When a virgin is pledged marriage to a man and another man comes upon her in the town and lies with her, you shall bring them both out to the gate of the town and stone them to death; the girl, because, although in the town she did not cry for help, and the man because he dishonoured another man's wife...If the man comes upon such a girl in the country and rapes her, then the man alone shall die...You shall do nothing to the girl she has done nothing worthy of death... When a man comes upon a virgin who is not pledged in marriage and forces her to lie with him, and they are discovered then the man who lies with her shall give the girl's father fifty pieces of silver and she shall be his wife because he has dishonoured her. He is not free to divorce her all his life long. Deuteronomy 22:23–9

This biblical passage reveals much about the foundations for historical and contemporary approaches to rape. Firstly; extramarital sex is considered sinful and in this culture, punishable by death; the notion of sex as a sinful and dishonouring practice is a constant in Western history and rape can be considered sex if there is insufficient corroboration for the woman's claims of rape. Note that the girl within the city walls could not have been raped because she did not cry out, whereas outside the city walls, it is believed her cries would never be heard so she is given the benefit of the doubt and this reflects the scepticism surrounding allegations of rape. Finally; the man who rapes a virgin must marry her as penance and never be divorced, as well as paying her father fifty pieces of silver; revealing that the woman is considered property which can be devalued. That the woman would be traumatized in the way we now understand it, is not even considered, if it was she would surely not be married off to her rapist for life who would then be given conjugal rights. This is actually protection of her reputation and thus ultimately her life. Dening suggests that the Christian church has never celebrated the female and notes:

> 'There is no denying that St Paul had no very great opinion of women. In his view, woman had been created for the benefit of man

and must therefore defer to him in everything, obedience being the price she must pay for Eve's sin in leading Adam astray.' (1996:144)

The biblical parable of Adam and Eve constructs Eve as deceitful with the power to lead Adam astray and this not only indicates the prevailing misogynistic beliefs about women at the time it was written, but has had a lasting legacy. This story is a metaphor for the danger posed by women's bodies and their sexuality. Eve convinced Adam to go against God; she was able to distract him from his own sense of morality with her unique and feminine powers of persuasion. History is littered with parables of dangerous seductive women leading men to destruction; the Sirens, for example, who lure men to their deaths on the rocky seas with their mesmerizing voices; Salome the dancing seductress who took the head of John the Baptist; Delilah the temptress who stole Samson's gifts of strength. Women are constructed in nearly all religious/cultural discourse as a temptation and danger to men. This is woman; she is dangerous, deceitful, seductive and mesmerizing, causing men to lose their good judgment and behave in a way that they normally would not; and this reflects another of the rape myths; men need protection from allegations of rape for they may have been seduced.

It is one of the documented rape myths that women who report rape are not to be believed (Rape Crisis 1999) for they may have lured the man to the brink of his own self control with their dangerous sexuality. This religious/cultural/mythological scepticism is entrenched also in legal discourse and the criminal justice response to allegations of rape, and has been for hundreds of years. In the 1600s Sir Matthew Hale, the then Lord Chief Justice of England, reinforced English common law with his famous cautionary rule, which has been used through the centuries to direct juries in cases of rape: 'It must be remembered that (rape) is an accusation easily to be made and hard to be proved, and harder to be defended by the party accused, though never so innocent' (cited in Cuklanz 1995:19). Clive Emsley illustrates that the same belief was present in medical discourse and reports that in an 1886 paper by Charles Routh presented to the Royal Gynaecological Society on the subject of 'nymphomania', the author is quoted as warning the medical profession about women who allege sexual assault: 'except upon the strongest corroborating evidence, the presumption is that they are liars, plausible liars, cunning liars' (2005:106).

It may appear from historical evidence that rape was not the phenomenon it is held to be today. The courts did not report many instances of rape with only half a dozen cases listed among the hundreds in the

Newgate Calendar (Wilson 1984); though the reasons for this could be easily speculated given the religious, legal and cultural approaches to rape and women; many women would probably not even report a rape for fear of the repercussions and the knowledge she would not be believed anyway; married women could not be raped by their husbands, so would have no legal redress in any event, and also women were defined as cunning liars and inherently deceitful by both law and medicine so many allegations would be lost in attrition. This is not dissimilar to the current situation where over 90 per cent of cases fail to achieve a conviction or are lost in attrition (Kelly *et al.* 2005, Harris and Grace 1999).

Porter (1986) argues that, historically, women weren't as fearful about rape and claims that this is supported by the fact that early feminists like Mary Wollstonecraft and Mary Astell did not agitate about it, even though they campaigned against other sexual issues like child prostitution and sexual diseases. However, according to Jeffreys (1984) the First Wave feminists did campaign against sexual violence, including marital rape and the sexual abuse of children. Bourke suggests that the discursive production of the concept of rape has changed over time and that women in the nineteenth century would have perceived and received the assault differently. She says that women would have been more aggrieved by the damage of a rape assault to their social standing or respectability. It should not be forgotten that the repercussions of a loss of social standing or reputation in the nineteenth century were not inconsiderable including a very real threat to her life. Also, it should be considered that rape is, and has always been, intertwined with multiple dangers to the victim which include the very real physical dangers related not only to the assault itself but the complications of pregnancy and childbirth. In the Victorian era pregnancy and childbirth were considerably less safe than they are now and the threat of miscarriage, more dangerous than a full-term birth (Jalland 1986). Mortality rates in this era were high and a routine cause for concern for women. There were no anti-biotics or blood transfusions to effectively deal with, especially miscarriage, and Jalland reports that the estimated five maternal deaths per thousand live births of the time, although much higher than today, fails to include many full term fatalities and all of those due to miscarriage which were much more prevalent (1986:159).

Diane Wolfthal (1999) also disagrees with the position of Porter (1986) that historically women were not as fearful of rape as women are now. Speaking of the Middle Ages and the Renaissance she comments on the historical depiction of rape in Art of the time, which is one of the few forums in which we may assess the meaning made of such violence. Wolfthal says that Art glorifies the crime with the aesthetic qualities of the paintings masking the reality of what they depict. Art and literature are powerful mediums with which to assess historical cultural life and are institutional sites in which discourses are constructed and reinforced. The discourses reflected or constructed in Art and literature have much authority and Foucault sees this medium as one of the 'great procedures' (1998:57) for producing the truth of 'sex'.

Rape in art and literature

Norman Bryson re-assesses two famous historical rapes depicted in Art to better understand their historical context and to question the contemporary perceptions of rape that may be projected on to the Art and therefore onto historical assessments of its meaning. Bryson argues that to understand the meaning of the Art we have to pay close attention to the narrative and ask 'what exactly occurred?' (1986:162). However, we must also consider that the narrative will only give us a partial version of what occurred. Bryson's first interpretation of an artistic story of rape is that of *The Rape of Lucretia* portrayed in oils by Titian. Bryson relates a narrative which sees a band of men competing to claim that their wife is the more virtuous. Lucretia, wife of Collatinus according to this story, wins the prize. Later that same night Sextus Tarquinius, the son of the King, enters the bedroom of Lucretia armed with a sword with the intention of raping her; he threatens to kill her if she does not acquiesce, and also to kill her black slave who he would lay alongside her after death creating a picture of what would be in that historical period, the worst kind of infidelity. Bryson describes this as a threat to her posthumous reputation, after which she submits to sexual intercourse. The narrative then tells of Lucretia calling the men of her house together the following day and using the sword of Tarquinius to kill herself in front of them, declaring she would 'never provide a precedent for unchaste women to escape what they deserve' (1986:163). This is what De Quincey (1847) might call a grand death and Bryson claims an equally grand motive for Lucretia as refusing to have her name become synonymous with indecency and a justification for shameless women. Her suicide and the manner in which it was done, he claims, was to protect her name from dishonour and to arouse her house to vengeance on another house (Bryson 1986). Lucretia's motives are also tied with the inference that she consented to sex albeit under duress, but which gives her the status of adulteress and this was a serious contravention which would have destroyed her reputation and status. The National Gallery (2003) in London describes the rape in more romantic terms stressing the sexual desire of Tarquinius and the beauty of Lucretia, though they too claim her death was the result of shame. This intelligible link between lucretia and her suicide is rationalized as the act of rape, a plausible explanation for the most brutal of self inflicted violence; to die is preferable to living with the stigma of rape. This is not an insignificant repercussion for Lucretia or for women.

In the second historical rape discussed by Bryson, which is that of the rape of the Sabine women depicted in oils and sculpture by the likes of Poussin and Bologna and named *The Rape of the Sabines,* again we see an act interpreted with a political slant. I use the term 'act' rather than 'acts' deliberately as this apparent 'mass rape' and we must consider it thus as it is titled as 'rape', is reduced to a single act. Bryson tells the story behind the art as Roman men carrying off Sabine women in a bid to 'reproduce Rome'; there was a significant deficit of Roman women with whom to complete this task. The Sabine men concocted revenge some years later when they scaled the city walls and attempted to kill the Romans who had abducted their women. Bryson notes that the Sabine women were by this time Roman matrons and their spokeswoman Hersilia said:

> Which shall we call worse, Roman lovemaking or Sabine compassion? If you were making war upon any other occasion, for our sakes you ought to withhold your hands from those to whom we have made you fathers in law and grandfathers. (1986:155)

Hersillia questions whether Roman lovemaking (rape?) or Sabine compassion (killing their now relatives?) is worse, indicating some trauma at least with regard to the physical act of rape itself. Bryson's assessment of the rape however, is that in historical terms 'it is hardly a crime at all', this is because according to Bryson it didn't transgress any of the laws of the Roman state except that permission to take the women was not sought from their male relatives. So here he assesses the story in reductionist terms; rape is sexual intercourse and women's legal status is that of property. The Sabine women were not raped then in a legal sense as they were married off to Roman men and the unions were thus legitimized; rape could not be committed by a husband against his wife. The story ends with the Sabine women apparently accepting their Roman mates, though how much choice they would have had is debatable. Bryson sees the question of identity more important to the

Sabine women than violation and he suggests that the upset caused to them was that they were not convinced of the validity of the marriage ceremonies and spoke of their injuries as tied with their legal status. The bigger inference here is that they did not suffer rape trauma as we perceive it today *or* as an individual rejection of a close and intimate violent physical assault. Whilst it is clearly accurate that there are differing historical constructions of female responses to rape, we cannot simply accept that there were no other less dominant discourses in circulation, or that the dominance of this legal discourse negated any more human, rather than purely female, responses. Such an explanation sanitizes the physical violence and the maltreatment of women, whilst simultaneously denying them any complexity. It also does not explicitly address that the repercussions for women of losing their social status could be appalling and even fatal. Bryson does however argue that the English term 'rape' is misleading. The Latin term *raptio* or *raptus* which was the original title for the work has a different meaning to Rape in that it suggests the mass kidnapping of women or taking of other types of property usually in time of war. It could be argued however, that the terms are not so dissimilar, especially not for the recipient of the violence and Wolfthal points out that Poussin leaves us in no doubt as to the terror and panic suffered by the women which is painted into their faces (1999:9). Bryson says the story is a 'fable of law, not of violence' (1986:158) and he may be right, but there is a sense in his discussions that 'rape' itself has been the subject of discursive violence; a once simple and straightforward concept made progressively more offensive by the complexities and multiplicities of the modern perspective. But this merely tells us that rape requires artistic sanitization only because of what it has become, and not because of what it was. In these terms rape used to be a simple affront to female reputation; it was unsullied by the ideologically constructed themes of brutality which dominate reasonable discussions and artistic interpretations of sexual violence now. However, in the case of Lucretia certainly, the repercussions of the rape were dire. Whether we believe they were caused by devaluing her legal status and reputation or a perverse *noblesse oblige* the outcome for lucretia was a brutal death.

Brownmiller (1975) sees that rape is often represented as a 'heroic' act and Wolfthal shows that after AD1500 a 'heroic' rape tradition emerged that served as erotica for the male viewer. The Rape of the Sabine Women has all the ingredients of a heroic rape depiction, according to Wolfthal, they are, aestheticization of rape, sanitization of the violence and sexual aspects, focus on the male point of view and the suggestion of a happy ending (1999:9). Vitz (1997) discusses the way rape was presented in medieval literature and claims that modern perceptions of rape and morality miss the meaning and cultural context of the times. 'Rape is sometimes ambiguous in the texts, or is treated humorously. The medieval view placed rape among the uncontrollable things that could befall a person' (1997:1). Vitz complains that feminist calls for rape to be more realistically represented as the ugly act it is, miss the 'fundamental aspects of medieval aesthetics; heroic literature must introduce evil so that its heroes can rescue others from it and 'without the menace of evil the true mettle of virtue (male or female) cannot be shown to shine' (1997:1). Detmer-Goebel (2001) in a critique of Shakespeare's *Titus Andronicus* shows how Lavinia is unable to speak of rape, 'Lavinia's chaste refusal to say the word "rape" reminds the audience that even to speak of rape brings a woman shame' (2001:75) and Roiphe (1994) reminds us how rape is an issue which threatens a woman's very life, for Lavinia having been raped, was then killed by her father Titus Andronicus. Roiphe says 'her virtue was so important, so vital, that once she was ravished, her life was worth nothing' (1994:70). The power of hetero/patriarchal discourses which create and reinforce the idea that the act of sex, irrespective of whether it is invited, removes femininity and therefore worth in the economy of heterosexual exchange, is a clearly running theme in Art. When the aesthetic of rape is argued to be spoiled by inconvenient reminders of its brutal realities, then Art fails in its claims to 'bring the spectator in closer touch with reality' (Wilkinson 2005:48) and in this respect critics also fail to consider whose voice is represented in the Art itself.

Detmer-Goebel argues that it is crucial to ask 'Who is telling this story of rape?' (2001:75) and this is a fundamental point for if the stories are mainly or wholly written and expressed by men then it is a male perception that is recorded. It is not in question that males dominated every sphere of life (Porter 1986) and it is also established that females have had little input in recording Western cultural historical life (Shlain 1999). It would seem to follow that women would have had little input in recording their perceptions and experiences of rape. The discourses may vary but there is one consistent theme – the representations are male and so can only effectively chart the male perspective. It is suggested by some that rape has been made progressively more offensive and traumatic over time: perhaps culminating in the aggressive and uncompromising representation of rape by the radical Second Wave feminists as a violent and brutal physical attack. But one thing we can say about the Second Wave perspective whether or not we find it provocative; it is a documentation of the perspective of women on the subject of rape.

Literacy has not always been the privilege of the many and because it is the main medium for passing cultural information, it must be considered that those capable of recording history were in a minority and Shlain says:

> Of all the sacred cows allowed to roam unimpeded in our culture, few are as revered as literacy. Its benefits have been so incontestable that in the five millennia since the advent of the written word numerous poets and writers have extolled its virtues. Few paused to consider its costs. Sophocles once warned 'Nothing vast enters the life of mortals without a curse. (1999:1)

Shlain (1999) asserts that writing has subliminally fostered a patriarchal outlook. His hypothesis that it is the written word that has caused the gender inequity in modern cultures cites the alphabetic form as diminishing feminine values and with that, feminine power in the culture. He describes feminine and masculine thinking characteristics as fundamentally different and asserts that once literacy is firmly rooted, it eclipses and supplants speech as the principal source of culture-changing information. Shlain tells us that archaeologists have discovered strong suggestive evidence that before the Old Testament the Goddess was the primary image, not the male Idol and Dening (1996) also holds that Goddess worship and its emphasis on feminine values was stamped out by the church in Europe and Shlain says: 'The Old Testament is the first alphabetic written work to influence future ages. The words on its pages anchor three powerful religions: Judaism, Christianity and Islam. Each is an exemplar of patriarchy' (1999:7).

In many patriarchal cultures women were (and still are) refused basic education or discouraged from following academic pursuits (Green 2001) which would have added to the disadvantage Shlain hypothesizes. The lack of female input in the recording of responses to sexual aggression makes it difficult to present an argument for what they did experience so the only definitive claim to be made about rape in Art and Literature is that it represents a perspective removed from those who were experiencing the assault: as Miss Elliott says to Captain Harville in Jane Austen's *Persuasion*:

> Yes, Yes if you please, no reference to examples in books. Men have had every advantage of us in telling their own story. Education has

been theirs in so much higher a degree; the pen has been in their hands. I will not allow books to prove anything. (1983:1279)

Art, literature and sexual murder

It is maintained here that representations of rape are consistently linked with death (either threatened, real or social); there are threats of murder, suicides and the death penalty, but Art and literature are also significantly concerned with representing the explicit sexual death of women. Maria Tatar's work *Lustmord* chronicles the cultural legacy of the depiction of 'sex murder' from Weimar Germany to the present and she comments that 'the sheer number of canvases from the 1920s with the title 'lustmord' (sexual murder) ought to have been a source of wonder for Weimar's cultural historians long before now.' (1995:4) Tatar notes that depiction of the violated female corpse is ubiquitous in Art, film, literature and across mass media, an artistic practice which suggests an unnerving cultural obsession with recording sexual violence against women as an aesthetic convention. But also she argues that this convention has links to truth in that Jack the Ripper is now more a 'cultural case history' (1995:7) than a literary construct and even the likes of fictional killer Norman Bates from Hitchcock's *Psycho* has found his way into 'legal arguments and psychiatric studies' (1995:7). In fact Tatar argues that such is the volume of art dedicated to depicting female sexual death that those images and women's position as victim have, to an extent become 'natural'. She quotes Brian De Palma as saying that 'using women in situations where they are killed or sexually attacked' is nothing more than a 'genre convention...like using violins when people look at each other' (1995:8). The normality of depicting female sexual death and its status as a 'genre convention' has, according to Bronfen (1992) caused a cultural blindness to its ubiquity. Such is the proliferation of depictions of female sexual death throughout history that it has become not only a genre convention but a culture convention; an unquestioned staple of human cultural life that is considered a natural outcome of our culturally prescribed heterosexual dynamic. Walter Sickert's macabre interest in female sexual death which he depicted in numerous paintings has seen him speculated to be Jack the Ripper by American crime novelist Patricia Cornwell. Though the claim is widely scorned the most offence was caused not by the sexual mutilations depicted in his paintings or the reverence of such images, but by Cornwell's apparently obscene act in causing damage to one of the paintings in order to complete forensic tests.

Some of the literature penned by the infamous Marquis de Sade describes truly horrific sexual violation of women and the notoriety of this particular individual is unquestioned. However, this notoriety did not come from his many acclaimed non-violently misogynistic outpourings. His literary brilliance is underpinned by the audacity of just four novels. Phillips argues that De Sade sees the female body as 'simultaneously a source of intense fascination and of immeasurable contempt' (2005:41) and that he has a desire to 'punish all women for their sexual inaccessibility' (2005:80). This conception reduces sexual murder to an extreme enactment of heterosexual frictions with 'woman' an object constructed through its discourses, and destroyed through them also. It is bizarre that women could be punished for their sexual inaccessibility when patriarchal custom dictates that they, as a matter of critical importance to their lives, restrict sexual access to their bodies. The ambiguous and contradictory rationalizations given by men who are excited by sexual violence sees women damned from all directions.

Tonic Immobility

Rape induced paralysis or 'Freezing' has been recognized as a common response to the threat of rape (Rape Crisis 1999). The condition, technically referred to as Tonic Immobility (Galliano *et al.* 1993) is observed commonly in more broad human responses to threat or panic. The 'freezing' of victims of rape is discussed by Wolbert Burgess and Holmstrom (1974) who identified and named Rape Trauma Syndrome, they characterize this as a more universal response to a threat to life and not a particular reaction of women when threatened with rape or sexual violence.

However, the connotation drawn from this by some has been that subconsciously women want to be raped and are naturally masochistic; psychoanalytic/psychological discourse has appeared to give support to this myth. Susan Brownmiller (1975) says 'we may thank the legacy of Freudian psychology for fostering a totally inaccurate popular conception of rape' (1975:192) and disputes psychoanalytic assessments of female sexuality which characterize women as masochistic by nature, an assessment which has been used to explain 'freezing', though many claim this is a misinterpretation of Freud's theory of the unconscious (Forrester 1986).

Historically police and others have searched for evidence of active resistance to support female allegations of rape, and screaming or fighting are commonly perceived to be indicators of that resistance (as far back as Deuteronomy as noted). There is even an enduring myth that it is impossible to rape a struggling woman (Galliano *et al.* 1993) the inference here being that uninjured women who report rape are lying. It is clear that there is limited popular understanding of the differing responses to a rape assault, and that in a criminal justice setting this can have significant effect. Juries, for example, who are made up from members of the public, may make assumptions as to the honesty of female victims if they fail to respond to rape in very particular ways and, in particular, if they fail to physically resist their attacker. There is suggestion by the Office for Criminal Justice Reform that jurors should be instructed to ignore rape myths and be educated on the realities of victim responses to rape (Home Office 2006). Research into this possibility has found that jurors do misunderstand rape victims and expect to see evidence that they fought and were injured in the process. It was found in mock jury trials that even when guidance was given and other beliefs were successfully challenged, this particular perception of what constitutes a 'real rape' remained (Ellison and Munro 2009). Freyd argues that jurors are generally required to use their 'common sense' when deliberating but that this is problematic 'when common sense and empirical reality do not coincide' (2008:15). She describes a case in which she acted as expert witness where the young victim had 'frozen' in response to sexual violence and that the inference drawn from this was that there was consent. Nearly all the rape myths invoke the accusation that the woman was really inviting and desiring the assault and the man was merely responding to her signals. It has been suggested that historically, psychological discourse, and especially evolutionary psychology has acted to defend rapists locating the violence within the individual and drawing from biological discourses which appear to mitigate for the rapist (Rose 2000, Brownmiller 1975). Despite the dominance of biological and evolutionary theories to explain rape, the idea that tonic immobility is 'an evolved defence mechanism to predation' (Ratner 1967 cited in Galliano *et al.* 1993) has been curiously absent in popular discussion. However, the apparent discursive divide existing between psychological and feminist discourses of rape does not define contemporary psychological theory and an inter-disciplinary approach is more usual. Polaschek and Ward (2002) propose several implicit beliefs that are often held by rapists which reflect some of the rape myths and include; ideas that women are fundamentally different to men and therefore heterosexual encounters are adversarial; that women are sex objects and are constantly sexually receptive to men's needs; that women cannot be injured by sexual activity unless physically injured; that male sex drive is uncontrollable and male sexual energy can build up to dangerous levels; that men can have the idea that that their needs should be met on demand; that they are justified in raping women as punishment for not being suitably subservient; and that the world is a hostile and dangerous place (cited in Ward *et al.* 2006:125). In more modern times the feminist position that situates sexual violence in a cultural frame is part of biological, psychological, anthropological, legal, medical and other discourses. However, even with these new discursive approaches being included across all disciplines the religious hetero/patriarchal discourses appear to have supremacy in rationalizing and responding to sexual violence against women in media and criminal justice narratives. The power of this approach and the repercussions will be discussed and explored in the following chapters, focusing on the way that the concept of rape has been linked to murder. The next chapter documents the feminist resistances to the historical/cultural discourses so that the relationship hypothesized as existing between rape and murder and central to this book is placed in context.

3
Feminism and Sexual Violence Discourse

Introduction

Whenever I have to speak on feminist discourse I feel a little apprehensive, and I have to admit there is an implied apology in my introduction. This is not because I feel I need to apologize for the theories or the research of feminist scholars, it is because I know that I am being resisted before I start. The feminist position has challenged practically all orthodox historical 'gender knowledge' and vigorously resisted the truths produced in religious, legal, medical and other powerful institutional sites which have disadvantaged women. Because some of the arguments of early feminism seriously sought to undermine the legitimacy of historical cultural discourses they attracted few allies, and accusations from those institutions that feminists were driven purely by a deviant political ideology or were disenfranchised, poorly socialized miscreants, made it very difficult for them to achieve legitimacy. There have been many attempts to disempower feminist theory and alienate the protagonists from the women they wish to speak for but despite this many of those theories are impacting cultural practices and beginning to permeate the stalwart institutions of power. In this chapter I will explore feminist discourse on the subject of sexual violence and rape although it should be noted that there is no one theoretical position which unites all feminists and given the vast body of work on the subject it would be impossible for me to effectively summarize all positions here. This chapter represents an overview of feminist discourse and merely seeks to identify key discursive positions on rape within feminism to illustrate the contested terrain of sexual violence discourse. Given that not all feminists agree, some of the frictions and disagreements that exist will be documented though it is important to note that these disagreements are not explored in the context of a critique of feminism, but to identify various discursive positions on the subject of rape and sexual violence which can be traced to the voice of women.

Women's inferior position in society and their apparently natural passive nature is a 'truth' that Haskell (1987) describes as 'the big lie' and Feminism was the first and perhaps only, serious challenge to this construction of women setting itself 'in opposition to virtually every culture on Earth' (Saul 2003 cited in Bourne and Derry 2005:54). Although there is now a feminist presence evident in all the disciplines, the theories have their roots in social science, though even social science has played a role in reinforcing the historical beliefs of female inferiority challenged by feminism. Friedan (1963), a pioneering Second Wave feminist scholar, argued that both psychoanalytic theory and functionalism undermined women's full participation in society. Feminism is, in this context, a distinct approach which simultaneously challenges and contributes to knowledge produced within all disciplines.

There are many categorisations of Feminist philosophy and theory but I will be using the broadly temporal ordering that sees three groupings described as the First, Second and Third waves of feminism. There is a significant discursive divide existing between the Second and Third wave which is clearly evident in their approaches to sexual and gendered violence. The Second Wave discourse, which is largely identifiable with a radical feminist philosophy, positions sexual violence as a significant method of oppression and equates all female subjugation with patriarchal practice; the Third Wave is less identifiable as a cohesive unified discourse and represents perhaps, the beliefs and approaches of women who have grown up in a world with a significant feminist agenda, questioning some of the more radical approaches. The term 'feminism' is itself problematic and some theorists have noted a reticence in many women to be associated with the term or to describe themselves as feminists. Rowe-Finkbeiner's title *The F-Word: Feminism in Jeopardy* illustrates the negative connotations attached to the term itself and the perceptions it creates:

> Clearly the word itself is quite problematic to this generation; otherwise it would not be so easily grouped into a list of disparate 'ism words having nothing in common but an attached suffix. (2004:5)

She found that of all the labels that could be attached to women, the label feminist grated the most. The term is perceived as representing a particular political approach that belongs to the radical theorists of the Second Wave of feminism which follows a tradition set by the suffragettes of militant activism and/or an uncompromising stance. These strategies certainly raised the profile of women's subjugation and achieved many freedoms and rights for women which are somewhat taken for granted now. It is also true that the Second Wave radical position had a significant impact on the way women and indeed men, perceive sexual violence and provided an alternative framework within which to begin interrogating the veracity of historical/cultural discourses. However, those women who have always known a feminist agenda are able to confidently construct their own new position, which because of the very presence of the Second Wave agenda can operate within a less radical framework. In this sense the Third Wave of feminism is a challenge and sometimes rejection of Second Wave ideals. The title of Christina Hoff Sommers (1995) publication *Who Stole Feminism?* succinctly captures the frictions and she clearly positions the Second Wave as unfairly and erroneously representing feminism with theories and strategies which she perceives as destructive both to feminism and to women.

The First Wave

As noted in Chapter 1 the Cross Government Action Plan on Sexual Violence and Abuse (CGAP 2007) explicitly states that sexual violence 'is a consequence and cause of gender inequality' and feminists have been campaigning against such inequality for centuries. Christine de Pizan could be considered one of the earliest feminist writers, born in 1363 in Venice, she challenged prevailing stereotypes of women and gave praise for their achievements. Her book published in 1405 *The Book of the City of Ladies* was a defence of women and their achievements and an advocation of equal rights for women in education. Mary Wollstonecraft's *A Vindication of the Rights of Woman* was published in 1792 and although she wasn't fundamentally opposed to differing gender roles she fought strongly for the education of women so that they could develop the solid virtues they were accused of lacking (Bourne and Derry 2005). Her work was considered radical at the time but did not give rise to any kind of female revolt (Brody 1992). According to Bevacqua (2000) it was in the middle of the nineteenth century that women began seriously campaigning against their unequal position and this period, covering the nineteenth and early twentieth century, encompasses what is referred to as the First Wave of feminism. The First Wave feminists focused on women's lack of rights exemplified in their legal status once married as 'feme covert', or *hidden woman*, a concept which has an equally powerful cultural presence. This status assimilated women into the legal persona of their husbands stripping them of individual legal rights; as a result women could not have their own money or property, they could be legally physically punished for disobedience by their husbands, they had no protection from unwanted marital sexual intercourse, they had no rights over their children and they could not vote or enter many of the professions (Bourne and Derry 2005). The Married Women's Property Act of 1882 gave married women equal property rights with unmarried women and allowed them some access to the legal system. However, this did not give them parity with men; women were not considered equal to men in any way and although the offence of petty treason was removed in 1828 it starkly illustrates where women sat in comparison to men in the social hierarchy. Petty treason was a form of aggravated murder with a more severe form of sentencing and was used in cases where individuals subverted the established and legally inscribed pecking order. If a servant were to kill a master, for example, or a woman her husband, this was considered an assault on the State as well as the victim. Women who killed their husbands were charged with petty treason rather than murder and burned at the stake for their sedition (Emsley *et al.* 2009). When women did begin to challenge their position in Victorian times they had few political or academic allies and those activists who were more aggressive in their approach, like Emmeline Pankhurst were accused of being 'unladylike', and even the more conventionally 'feminine' feminists like Millicent Fawcett argued that their activities were detrimental to the cause.

The positions of the First Wave feminists on the subject of rape and sexual violence are largely unrepresented in much literature, and it is even posited by some writers that the First Wave feminists did not campaign a great deal about sexual violence or more particularly, rape. As noted in Chapter 2, Roy Porter (1986) states that early feminists like Mary Wollstonecraft and Mary Astell did not agitate about rape, even though they campaigned against other sexual issues like child prostitution and sexually transmitted diseases. However, Jeffreys (1984) argues that the First Wave feminists were concerned with these issues and in an effort to transform male sexual behaviour, they campaigned against the abuse of women in prostitution, the sexual abuse of children and marital rape but this campaign is largely undocumented in historical texts which focus on suffrage. Bevacqua (2000) suggests that members of the suffrage and women's rights movements did allude to issues of sexual violence and the emerging discourses saw the problems as rooted in women's lack of sexual autonomy and 'ownership' of women via marriage. She suggests that 'the first outcry against sexual assault as a systematic abuse of women came in response to the rule of 'lynch law in America' in the years following the emancipation of slaves.' (2000:21). In fact Bourke notes that it was not until 1883 that the term 'rapist' was first used and this was in an article in the *National Police Gazette* referring to a 'nigger rapist' (2007:409). It was activist Ida B. Wells in 1892, who, after investigating and reporting on extralegal lynchings of black men, first 'articulated a political understanding of sexual assault' (Bevacqua 2000:21). Wells' particular position was that rape and sexual assault were being used to achieve more general political aims; specifically that a fallacious chivalry was being used to justify the lynching and killing of black men who were often spuriously accused of raping white women. She argued that this masked the true reasons for the racist violence which were in reality rooted in fears of black economic progress. The idea that rape could be understood as a political rather than a purely sexual assault was to become a significant approach of the Second Wave feminists. The sexual double standard was positioned as a social practice which disadvantaged women and the disadvantages suffered by women were exemplified in the powers conferred in the Contagious Diseases Acts of 1864, 1867 and 1869. Powers were granted to police that allowed them to remove women suspected of infection with a sexually transmitted disease or prostitution, in named garrison towns, and to intimately examine them for signs of infection and then forcibly incarcerate and treat them. Sexually transmitted diseases were of epidemic proportions and in the culture of the time discourses of female sexuality dictated that female prostitutes were the cause of the problem, not the males who used their services. The inspection of women erroneously or maliciously described as potentially infected was reported to be a fairly common practice and in this way the Acts sanctioned a form of sexual violence against women. There was no forcible examination of soldiers and sailors as it was thought that this would be bad for morale and according to Bourne and Derry (2005) senior military officers and doctors felt that servicemen *needed* access to healthy, uninfected prostitutes and certainly one of the driving forces for implementation of the Acts were 'fears that venereal disease would make male bodies too weak for military purposes' (Mottier 2008:51). This approach reflects the scientific discourses that constructed male sexuality as biologically determined, static and driven by uncontrollable urges, but also the religious moral discourses that constructed a code of sexual behaviour for women that revolved around virginity, abstinence and purity.

In 1871 the report of the Royal Commission upon the Administration and Operation of the Contagious Diseases Acts made it clear that women were to be held morally responsible for the spread of sexually transmitted diseases and Walkowitz says that they used pseudoscientific language to transform 'a time honoured male privilege into a physiological imperative' (1992:71) and it was stated in the report that:

> We may at once dispose of any recommendation founded on the principle of putting both parties to the sin of fornication on the same footing...there is no comparison to be made between prostitutes and the men who consort with them. With the one sex the offence is committed as a matter of gain; with the other it is an irregular indulgence of a natural impulse. (cited in Walkowitz 1992:71)

Vociferous opposition to the Acts mobilized working and middle class women to join forces and occupy public spaces to speak openly about their sexual subjugation and the outrage they felt at the powers conferred in the Acts. Christian Feminist Josephine Butler was the most prominent leader of the resistance to the Acts which were finally repealed in 1886. Although this campaign was not specifically directed at the offence of rape, the forced removal and inspection of women allowed under the Acts represented the tacitly sanctioned use of sexual violence by men and was the driver for determined female opposition. Another controversy of the 1880s which marshalled widespread revolt and action was the publication in 1885 of W.T. Stead's *The Maiden Tribute of Modern Babylon* in the *Pall Mall Gazette*. This series of reports documented Stead's purchase of a young virgin girl for the purposes of sex and revealed the extent of the sexual exploitation of working class girls in the East End. These actions were a direct and radical challenge to the legal operation of the double standard which is a premise that features widely in later radical feminist approaches to sexual violence. In referring to the double standard as politically constructed, the First Wave feminists laid the groundwork for the emerging Second Wave feminist discourses which were to re-define rape as political and not sexual violence.

The Second Wave

In 1963 Betty Friedan published *The Feminine Mystique* and Bevacqua sees this as a 'critical mobilising event'. She describes this book as the:

> first to articulate the sense of alienation middle class American women often experienced in their role as housewives in the 1950's and early 1960's...and helped establish the women's rights branch of the second wave of feminism. (2000:54)

Friedan exposed what she described as a hidden problem amongst American women; a lack of fulfilment in their prescribed gender role. She argued that women who aspired to achieve access to political rights, higher education, professional careers or artistic recognition were represented as if they were to be pitied, with the dominant discourses of femininity constructing them as abnormal and unfeminine. This powerful belief system sought to undermine the achievements of the First Wave feminists and reinforced the idea of a natural and biological female inferiority which Freidan explicitly denounced. In a critique of Freud's work which she characterized as a belief that had hardened into fact; she argued that American women had been trapped into believing a myth of femininity. She also asserted that Freud's theory of 'penis envy' was interpreted as having a biological, rather than a cultural aetiology and was applied too literally, again reinforcing male superiority (1963:104). Social science was relatively unexplored at the time and according to Friedan the emerging social science approach failed to distance itself from biological determinism but that this is often missed in the interpretation of Freud's work:

> Instead of destroying the old prejudices that restricted women's lives, social science in America merely gave them new authority. By a curious circular process, the insights of psychology and anthropology and sociology, which should have been powerful weapons to free women, somehow cancelled each other out, trapping women in dead centre. (1963:117)

Friedan also attacked sociological functionalism and argued that by attempting to make itself more 'scientific', social science had borrowed from biology and studied institutions as if they were comparable to a human body in terms of their structure and function.

> By studying an institution only in terms of its function within its own society, the social scientists intended to avert unscientific value judgements. In practice functionalism was less a scientific movement than a scientific word-game...By giving an absolute meaning and a sanctimonious value to the generic term 'woman's role', functionalism put American women into a kind of deep freeze. (1963:118)

In this sense second wave feminism was challenging every accepted and orthodox discourse of gender and this was never going to be an easy position from which to further a political ideal. Again Feminism was being represented as the political goal of 'unfeminine', ill-adjusted women rather than a scientifically or empirically sound position. Feminists were in the position of attempting to resist the knowledge produced in multiple dominant discourses and they were in Mills (2003) terms represented as 'incomprehensible' as a legitimate voice.

Susan Brownmiller's *Against Our Will* published in 1975 was a seminal work which reconstructed rape as political violence. She unapologetically positioned rape as a political process of intimidation, an act tacitly endorsed by all men, and perpetrated against all women. She directly challenged the idea that rapists suffered from mental illness or an overwhelming sexual desire and re-constructed them as quite ordinary individuals who identified with a patriarchal and misogynistic culture. She also challenged the prevailing belief that only certain types of women get raped, arguing that any woman irrespective of age or any other characteristics could become a victim. This radical position exposed the normality of the offence and challenged the assumption that male sexuality was static and biologically driven. What made her new discursive approach so controversial was the accusation that rape was used as a process of intimidation so that the social elite (of males) could maintain their dominant position.

The developing discourses were given focus by forming an anti-rape ideology and rape was re-conceptualized. The poor criminal justice response to rape became a verification of the arguments and the high attrition rates, low reporting and low conviction rates were made visible and became the rallying call of the movement. By challenging the dominant perceptions of the 'rape victim' and the 'rapist' and presenting evidence to support the claim that all types of women were represented as victims the arguments resonated with women everywhere.

Pornography too became a significant focus and was implicated by the Second Wave in reinforcing rape myths and encouraging a rape culture. Andrea Dworkin (1999) suggested that pornography was a form of propaganda and stated:

> The character of pornography and its relationship to actual violence against women, if it's analogous to anything is analogous to the way anti Semitic literature blanketed Germany and enabled what occurred to be justified, encouraged it, incited it, promoted it. (1999:141)

This is a powerful statement, though Dworkin is not alone in likening pornographic literature to propaganda. Russell (1993) presented a causal model of pornography and rape and her use of Finkelhor's (1984) model for child sexual abuse characterizes pornography as a forum to undermine the assailant's inhibitions against committing such an act. Harstock (1999) implicated pornography in the sexualisation of victimized women and the normalisation of the brutal, sexually aggressive male; she states that: 'there is a surprising degree of consensus that hostility and domination as opposed to intimacy and physical pleasure are central to sexual excitement' (1999:97). This approach to pornography was given some clarity after the death of Jane Longhurst in March 2003. The man convicted of her murder, Graham Coutts fallaciously claimed that his murder of Jane was a sex game that had ended in tragedy. After his arrest police found hundreds of images of strangulation and necrophilia on his computer. This man's obsessive interest in violent pornography led to a campaign by Jane's mother Liz Longhurst to outlaw possession of violent pornographic images on the premise that they can lead to sexual violence. The campaign enjoyed some success and the police can now prosecute those in possession of violent pornography but opinion on whether this is a victory for women's rights or an infringement of civil liberties rages on. Feminist activist and journalist Julie Bindel tells of extreme pornography and the existence of 'snuff movies' (movies which show the real rape, torture and murder of women). Having watched one of these movies herself in an anti-pornography forum attended by journalists, special-effects experts and activists, she can personally attest to their existence and dissemination in domestic environments. The movie, which depicted a South American woman being tortured, raped and murdered and was sourced from an English porn shop and was kept 'under the counter' (*Guardian* 2006). Others however, like Holly Combe from the organisation Feminists Against Censorship states that the government should not place limits on sexual preference and that implicating violent pornography as a cause of sexual violence merely gives the abuser an excuse and may discriminate against the apparently non abusive S&M community (*Guardian* 2006).

The 'sexually dominant male' and the 'sexually passive or submissive female' often depicted in violent pornography were argued by the Second Wave to be an erroneous representation of 'natural' stereotypes of men and women which reflect a certain dominant discourse of heterosexuality which excuses enjoyment of such imagery; Dworkin and MacKinnon argue, for example, that:

What would it say about one's status if the society permits one to be hung from trees and calls it entertainment – calls it what it is to those who enjoy it, rather than what it is to those to whom it is done? (Dworkin and MacKinnon cited in Russell 1993:1)

Lees (1997) research describes the passive/aggressive nature of hetero/ sexual relations operating in Western culture as pivotal to the maintenance of the double standard; the double standard could not operate without the normalising of the passive woman and the aggressive man. According to Lees males are expected to aggress and females to respond or not, and her research graphically depicts the foundations for the support of the double standard: 'A girl's standing can be destroyed by insinuation about her sexual morality. A boy's reputation in contrast is usually enhanced by his sexual exploits' (1997:17). She effectively established the importance of reputation in the life of girls illustrating how both males and females police female behaviour using reputation as a control. Consequently use of insulting terms like 'slag' can steer girls into accepted roles and behaviours. Although the term 'slag' appears to have no stable definition the inference in the term is that the female is promiscuous irrespective of what initially attracted the insult and this could be anything from swearing to speaking with boys. The concept of reputation is critically important and more poignant than it at first appears for a female with a bad reputation can actually be left with little protection in law for many offences which may be committed against her by a sexual aggressor. This is vividly demonstrated in the criminal justice system where any slur on the reputation of the victim may precipitate a not guilty verdict (Lees 2002). Even now when women are urged to enjoy more sexual freedoms the spectre of their sexual reputation will be of crucial significance in the way they are treated in many contexts, including in the criminal justice system. Sex then is an issue to be treated with some caution outside the risks of unwanted pregnancy or sexually transmitted diseases. The discursive practice of controlling female sexual behaviour in this way is illustration of Foucault's proposition that discourse has real effect and can produce the objects of which it speaks, namely in this context 'the slag'. A 'slag' cannot exist as a morally deviant 'object' without a framework to support the belief that the behaviour attracting the label is unnatural or deviant. Foucault (1998) discussed the entry into sexual discourse of the 'homosexual' as a 'species' and the production of names for 'heresies' (1998:43). The homosexual was variously constructed in discourse and became an 'object' to be described and recognized. The 'slag' in similar fashion, is a discursive object, produced by and constructed in, discourses of gender and hetero/sexuality. More recently Tanenbaum (2007) found that such terms are still used in the control of women's behaviour.

French sociologist Emile Durkheim (1858–1917) described all human behaviour as being on a continuum, at one end a particular behaviour may be perceived as criminal or deviant but similar behaviour at a different point on the continuum may be seen as acceptable or normal. Radical criminologist Steven Box (1992) referred to the theory to illustrate how normalized aggressive sexual behaviour and rape are at different points on a single continuum. He argued, for example, that in patriarchal cultures men are expected to apply pressure on women to agree to sexual intercourse but women, conversely, are expected to resist that pressure. He cites Clark and Lewis's (1977) proposition that 'the socialisation of both men and women takes coercive sexuality as the normal standard of sexual behaviour' (cited in Box 1992:141) and that those men who identify strongly with patriarchal culture can perceive sexual aggression as a kind of seduction where it is possible to see rape as 'not only normal but even desired by the victim' (1992:146). Brownmiller (1975) also exposed rape as a culturally sanctioned behaviour and strived to show that the stereotypical view of a rape assault is flawed. In embracing the idea that rape can occur in circumstances other than a violent stranger attack Brownmiller brought the idea of acquaintance, marital and date rape to centre stage, and this has been the cause of some of the most vigorous disagreement between feminists. Brownmiller and others used statistics like those of the Koss (1985) survey to illustrate how widespread the problem of rape was. The Koss survey suggested that one in four women had been victims of rape and this statistic was used to illustrate how sexual violence and rape were a significant social problem. The inability of the criminal justice system to deal with allegations of rape was exposed as well as the prejudices that were apparent that saw women scrutinized for blame in a culture that disbelieved their allegations. Sexual violence and rape became a forum for exposing what they saw as the consistent subjugation of women by a patriarchal culture. Although the campaign did much to change practices within the criminal justice system and reveal its inadequacies, conviction rates have not improved and the amount of rapes reported has not diminished, they have in fact increased (Kelly *et al.* 2005). These findings have fortified radical feminist discourse and the fact that most sexual victimisation occurs in the private sphere illustrates the foundations for the feminist slogan 'the personal is political', which encourages examination of domestic as well as more traditional politics. However, this position has attracted harsh criticism with many younger feminist writers, reflecting a perception of radical feminism as reductionist and judgemental (Bourne and Derry 2005).

The Third Wave

It is suggested by some that the Third Wave are concentrating less on the subject of rape than their Second Wave peers and Bevacqua states that: 'by the beginning of the 1980's, rape was not the 'hot' issue it had been in 1972' (2000:152). Other forms of violence like domestic assault, sexual harassment and child sexual abuse were receiving more publicity. However, work was continuing in the background and the 1980's saw the growth and consolidation of rape crisis centres and anti rape coalitions (Bevacqua 2000). The third wave in this respect was formed of both those younger women who rejected the Second Wave ideology and those who were motivated to take it forward. The differences between the politics of Katie Roiphe, for example, and her uncompromising stance against the Second Wave, and the politics of Jennifer Baumgardner and Amy Richards whose position is more a political vision of evolvement of Second Wave fundamentalism, is not necessarily as adversarial as the rift between the likes of Roiphe and the Second Wave. The disparities between the Second Wave and the new Third Wave are effectively articulated in their positions on the subject of rape. Despite the subject of rape losing its high profile in the nineties, it was nonetheless still the subject of vigorous debate particularly those issues surrounding the representation of the typical rapist and the movement to classify different categories of rape. Different 'types' of rape were named depending largely upon the relationship between the victim and assailant and produced new terms like 'acquaintance rape' or 'date rape'. However, the terms seemed to create a spectrum of rape offences delineated by the perceived seriousness of the assault which was directly related to the victim/offender relationship. This was challenged by the Second Wave who claimed that all rapes were of equal seriousness. Some of the Third Wave feminists like Katie Roiphe (1994) argued that a failure to classify different sorts of sexual aggression was creating a feeling of victimisation in women that was inappropriate. This high profile discussion made it clear that rapes did occur in the private sphere and gave women a language with which to rationalize their experiences of sexual aggression or violence. Kitzinger's (2004) study of child sexual abuse shows how having the language to rationalize an experience may transform the perception of that experience: 'Prior to 1986 incestuously abused children and adult survivors had to process their experiences in an almost total cultural vacuum. Some grew up thinking it was perfectly normal.' (2004:37). This new expressive language and conceptualisation of the offence is said to have resulted in an increase in reported rapes and women were accused of reconstructing bad sexual experiences as rape (Roiphe 1994). The accusation against the Second Wave was that they were 'creating victims' in the name of politics and this practice was described as 'victim feminism'. The backlash from the Third Wave presented an argument that rape was being redefined in too broad terms. The most significant backlash commentary came from Camille Paglia (1990), Katie Roiphe (1994) and Christina Hoff Sommers (2001). Paglia has long challenged the Second Wave especially on their position on what has been called date rape and states:

> My position on date rape is partly based on my study of the faerie queene. ...In 1590 the poet Edward Spencer already sees that passive, drippy, naïve, women constantly get themselves into rape scenarios, while talented, intelligent, alert women, his warrior heroines, spot trouble coming or boldly trounce their male assailants. (cited in Bevacqua 2000:185)

Paglia claims that the Second Wave oversimplifies the problem of sex by reducing it to a social convention. She claims that sex is a point of contact between man and nature and cannot always be reduced to a social model. Her claim that sex is daemonic, as is all nature, seems to be explanation for the problematic nature of hetero/sexual relations. She shows sympathy for men and the problems they have with sex, claiming that women have no fundamental problem with which to deal, in the way that men do. She also claims that women do not have to prove themselves women, in the grim way that men have to prove their masculinity. This is in direct contradiction to Second Wave arguments like that of Simone de Beauvoir who famously stated in *The Second Sex* (1952):

> One is not born, but becomes a woman. No biological, psychological, or economic fate determines the figure that the human female presents in society: it is civilisation as a whole that produces this creature intermediate between male and eunuch, which is described as feminine. (1952:295)

Brownmiller similarly asserted that: 'Femininity always demands more. It must constantly reassure its audience by a willing demonstration of difference, even when one does not exist in nature' (1984:1). Femininity, from this perspective is something to be performed and in this sense it is a discursive practice. Katie Roiphe (1994) echoes some of

Paglia's points and claims that incidence of victimisation that (Second Wave) feminism claims exists, could be eradicated if women took more care to observe when they may be in danger, and that women should pay attention to rape myths instead of rejecting them. Paglia too, is at odds with traditional Second Wave feminism and she asserts that society is woman's protection from rape and not the cause of it. This is a claim that would turn a good deal of Second Wave argument on its head. The double standard that is said to impede prosecutions and nurture an aggressive sexual style from men, according to Paglia, is actually protecting women from the realities of a more pagan life. Roiphe claims that rates of sexual assault are exaggerated or created by political manipulation of potential victims suggesting that the Second Wave not only exaggerates the prevalence of rape, but creates fear in women, causing them to dwell on their perceived violation and re-classify bad experiences as assaults. It is further argued that this retrospective re-classification of experiences caused a false rise in rape statistics and created a feeling in women of vulnerability. In short Roiphe states that: 'If you don't tell the victim that she's a victim, she may sail through the experience without fully grasping the gravity of her humiliation' (1994:109). In contrast feminist lawyer Catherine MacKinnon (2002) suggests that when women accept rape as a bad sexual experience their oppression is complete. MacKinnon sees violation in women's acceptance of aggressive sex, whereas Roiphe would see 'bad sex' and nothing more. MacKinnon asserts that the violation is there masquerading as sex, Roiphe holds the sex is there masquerading as violation.

Shanahan (1999) argues that the harm of any rape is harm to all women because of the fear all women may have as a result of the violation of others. Ward *et al.* interpret this position as arguing 'that all men somehow share in social and material 'benefits' which result from other men behaving in sexually abusive ways' (2006:171). It is established that women suffer high levels of fear of crime and research has shown that this is three times higher than that of men (Stanko 1996). It is established that women's fear of crime is largely fear of sexual assault or more importantly, rape (Warr 1984). Stanko too, argues this point and sees part of the reason for the high levels of fear of sexual assault being the commercialisation of women's victimisation. She talks of the way women's fear of crime has precipitated a commercial response. Personal attack alarms are sold mainly to, and aimed at women. Advice from legitimate agencies focuses on women, like not walking home alone at night and keeping to well lit areas and keeping a tank full of petrol (Stanko 1996). Lees (1997) also theorizes that cultural and social supports promote a climate of fear in women and research supports the notion that women are manipulated into a state of fear of sexual assault. This climate of fear manipulated by culture or society is seen by some Third Wave feminists as exacerbated by the ideals and theories of the so-called 'victim feminists'. This is a point of divergence in feminist politics which sees little hope of reconciliation but it should not be assumed that these divergences dominate contemporary feminist theory. Astrid Henry states that there is also an 'explosion of independent feminist publications...and cultural movements such as the Riot Grrrls and the Radical Cheerleaders' (Henry 2004:31). Henry describes this brand of Third Wave feminism as different to that presented by commentators like Roiphe which is described as unselfconsciously and narrowly focused on the experiences of white women, failing to engage with the multicultural nature of American society and women across the world. There is also an explicitly political strand exemplified in Jennifer Baumgardner and Amy Richards' 'ManifestA' (2000), this book begins by describing a world without the changes wrought by the Second Wave and advocates continuing political activism with a vision for a way forward. The arguments are not a rejection of Second Wave ideals and incorporate the new forums and milieus of the late twentieth and early twenty first century, like the internet and AIDS and also nod to the new manifestations of particular brands of female power like that espoused by the likes of the Spice Girls and others. However, Tanenbaum's (2007) work echoes the work of Sue Lees and her research into the sexual double standard and the importance of sexual reputation in the life of women. It seems from this research that little in this area has changed though this work expands Lees original focus and incorporates the effects of sexual reputation on the lives of women of all ages.

Postfeminism

For my purposes Postfeminism isn't to be considered as that which comes after Feminism or even after the Third Wave, but like postmodernism, it is concerned with a particular way of assessing or conceptualising reality and has been around since the 1960's interrogating and deconstructing patriarchal discourses (Phoca 1999). Strands of postfeminist theory can be seen running through the second and third waves in the way they both question the nature of gender and the interests of the institutional sites which produce knowledge about gender. There has been a move in some recent feminist writing on rape which embraces a melding of the postfeminist tradition with an inter-disciplinary focus to critique the social construction of rape and sexual violence. Anderson and Doherty's (2008) examination of the social construction of rape from a psychological position, for example, locates rape within a wider social frame and claims that rape is 'socially produced and socially legitimated' (2008:123) building bridges between the traditionally micro level theorising of psychology and the macro level theorising of sociology. This inter-disciplinary approach is more characteristic of modern feminist approaches to rape and sexual violence where the hetero/patriarchal culture is now established as implicated with little serious dissent within feminism. Having said this, representation of Second Wave feminists as driven by a man-hating political ideology has remained in the culture as a stick to beat the new generation of feminists with, despite the now wide acceptance of their fundamental arguments. This is perhaps illustrative of Foucault's ideas of discursive constraints; a movement to discredit them as those authorized to speak has left its legacy as an effective weapon against those who challenge discourses of male authority.

4
Jack the Ripper Narrative

Introduction

When writing of the death of Joan of Arc, Thomas De Quincey (1847) declared that despite the female gender failing to distinguish themselves in the arts and history, there was one thing they could do that surpassed even the achievements of the Masters; women could 'die grandly', as grandly as any man. Certainly the violent death of females has been a staple of cinema and television over the last century especially at the hands of psychotic strangers or mythic monsters, giving many of the victims ever more graphically eroticized deaths which are perversely grand. These murders are often highly sexualized and it is a convention that most female victims will be young and/or attractive; film director Dario Argento states: 'I like women especially beautiful ones. If they have a good face and figure, I would much prefer to watch them being murdered than an ugly girl or man', and Schoell a film historian notes: 'Other filmmakers figured that the only thing better than one beautiful woman being gruesomely murdered was a whole series of beautiful women being gruesomely murdered' (cited in Clover 1992:32). These comments reveal that in the years since De Quincey's declaration, female death retains its potential to distinguish the victim allowing her to die spectacularly. But it is a feminized death; it is a death closely associated with another form of feminized trauma, the trauma of rape, and in certain contexts in film, not only are murder and rape concomitants, they are conflated.

Joanna Bourke (2007) states that there is a rape scene in one out of every eight Hollywood movies and there are models of narrative which excuse brutal violence and murder in the name of 'rape revenge' (Clover 1992), as well as the enormous amount of art, literature and film which routinely depict the sexual murder of women (Tatar 1995). The concept of rape seems to stalk our entertainment and news media, and has a potent connection to the death and/or murder of women in films; one such genre of films is the focus in this chapter; the crimes of Jack the Ripper.

As noted in Chapter 1, Jack the Ripper has been described as the 'archetypal rapist', despite the absence of any evidence to suggest that he raped or even attempted to rape any of his victims. To explore how the concept of rape is embedded in Jack the Ripper narrative, the representation of his crimes in film is a particularly rich source for data as there is in existence what Soothill (1993) and Cook (2009) refer to as the 'Jack the Ripper industry' which embraces all forms of media. With over 120 films made using the Jack the Ripper name or drawing from the events (Kelly and Sharp 1995) this is an enduringly popular and fertile forum for presenting speculations about the killer and his motivations. The films are not only a genre of their own, they also adhere to many of the conventions of both horror and 'slasher' films which sexualize violence against women making strong links between sex, seduction, violence, rape and death. Harper (2004) when discussing the 'slasher' genre, suggests that the film-makers rely on the presentation of images of sex and death to tell their stories with a growing concentration on female nudity rather than graphic bloodshed to create spectacle; a feature which he suggests is easier to get past censors than gore and cheaper than special effects. He further claims that because of this an increasing number of female roles in these films are given to 'sub playboy, silicone enhanced starlets' (2004:22). The ease with which slasher movies are able to mix up sex in the form of pornographic images and death in the form of serial killing is testament to the way the discourse of sexual murder makes meaning of violence against women.

Clover (1992) argues that the film most influential to the 'Slasher' genre is *Psycho* (dir. Alfred Hitchcock, 1960) and it is interesting to note that as well as being the director of the most influential 'Slasher' film, Hitchcock was the director of what is claimed to be the first serious interpretation of Jack the Ripper and his crimes with *The Lodger* in 1927 (Meikle 2003). The similarities between the two films are apparent in their adherence to a model now very familiar; a stalking and sexualized form of violence predominantly against women. It is entirely possible that the making of *Psycho* was influenced by the crimes of Jack the Ripper and a particular interpretation of gendered violence that framed the narrative of *The Lodger*.

Serial killing and the FBI

The crimes of Jack the Ripper have been endlessly re-visited in an apparent attempt to identify the killer and to create entertainment media, and because of this he has blended into British folklore (Cook 2009). Tatar states that: 'Because Jack the Ripper lacks a stable social and historical identity, he can be reinvented by each age to stand as the most notorious example of male sexual violence' (1995:22). He has become as Tatar posits, 'more fictional construct than historical figure' (1995:23) but despite his questionable credentials, an authoritative discourse emerged from the foggy streets of late nineteenth-century Whitechapel based upon his acts of violence. These crimes as noted, exemplify a conflation of rape and murder but their significance extends beyond this, the modern dominant discourse of sexual murder is widely regarded as having originated from these crimes (Caputi 1987, Boyle 2005, Schmid 2005). Sexologist Richard Von Kraft-Ebing however, identified mutilation murders as a distinctive form of sexual psychopathy in his *Psychopathia Sexualis* in 1885 (Tatar 1995:22) and Jack the Ripper came to exemplify the psychopathy described, becoming the poster boy for the serial killer industry which was to emerge in the 1970s.

It was the FBI who claimed serial/sexual murder as their own in the late 1970s and Schmid argues that they became central in producing the 'official' definition and are now the 'pre-eminent source of expertise on the subject of sexual homicide' (2005:77). It was more than merely fortuitous that this new and visceral threat had its nemesis in the FBI, an organization newly free of the autocratic yet charismatic J. Edgar Hoover, and seeking to consolidate and justify their existence as champions in the fight against America's domestic enemies. Stephen Milligen describes the re-building of the FBI after Hoover's death, claiming that a 'new area of specialization was needed to justify the Bureau's budget and continued existence' (2006:97). Vronsky (2004) too notes that the 'serial killer epidemic' (2004:23) which gathered pace in the 1970's coincided with the FBI lobbying the government for more funding. The FBI certainly had a history of successfully manipulating media to their own advantage, but Milligen goes further in suggesting a history of inventing domestic enemies and creating moral panics. Their peculiar ability, brought about by Hoover's careful manipulation of the Bureau's public image, to 'shape attitudes towards crime and crime control' (2006:15) and to define reality for legislators, police and bureaucrats (2006:25), positioned them perfectly to promote the dangers posed by the serial killer and represent themselves as the only organization equipped to neutralize the threat. In 1979 they conducted the highly publicized Criminal Personality Research Project, a study exploring the problems of serial murder by such killers as Jack the Ripper. The initial findings were based on a research sample of just 36 serial killers (Purcell and Arrigo 2006) but this is the seminal study in the area and the precursor to a larger Institute of Justice funded project in the early 1980s (Petherick 2005). It was at this time that the 'serial killer' materialized as a morphology. He was now identified and defined and the dangers he presented were formally articulated to the public on 26 October 1983 in a press conference held by the Justice Department (Schmid 2005). The serial killer was defined as a sexual sadist who preyed on random victims with the inference that prevailing liberal attitudes to sexuality were to blame for his emergence. (Schmid 2005:78)

Bringing together the FBI and Jack the Ripper, according to Schmid, made perfect sense and each further enhanced the fame and authority of the other, allowing the FBI to construct a discourse of sexual murder based on his 'foundational place in the pantheon of serial killers' (2005:67). Their practice of constructing 'offender profiles' coupled with their high profile status as 'experts on the phenomenon' allowed them to construct an authoritative and dominant discourse which, to cite Schmid, reinforces an 'extremely limited and distorted image of what serial murder is, who commits it, who is victimized, how they are victimized and why they are victimized' (2005:79).

The FBI certainly provided powerful authority for interpreting Jack the Ripper's crimes as sexual, or more importantly perversely hetero/sexual. Milligen states that 'the FBI went looking for sexual criminals and, using Freudian interpretation, they found sexual criminals' (2006:102). He further states that the BSU studies were based on a specific type of sex crime which updated 'Jack the Ripper for late twentieth century America' (2006:102) promoting a right wing political morality. This practice feminizes the victim and even though it is rarely acknowledged, eliminates male heterosexuals as potential targets, creating a forum for terrorizing and marginalizing those who are potential targets. Given that potential victims are those who deviate from the category adult male heterosexual, and include women, children and homosexuals, the most powerful societal group maintain their freedoms in public spaces. A ritualized panopticism ensues which sees the behaviours and practices of those who are not heterosexual males policed both by themselves and by others. Given the symbolism and rhetoric surrounding serial killing, victimization will always serve as a warning to other potential victims to curb their choices and restrict their sexuality. The serial killer is a spectre who stalks the freedoms of women, embodying all the symbolic values of the rapist, but much worse, the perceived sadism of the mutilator. This narrow definition of serial killing eclipses any focus on other types of multiple murder and according to Schmid 'increases the public's level of fear...partly because the crimes are so vicious, and partly because the victim selection... seems so random (2005:79). However, Schmid's assessment masks the fact that random does not mean random person, as will be discussed at length in Chapter 5, but largely means random female. By limiting the dangers posed in the public space to those dangers which face women and being explicit that those dangers are sexual in nature, an insidious form of power is reinforced.

Modern techniques like those pioneered by the FBI are employed to seek to 'know' the serial/sex killer and to comprehend his madness. The criminal justice system is increasingly embracing the use of psychological and psychiatric discourse in the courtroom and the prison, medicalizing the deviancy of sex offenders and creating the idea that in the end we can know 'who' they are. Foucault (1994) argues that it used to be enough that the offender committed a crime, he was identified and we applied a sanction, but in a modern judicial system this is no longer the case; the focus on the crime is superseded by an intense desire to 'know' its author. This has special resonance in the apparently senseless and insane sex killing; the motive must be established, what Foucault describes as the 'psychologically intelligible link between the act and the author' (1994:188). The disciplines of psychology, psychiatry and criminology are increasingly contributing what is considered orthodox knowledge to the subject of sex killer motivations. However, the failure of popular media and some psychological interpretations of motivation to locate the pathology of the offender at least partially in its societal or cultural context leaves these crimes represented as purely 'sexual' and biological. Often the 'cause' is traced back to unresolved childhood trauma (Purcell and Arrigo 2006) but rarely explicitly explains why the violence is sexual, why it is often committed against women and why it is almost exclusively a male pursuit. This failure to embrace structural explanations typifies the importance given to individualized medical interventions. Soothill *et al.* (2009) in a discussion of criminal offending more generally, consider the possibility that structural changes may have more impact in reducing offending than individualized treatments. Roger Depue argues that the FBI in particular have little interest in exploring the social causes of crime (cited in Milligen 2006:112) focusing almost entirely on individual psychopathology. The construction of technical and scientific knowledge systems to isolate and characterize the criminal mind is one of the most widely hyped psycho/criminological practices. So-called criminal profilers have achieved an almost mythical status as demon hunters in the popular imagination personified in characters like Fitz (played by Robbie Coltrane) in TV series *Cracker* and Dr Tony Hill (played by Robson Green) in TV series *Wire in the Blood*. The FBI are popularly, though wrongly, believed to have established this practice (Milligen 2006, Purcell and Arrigo 2006, Schmid 2005) at their Behavioural Science Unit (BSU) in Quantico, Virginia crediting them with 'being world experts in serial murder and the originators of the term "serial killer"' (Milligen 2006:98). The BSU aligned itself with scientific disciplines and methods which enhanced the credibility of their practices but the reality of these knowledge systems is very different from the depictions of psychically gifted individuals doing battle with monsters that we see in the media and may even read about in certain autobiographical accounts of practising profilers. However, practitioners have much invested in this conception of their work and Warwick (2006) suggests that there is also much money to be made; especially given the strong links and shared discourses of serial killing between the UK and the USA. The serial killer industry is burgeoning with enormous income streams from both popular and academic sources and consequently resistance to the dominant discourses is piecemeal and often scorned. The narrative now offered based on killers like Jack the Ripper, as Walkowitz notes, 'presents a far more stabilized account than media coverage offered at the time' (1992:3) and this may be partially the result of powerful authorization of particular perspectives and interpretations as both informed and durable.

There is a growing cynicism, however, which questions whether Jack the Ripper existed at all as a single serial killer which could potentially undermine the veracity of the knowledge produced in his name, or at least reveal the omissions. It has been suggested that enthusiastic case linkage to calm panics, improve clear up rates or even create panics is not unknown (Milligen 2006). There were at least eleven murders of women in the Whitechapel area at the time Jack the Ripper is documented as operating. Though not all of them are popularly attributed to him some would argue his victims numbered far more than five. It is speculated that these murders could have been committed by numerous killers, and that even the so-called canonical five were the work of at least three different individuals. The linking of certain cases with claims that just one individual was responsible is speculated to have been the work of enterprising Fleet Street journalists. Cook (2009) presents a convincing argument that the birth of Jack the Ripper as a single serial killer was a media hoax. He also claims that police surgeons and police investigators of the time believed that due to the differences in *modus operandi* and offending signatures noted in the post mortems, that the killings must have been the work of more than one person; there is even suggestion that these experts believed some of the murders were copycat killings even at the time. If this was the case then the interpretations of the motivations would be significantly undermined; they could be based on a serial killer who didn't actually exist, using the interpretive fantasies of journalists, malicious or mischievous letter writers and copycat killers. However, it should be noted that the dominance of the 'sexual' element speculated to have driven these crimes was not dominant in 1888 in the form that it is now, though Dr Thomas Bond a police pathologist, according to Rumbelow 'inferred that the offender may have been suffering from a condition known as *satyriasis* – excessive and uncontrollable sexual desire in males' (Rumbelow cited in Norris 2005:1).

A history of the story

Jack the Ripper's crimes occurred at the same time as a popular mass press was emerging and so received unprecedented coverage coupled with a highly stylized representation which has obstinately stood the test of time (Diamond 2003). Diamond states that the Victorians had more opportunity than their predecessors to enjoy sensations, and that certain legal changes like the abolition of tax on newspaper advertising in 1853, the repeal of stamp duty on newspapers in 1855, and the dropping of paper duty in 1861 aided in the availability of printed news media for the masses; he also sees the development of the railway system as aiding distribution (2003:1). With the most important newspapers concentrated in London, Diamond asserts that sensations were easy to create in the city (2003:2). Cook (2009) suggests that the birth of the *Star* newspaper which was launched in January 1888 represented a move towards a new style of journalism which was particularly suited to sensationalist crimes. He further suggests that the paper was designed to appeal to the newly literate (thanks to the 1870 Education Act) middle and working classes and deliberately presented news in a sensationalist way subverting many of the more ethical journalistic ideals and pricing itself at half the cost of its rivals at one halfpenny (2009:15). It was the *Star* which first proposed the idea that the Whitechapel murders were the work of a single killer who lived in the East End, an individual who was known as 'leather apron'. This was a move which was based entirely on unsupported speculation and which apparently cost them financially after 'leather apron', a man called John Pizer was exonerated, but this was a move which saw the paper's circulation increase by over 60 per cent (2009:71).

Speculation at the time was hampered by a dearth of evidence and conflicting and vague eyewitness accounts. There appeared to be no historical precedent for such offending, so no framework within which to begin rationalizing the violence. Local political and economic conditions began to situate the potential motivations with a mix of racist and mythical constructions of the type of offender Jack the Ripper might be. The divisions between rich and poor, the abusive treatment of women by men and the idea of a homicidal maniac were all speculated as implicated in these murders; an explicit sexual motivation was not the dominant framework within which these murders were generally rationalized at the time. The idea of sexual danger for women was however, at this time a subject of wide public concern and Walkowitz argues that after the publication in the *Pall Mall Gazette* in 1885 of W. T. Stead's infamous *Maiden Tribute of Modern Babylon* which documented the trafficking in underage girls for the purposes of prostitution, that women added their voices to the circulating debates on prostitution and sexual deviancy. This piece was in fact 'one of the most successful pieces of scandal journalism of the nineteenth century' (1992:81) exemplifying the power and reach of tabloid style journalistic practice. Walkowitz even suggests that Stead's obsessive discourse around sexuality remains a legacy for the modern era (1992:85) simultaneously amplifying fears of sexual danger for women whilst mobilizing public outcries against it (1992:95). He was perhaps the first journalist to explicitly suggest a sexual motive for the crimes of Jack the Ripper likening the unknown killer to a lust driven homicidal man/beast in the style of Dr Jekyll and Mr Hyde. There was an idea that the mutilations were the work of a skilled medic and this fuelled speculation that the killer was a doctor and a gentleman though there was scant evidence to support this speculation. The story of *Dr Jekyll and Mr Hyde* was running in a London theatre at the time and Robert Louis Stevenson's character became a focus, with the actor playing the lead, Richard Mansfield listed as an official suspect because of his realistic portrayal of the change from 'normal' man to 'homicidal beast'. The original meaning of Hyde's monstrous psychopathy was lost in the more accessible and exciting sexual subtext which has become a staple of the story. Frayling suggests that this model of offender was 'the most accessible explanation for newspapers to exploit' (1986:197) and the early Jack the Ripper narrative began to form.

The modern narrative

The popular modern telling of the story is illustrated by use of iconic images that have become synonymous with the crimes, the thick London fog, Hansom cabs, a cloaked faceless stranger with a Gladstone bag and poverty stricken whores butchered in the dark cobbled streets. The seediness and omnipresent, all encompassing abject poverty and darkness of the East End is juxtaposed with the affluent and light West End, creating a lasting image of the East End as a cesspit containing the worst kind of human low life imaginable. These polarized images are constructed for media effect and are somewhat expected in any dramatization of the events, and to an extent all the imagery and myth that surrounds the story is probably part of the attraction for viewing Ripper films. The popularity of the story really gained momentum in the 1970s and the bulk of literature and films have been produced since then. To illustrate the ever-expanding volume of publications dedicated to, or inspired by, the crimes of Jack the Ripper, I will offer some numbers: up to 1995 there have been over 470 serious publications; over 60 biographies of individuals involved in the investigations; over 190 fictional publications; over 120 films (Kelly and Sharp 1995) and nearly 200,000 web pages (Cook 2009). These figures do not include the serial publications like *Ripperologist* or *Ripper Notes* or magazine articles, or in fact, any of the films and books published since 1995 which are countless. Between 1972 and 1995 it is stated that at least 400 books and articles were published with something to say about Jack the Ripper (Kelly and Sharp 1995). Kelly and Sharp capture the diversity and tone of much Jack the Ripper literature in saying:

> The books devoted to the Ripper are usually characterized by a painstaking build up of facts and theories followed by a vertiginous leap into fantasy in the closing chapters...Theories about the ripper's identity are legion and range from an escaped orangutan to the poet Swinburne and from Jill the Ripper to most members of the Royal household. (1995:52)

The 2003 publication *Jack the Ripper: Crime Scene Investigation* illustrates the nature of the narrative used routinely in many modern films and publications in its synopsis: 'Just the facts Jack! A must read for anyone with a serious interest in Jack the Ripper...a horrific series of sex-lust murders and mutilations in the autumn of 1888...'(Speare 2003). It is fair to say that many so-called Ripperologists take their investigations and speculations very seriously and often painstaking and intricate research has informed their work. Whilst the above quote may serve to demean the rigour of their research, its purpose is to illustrate how the discourse, which is creating the meaning made of these crimes, may be constraining serious debate and reproducing Jack the Ripper as a form of sexually motivated rapist, which is wholly inaccurate. Many authors have tried to convince a cynical but fascinated audience that they have the final solution to this mystery and the identity of Jack the Ripper has been endlessly re-written. Whilst the speculated identities are diverse and sometimes bizarre, the speculated motivations are not. Most authors are reproducing the dominant discourse of sexual murder, relying on myths that have emerged from the East End fog as definitive truths and as Odell suggests 'Ripperology combines historical fact and pseudo science in ways that blur the truth' (2006:239).

Marriner (1992) however, makes clear the perceived motivations for Jack the Ripper's mutilation of his victims: 'he disembowelled his victims in a mad frenzy to reach the womb' (1992:20) and this is a position reflected in both serious and fanciful re-telling of the story. Marriner speculates further, reproducing the misogyny and institutionalized sexism apparent in most narratives:

> The secret, morbid interest in sex was exposed when the Ripper committed public deeds which many of those Victorian fathers and brothers, working in respectable offices, perhaps secretly envied. They read with shudders of horrified envy about the maniac who was committing what seemed like the ultimate rape. (1992:26)

Marriner's narrative positions these crimes inescapably and elaborately within the dominant discourse of 'sexual murder' and the hetero/ sexual frame. The womb, speculated as so central in the killer's desire is analogized as eroginic, and the symbolism of the violence is positioned as sublimation for non-consensual hetero/sexual intercourse. This is illustrative of the semiotic practices which have constructed the motivations behind these crimes. It is precisely the position of some feminist writing that killers like Jack the Ripper are merely at an extreme point on a continuum of recognized male violence. Marriner's enthusiastic slavering, which is not unusual in the more popular end of the market, reveals in its narrative what Tatar says of the Germanic Weimar *Lustmord* tradition 'it so clearly captures Western notions of what drives men to murder women' (1995:7).

Uncle Jack (Williams and Price 2005) begins by describing the finding of Jack the Ripper's (apparent) last victim: 'The 25-year-old prostitute, regarded locally as something of a beauty, was lying lifeless on her blood soaked bed, her body savagely mutilated' (Braid 2005). There is little evidence to suggest that the narrative framing of this story differs in any respect from the framing of previous narratives. Meikle (2003) notes that similarly, the screen image of Jack the Ripper has remained relatively constant over 75 years, even though his identity has been reappraised and revisited in many books and films. The visual image of Jack the Ripper is a powerful one, as are the visual images of the victims, the East End and the other iconic artifacts related to this story. They are as much a part of the discourse as the language employed and their relatively static representation indicates the limitations and conservative nature of this genre. The narrative is embedded in the cultural imagination, its truths of sex killer psychology axiomatic and its warnings absorbed into the droning routines of feminine security. In the century since these crimes occurred they have been referred back to, to give meaning to subsequent and apparently similar crimes, like those of Peter Sutcliffe, the so-called Yorkshire Ripper between 1975 and 1980, and Steve Wright the so-called Suffolk Strangler in 2006. A practice which reinforces the status of the Jack the Ripper narrative as 'truth' and, at least in the case of Sutcliffe, significantly and negatively distracted the investigation (Ward Jouve 1988).

Overview of the events

The murders occurred over one hundred years ago in 1888 in an area of the East End of London referred to as Whitechapel. Though not all the murders fell within its boundaries there is a general consensus among Ripperologists that there were five murders though some say only four there is speculation of many more. The so-called canonical five victims were all killed between the hours of midnight and dawn in the East End of London; all were attacked to various degrees with a sharp knife, except one where it was speculated the killer had been disturbed before he could carry out any mutilations, and they were: 31 August 1888 – Mary Anne Nicholls; 8 September 1888 – Annie Chapman; 30 September 1888 – Elizabeth Stride; 30 September 1888 – Catherine Eddowes; 9 November 1888 – Mary Jane Kelly.

It is probably the nature of their injuries that has been subject of most graphic representation and description, leading to much speculation as to motive. All the victims had their throats slashed with some force and this is given as the cause of death on the death certificates of all victims, though there is evidence to suggest that at least three may have been strangled or asphyxiated first. There was no evidence of conventional sexual assault or rape of the victims. It is believed that organs were removed from some of the bodies including a kidney and a uterus; there is some question as to whether a heart was taken from the last victim (Yost 2009) though news reports of the time refute this. The violence on the 'post mortem' bodies was extensive and directed at the face and abdomen. The modus operandi of the Ripper has since been hotly debated but Barbee (2009) suggests that it is generally accepted now, with a new medical reading of the injuries, that the victim and assailant were facing each other just prior to death and the victims were killed by asphyxiation and then laid, rather than thrown on the ground with their heads to his left, this being established by the lack of injury to the back of the head and the positioning of the bodies. This contradicts the popular narrative in which the victims were approached from behind and killed by having their throats slashed; their throats were slashed, but apparently whilst they were on the ground, this being indicated by the pooling of blood beneath and behind the neck. Because the heart had stopped beating there would have been no pressure to spurt the blood and the killer could have been relatively blood free. No sign of sexual assault was ever found, neither did the Ripper ejaculate over the bodies (Barbee 2009). However, this new reading is not universally accepted and those who believe that Jack the Ripper was not one individual, point to differences in *modus operandi* which undermine the apparent consistency of the methods used to kill and mutilate the women (Cook 2009).

Much Ripper literature speculates that the killer was obsessed with the womb and it is noted that this organ was targeted in two of the assaults, yet it is a kidney that was the subject of huge media attention when a parcel received by George Lusk, the president of the vigilance committee, claiming to be from the killer and addressed as 'From Hell', contained a human kidney. It appears that because reproductive organs could be documented as targeted in the assaults that this is crucial. If five kidneys had been removed and one uterus, one could assume that the uterus would be the most significant in creating meaning. Jack the Ripper eviscerated the entire body of his final victim, but when this violence is visualized, what we appear to see is rape and genital mutilation.

Jack the Ripper in film

Representation of these crimes in film has a long history; according to a list compiled by Meikle the first film to star Jack the Ripper was a novelty item released in 1915 named *Farmer Spudd and his Missus Take a Trip to Town* (dir. J.V. Leigh, 1915). However, the first influential release was in 1927 and was a film version of a story by Marie Belloc Lowndes (1927) named *The Lodger* (dir. Alfred Hitchcock, 1927) which started life as a short story in a magazine. It was said to have been inspired by a conversation heard by Lowndes telling the story of a couple who were convinced they had Jack the Ripper as a lodger in their home at the time of the murders (McCarty 1993). There were three versions of this story alone (*The Lodger*, dir. Alfred Hitchcock 1927, *The Lodger*, dir. Maurice Elvey 1932, and *The Lodger*, dir. John Brahm 1944). Subsequent titles like *Room to Let* (dir. Godfrey Grayson 1950), and *Man in the Attic* (dir. Hugo Fregonese 1954) indicate the influence of this particular narrative. Since these early productions there have been many attempts to tell the story with many representations merely using the name to frame a 'horror' type story, for example, *Jack the Ripper* (dir. Jesus Franco 1976) is apparently set in Whitechapel but the individuals involved in the original events (except the killer) are not referred to and the killer is graphically depicted as a rapist who removes the breasts of his victims. Both *Jack the Ripper* (dir. David Wickes 1988) and *From Hell* (dir. Albert Hughes and Allen Hughes 2001) make a serious attempt to recreate the events and engage with history. Several films set the crimes in the present and this is achieved either by a copycat killer as in *Ripper: Letter from Hell* (dir John E. Eyres 2001) and *Jack's Back* (dir. Rowdy Herrington 1988) or a time travelling machine as in *Time After Time* (dir. Nicholas Meyer 1979). In *Hands of the Ripper* (dir. Peter Sasdy 1971), the killer is the daughter of Jack the Ripper possessed by his spirit. There are versions where the fictional unashamedly meets the real as in *Dr Jekyll and Sister Hyde* (dir. Roy Ward Baker 1971), and *Murder by Decree* (dir. Bob Clark 1979) which sees fictional detective Sherlock Holmes solving the case.

In addition to the many formats which see the Jack the Ripper story being told there are many documentary/docudrama type films including *The Whitechapel Murders* (1997), *The Jack the Ripper Conspiracies* (2003) and *The Diary of Jack the Ripper* (1999). Like the films, the documentary style is significantly geared towards speculating the identity of the offender. The most recent offering is a TV mini-series named *Whitechapel* (Dir. S.J. Clarkson 2009), this film closely adheres to the popular Jack the Ripper story presenting a copycat killer duplicating the murders of the original Jack the Ripper. Though this film does speculate who the original Jack the Ripper was, the narrative is more about a replication of events culminating in the modern killer held physically captive by the police, but impossible to identify by name or personal history which in this respect again parallels the events of 1888 in that the killer remains unidentified.

A list of Jack the Ripper films compiled by Meikle (2003) was consulted to select films/TV suitable for this analysis. Meikle's list incorporated film/TV with any reference to Jack the Ripper and included 65 separate listings, The sample was first limited to films produced post 1970, as this is the time when most Ripper films and other Ripper media were produced and reflects a growing interest in the crimes, but is also a time when discourses of sexual homicide were being formally constructed by agencies like the FBI (Schmid 2005). Vronsky states that this time scale represents the 'postmodern age of serial homicide' (2004:3) and a time when the term 'serial killer' was first used. The discourse of sexual murder as it is today was in this sense, constructed after 1970 and the meanings and knowledge it produced are back projected onto the events of 1888. However, it was decided to include 'The Lodger' (dir. Alfred Hitchcock 1927), as this is considered to be the first serious interpretation of the events (Meikle 2003). Films that were indicated to be of minor importance to the genre by Meikle were discarded, also films that were part of television serials normally unrelated to Jack the Ripper, for example, episodes of *Fantasy Island* and *Star Trek*. There were no docudrama style films in Meikle's list so these titles were selected from an online retail agency (www.Amazon.co.uk) which provided the most comprehensive selection available. The TV series *Whitechapel* was made after Meikle's list was compiled but is included in the sample. It is the commonalities present in the different ways of 'telling' the story that are of importance; the common themes, the discursive strategies and the objects of the discourse. In this way whether the story is being told in a cinema film style, a made for TV style or a docudrama style, is of less importance than the consistency of the techniques, themes, silences and objects used and produced. The twenty films in the final sample that were available and used are listed in the Appendix.

Three dominant characteristics to Ripper films were identified which are exploited to sexualize the narrative and these are: the speculated sexual motivation; the representation of the victims and the representation of the killer. These three themes are discussed separately and organize the data and the analysis. There are of course many more sexualizing processes and conventions than I document here. I confine myself to identifying how, through these three particular mediums, the narrative is dominated by sexual semiotics.

The primacy of sex as motivation

The use of female nudity and male sexual menace in Ripper film often borders on the pornographic and *New York Ripper* was refused certification by the BBFC (British Board of Film Classification) in 1984 and then certified as '18' with cuts to the original in 2001 (BBFC 2005). The principal objections were to scenes of naked women being graphically mutilated. Even Harper (2004), a fan of the 'slasher' genre, which shares many of the conventions of serial killer film, berates this film as plunging 'headlong into cruelty against women' with gore and lengthy soft core sex scenes that are difficult to get past. (2004:17) There is an underlying sexual menace in all Jack the Ripper film and the extent to which that sexual aspect is exploited varies, for example, in *From Hell* (Dir. Albert Hughes and Allen Hughes 2005) the image of a knife put to the breast of a female, or cutting the buttons from the bodice of a dress with the suggestion that the breast will be exposed or cut, powerfully links male violence, weapons and sexual excitement. The character of Abberline, in this film portrayed by the actor Johnny Depp, is presented as opium-addicted and it is in the guise of creating his drug-induced hallucinations that female nudity is again exploited. The entire film manipulates conventional male-centred hetero/sexual desire at the expense of the plot, or conversely it defines the plot.

Jack the Ripper (dir. David Wickes 1988) is less obviously and overtly concerned with female nudity but the victims are highly sexualized as are the representations of Victorian East End brothels as sanitary, romantic and genteel places. In *Jack the Ripper* (Jesus Franco 1976) there are two graphic depictions of rape of victims, the women are seen stripped and raped and the 'Ripper' also kills a woman as she performs an oral sex act on him. In *New York Ripper* (Lucio Fulci 1981) prostitutes are being mutilated in modern day New York and the sexual framing of this story is inescapably explicit. Although the killer does not attempt to have sexual intercourse with his victims, the use of females committing sex acts and female nudity throughout the film coupled with shots of naked women being attacked, makes the description 'pornographic' more appropriate than anything else it could be described as. The juxtaposition of extreme gratuitous violence, sexual acts and female nudity, explicitly centre the motivations of the killer in a sexual frame, conflating sex and violence. Although the sexual messages are clearly there, sexual intercourse is not always explicitly presented and Clover (1992) says 'actual rape is practically nonexistent in the slasher film, evidently on the premise that violence and sex are not concomitants but alternatives, the one as much a substitute and prelude for the other' (1992:29).

In *Ripper: Letter from Hell* (dir John E. Eyres 2001) the female victims are not Victorian prostitutes but sexually confident modern-day college students and a scene depicting one of the victim's indulging in a sex act with the killer, believing him to be someone else (he is masked), highlights two points – first, we are actually witnessing a rape and, secondly, we are also witnessing an act of casual sex in a public place. This could be seen as drawing parallels with the behaviour of prostitutes, who indulge in acts of casual sex consensually with men, with whom, in other circumstances they probably would not. *Whitechapel* is set in modern London but there is little attention paid to the victims, even the female Police Community Support Officer who appears in the first scene and is murdered later in the film is peripheral to both the male characters and the story being told. This is a significantly masculine film, the female characters are stereotyped feminized characterizations – the prostitutes, the heavily pregnant pathologist and the mutilated victims. This is a film about men.

In *The Jack the Ripper Conspiracies* (2003) which is a docudrama style, there was no dramatized re-enactment of a story or reference to rape. The visual reference to sexual motivation largely consisted of scenes depicting a male hand rubbing and caressing the bloodied and naked abdomen of a female, or caressing internal bloodied organs across the naked abdomen of a female whilst the sound of frantic and heavy breathing getting faster and faster as if in the throes of orgasm, dominates the soundtrack. This creates a very powerful message, where the bloodied, passive and naked female is a sexual stimulant for the orgasmic male. 'This linking of a normal sexual desire to an aberrant violent act of murder makes Jack the Ripper a particularly disturbed "rapist"' (Caputi 1987:14)

The primacy of sex in representing victims

The victims represent the 'serial' nature of the crimes, they can be grouped, categorized and counted. Simpson sees Jack the Ripper as the first serial killer 'simply because the Ripper's advent on the stage of media happened to coincide with the serial format as popularized in the Victorian press' (2000:36). His victims are remembered as prostitutes, this is how they are described and categorized in all Jack the Ripper media. Their prostitution is an important part of the narrative creating some of the meaning for the crimes and also making easy links between sexual acts and violence. It should be considered that indulging in acts of prostitution was not unusual for poverty stricken women of the time. Placed in its historical context, it is possible that most women in that particular part of London, at that time in history and at those times of night would have participated in prostitution at some point in their lives. In 1888 the Metropolitan Police documented twelve hundred prostitutes of low class in a specific area of the East End. According to Meikle (2003), Mayhew and Hemyng both disputed the official figures and felt that the true picture required them to be incremented by a factor of ten. This would put the figure at closer to twelve thousand casual prostitutes operating in the area. W.T. Stead (1885) in his series of articles in the *Pall Mall Gazette* speculated the number to be 50,000 or more. A killer attacking poverty-stricken women who had little means of support, especially in the culture of the time, would have been statistically likely to have attacked a prostitute, or a woman who had at some time indulged in prostitution, or even been labelled a prostitute merely because she had been arrested; Clive Emsley (2005) notes that often arresting police would catalogue drunken women as prostitutes regardless of whether they had any evidence to support this. Also the powers conferred in the Contagious Diseases Acts had seen many unaccompanied women removed to police stations and erroneously catalogued as prostitutes. In Victorian England prostitutes were considered the female equivalent of the male criminal class and the bodies of the victims left displayed in the street offered an 'awful warning of what happened when the natural order of things was broken' (Emsley 2005:96). In many films Jack the Ripper's motivations are speculated to be intimately related to the sexual transgression of the victims, a kind of moral crusade to 'clean the streets' (Ward Jouve 1988) and his methods reflect the potency of spectacle in expressing and reinforcing power. Jervis suggests that 'power existed through spectacle' (1998:55) and the era had a close historical relationship with state exercised public punishment and torture.

Clover (1992) sees the modern horror film as clearly drawing a cause-and-effect relationship between illicit sex and death. 'Killing those who engage in unauthorized sex amounts to a generic imperative of the slasher film' (1992:34). The intimation that femaleness is diminished by illicit sex and prostitution removes the burden from the film-makers and directors of representing Jack the Ripper as a killer of women, a blunt and brutal social statement that may alienate half the potential audience and require some kind of unpalatable story resolution.

In many of the films the prostitution of the victims is used to introduce both a purely sexual element as well as an element of sexual transgression. In *From Hell* a film which Meikle notes is 'scripted and dramatized in the formulaic manner of the typical Hollywood serial-killer thriller' (2003:191), a scene depicting the body of Martha Tabram (not universally considered a Ripper victim) in a mortuary, shows her surrounded by males, a police sergeant roughly lifts her skirts to reveal the groin area and says 'he removed her livelihood as a keepsake'. The exposing of the genital area of the victim and the accompanying words place female sexual anatomy and prostitution at the very centre of the motivations behind the crime. It should also be considered that although there were some 39 stab wounds to Tabram's body listed in the original post mortem report, no organs were missing and mention of specific injury to genitals is absent, though injury to the groin area is accepted as part of the abdominal injuries, most of the stab wounds were apparently to her chest. The 'soundbite' comment that the killer had removed her livelihood could be described as artistic licence by the scriptwriters, but the powerful message included in this scene transcends artistic interpretation. It is clearly stated that the prostitution of the victim is central to her injuries, that her 'unauthorized sex' is implicated in her death and mutilation.

Martha Tabram is speculated, in the film *From Hell*, to be the victim of a gang terrorizing prostitutes, and in this film Jack the Ripper is described by the Inspector Abberline character as 'altogether a different breed of killer' from Tabram's assailants, yet the genital mutilation or injury allegedly perpetrated by both killers is accepted as central to the modus operandi. The difference in the murders is seen as a matter of approach and method in the killer, not the nature of the injuries or mutilation suffered by the victim. The implied methodical and controlled technique used by Jack the Ripper in his disembowelment and display of the corpse is what sets him apart. It is interesting to note that although Jack the Ripper is represented as more 'evil' than Tabram's assailants in this film and others, her injuries are documented as 'committed in life' (*The Times 1888*) and this is alluded to in the film, whereas the mutilations on Jack the Ripper's victims were committed after death. It could be considered that a violent and prolonged attack 'in life' would be more sadistic and depraved than the violence perpetrated on a corpse. However, the symbolic value of Jack the Ripper's violence transcends the realities of the experience for the victim.

In *Love Lies Bleeding* (dir. William Tannen 1998) a female character asks why the Ripper is killing prostitutes in particular, the reply is:

> "Why not? They are easy targets, they walk the streets in the middle of the night when there's no-one around, they're defenceless, he was probably making a statement"

This quote appears to resist the dominant discursive constructions of sex and punishment as central, and places the victim's prostitution as relevant because it would make the women more easily available. However, when asked to elaborate on what type of statement the Ripper may be trying to make, the reply is: 'a moral statement, you know, rid the streets of this degrading form of life'. Later in this film the killer himself in answer to the question 'what is it do you think that drives a man like that?' replies 'Maybe he's heard the voice of God or perhaps he's trying to keep the world clean' exemplifying the relevance of prostitution in many of the films.

Jill the Ripper (dir. Anthony Hickox 2000) is a kind of resistance in that the Jack the Ripper character is female and is killing males. However, even in this inverted narrative the importance of prostitution and sex is evident. The killer is a prostitute who kills her male clients whilst they are tied and bound for sado/masochistic sex. She appears to remove their genitals. However, the female is a prostitute, the settings are sexual, the female is very attractive and the male victims are men with 'perverse' sexual desires. The killer turns out to be motivated by revenge. She is not directed by God or acting on her own sexual fantasies when she kills, neither is she on a moral crusade to clean the streets of men with perverted sexual desires. In this sense, although the genders have been reversed as regards victim and killer, the gendered conventions remain. The dominant discourse of sexual murder normally prescribes that the victim is female and the killer male. It would appear that this is the only element to be changed, it is not challenged or resisted and this is important. The film does not speculate that the original Jack the Ripper was female, neither does it speculate that a female killer would behave too far outside her expected gender behaviour. The woman is a prostitute, she is attractive and she is a victim of male sexual abuse. She seeks revenge for her victimization and is eventually killed by the male forces of law and order. No gender roles are challenged here. The male leads in this film brutally kill at least two other prostitutes senselessly and in this sense the narrative is merely 'adjusted' slightly to allow for a coherent story of a female Jack the Ripper. The men are still powerfully killing the women who are transgressing the code. In *Whitechapel* (dir. S.J. Clarkson 2009) it is briefly speculated that Jack could be Jill, but not a woman who would have sexual or 'masculine' drives; she is speculated to be stealing wombs because of her inability to conceive. In these films convention is followed in that women who kill have extrinsic rather than intrinsic motivations.

The docudrama 'Diary of Jack the Ripper' (1993 Image Entertainment) is a defence of the authenticity of the so-called diary of Jack the Ripper (Harrison 1998). In this version of events the prostitution of the victims is absolutely central to their victimization and this is clear. The language employed by the diarist is misogynistic in the extreme and the motivation is apparently the 'whoring' of his young wife. The diary is apparently written by a cotton merchant named James Maybrick who was known for his 'womanizing' and abuse of arsenic. To describe his wife's alleged infidelity as 'whoring', when he himself was reputed to be a 'womanizer' is a clear example of the gendered subjectivity employed, irrespective of whether it was written in 1888 or 2008. Not only are the victims killed because they are prostitutes or whores, it is also claimed by the diarist that God is compelling him. This construction of events is similar to the defence of Peter Sutcliffe who also claimed he was acting on the word of God. Ward Jouve (1988) comments on this aspect of the Yorkshire Ripper story:

> But tell me. Why was it that Sutcliffe could believe that God was ordering him to clean the streets by killing women? It's no good saying 'he was mad'. That explains nothing...and how come the reverse is not true? Why is it that no women go about murdering 'punters', convinced they're on a mission to rid the city of its litter? It's not just that the case is never reversed: we can't even imagine it being reversed.' (1988:33–4)

Ward Jouve's point illustrates that this particular aspect to the crimes of Peter Sutcliffe and Jack the Ripper is part of the discourse of sexual murder. Not only do self- appointed avengers of public morals principally target women, according to the definition of serial murder it is in an orgasmic rage; a motivation as contradictory as it is spurious. Whilst we allow these killers to simultaneously demonstrate offence at deviant sexuality whilst practising it, and call the inconsistency madness, we sidestep the only framework within which this inconsistency is given clarity; the hetero/patriarchal passive/aggressive, double standard, practice of sexual relations.

Within this framework women who transgress the moral code as it applies to female sexual behaviour are able to be represented as immoral, ungodly, dirty, non-feminine, debauched, evil and a danger to the fabric of society. Thus the framework allows or even encourages inspection of the sexual behaviour of female victims because it is potentially the reason for their violation. There is powerful resistance, or more particularly a constraint, within the discourse that disallows conceiving of male sexual behaviours in this way. In *Love Lies Bleeding* the hypocrisy of this position is commented on when the character who turns out to be the killer, blames the clients of prostitutes equally for spreading venereal disease in a debate on the wickedness of prostitution. It is a constant through all the films that the victims are prostitutes first and women second. It is also consistent that the victims are portrayed as wholly defined by their prostitution, they are one-dimensional in this respect. Only Mary Kelly, the final victim, is given extra dimensions to her character in some of the films, but having said that, even though she is portrayed as hating her 'work', she, like the other women is portrayed as having a life that wholly revolves around her identity as prostitute.

Not only are the victims in Jack the Ripper film sexual in that they are prostitutes, they are consistently represented as young and attractive, though it is clear from their descriptions and histories that they were not. All, apart from Mary Kelly were in their forties, all had alcohol problems and most had teeth missing. I note this to illustrate how culturally unattractive these women probably were, due to their abject poverty, poor health, lack of resources and possible alcohol addiction. Douglas and Olshaker describe the victims as 'relatively old, beaten down by life and fairly unattractive' (2000:65). In these films the actresses used to represent the victims are usually young, attractive and highly sexual. *The Secret Identity of Jack the Ripper* (2003 Harmony Gold USA) portrays the women far more realistically than most films but prefaces their appearance with an explicit denial of their beauty. However, where the victims are cast, they are invariably cast as that which they were not. In sanitizing the appearance and behaviour of the victims, more sympathy may well be elicited, but this sanitization and 'sexing up' of their appearance strengthens the sexual aspects of the story being told. The attractiveness of the victims is presented as central to their victimization, especially as sexual lust and sex acts form the body of the narrative; it is an important element in the story. In the interviews discussed in Chapter 5 I asked police officers about the murder of a teenager, all commented on her beauty. Several of them commented that it was unfair that in the *Crimewatch* reconstruction of her murder, the female cast as her was not as attractive as the victim, as if her beauty was an element that *needed* portraying.

In such films victim beauty sanitizes the violence against them, giving it an aesthetic which not only justifies enjoyment of the violence but turns it into edgy erotica. An advertising poster for *Jack the Ripper* (dir. Robert S. Baker and Monty Berman 1959) illustrates graphically in image and words the focus on male sexual stimulation; the victim is seen lying on her back apparently dead but still sexually 'posed' with one shapely leg lifted, bent and visible, the shape of her breasts accentuated beneath the legs of her killer and her long blonde hair strewn about the ground around her. She clearly is wearing high pointed heels and her dress is dishevelled. The words 'The swinging purse...the painted lips...the languid pose against the lamp post' position this victim, or all the victims, as one-dimensionally sexual and objects of male lust.

In *A Study in Terror* (dir. James Hill 1966), a young Barbara Windsor plays the part of Ripper victim, Annie Chapman. She appears as well-dressed, with immaculate make-up, jewellery, curly coiffed blonde hair with her cleavage clearly visible in a low- cut dress. Barbara Windsor, in her youth and perhaps still now, was or is considered something of a sex symbol. *From Hell* has final victim Mary Kelly played by Heather Graham, an actress with a lucrative modelling contract and so attractive she gains the love and respect of the chief police officer in the investigation; Annie Cook, a prostitute involved with a royal prince and played by actress Joanna Page, appears as young, slim, innocent and beautiful, and misted shots of her long and flowing blonde hair are combined with her air-brushed nudity when recreating a coitus with the prince. In *Whitechapel* the victims are largely invisible except the Mary Kelly parallel and she is a young, slim, intelligent and attractive nurse who escapes death and mutilation. In a modern re-telling of the story, *Letter from Hell* the victims are all young sexually precocious college students. The importance of these portrayals of female victims cannot be overstated, not only in that they accentuate the sexual dimension of the narrative, but in that they link beauty and sexual attractiveness to victimization. This frames the crimes as lust driven and makes representation of dead and mutilated women highly sexual, displaying some consonance between killer, film-maker and voyeur that this is a legitimate forum for sexual excitement.

The photographic images of the post mortem bodies of the victims of Jack the Ripper have become as iconic as the London fog and the

Gladstone bag. Sturken states that 'memory appears to reside within the photographic image to tell its story in response to our gaze' (1997:19). The sad and mutilated bodies of the canonical victims are the most powerful genuine artifacts that remain from these violent crimes. They evoke a kind of reality that brings the crimes away from the mythical, but as Sturken notes:

> They can lend shape to histories and personal stories often providing the material evidence on which claims of truth are based. (1997:20)

No one alive has a true memory of the crimes of Jack the Ripper – we must all rely upon historical text – yet these photographs are a direct link with the actual events, and those bodies forever captured at a particular moment in time and displayed alongside the current representations of the events, add an authenticity to the myths; the very few images, being forever associated with the stylized re-telling of the story. The photographic images of the bodies are displayed as spectacle, the corpses, naked and mutilated, are powerfully suggestive of passive sexual suffering. This acts to elevate their feminine status, but is also an inconvenient reminder that this isn't erotica and it isn't sexy. That they have died a 'grand' death mitigates for their transgression of the moral code and we, as voyeurs can feel profound sympathy for them.

The primacy of sex in representing killers

What is apparent in all types of Jack the Ripper film is that the killer is represented as sexually attractive and sexually obsessed and/or psychotic or psychopathic. Characteristics that may make a male sexually attractive are not necessarily related to his physical appearance as they are with women. In some of the films Jack the Ripper is played by tall, slim, young and striking looking actors as in *Love Lies Bleeding* (played by Paul Rhys), *Dr Jekyll and Sister Hyde* (played by Ralph Bates) and *Jack the Ripper* (played by Klaus Kinski) and *Whitechapel* (played by Paul Hickey). Other films use the wealth and power of the speculated killer to denote his sexual appeal, for example, in *From Hell* he is the Royal surgeon to the Queen, respected and admired by his peers with political and Royal influence. The classic image is somewhat sinister in a possibly attractive way, and is that of a tall, slim 'gentleman', wearing a long cloak, face shaded and carrying a Gladstone type bag, an image denoting class. In *Jack the Ripper* (Franco) he is played by veteran actor Klaus Kinski, and is portrayed as a man relentlessly sexually pursued by his landlady and various attractive prostitutes. In *From Hell* the possible suspects are all educated and privileged; there are two surgeons, one being the Queen's surgeon and a senior Special Branch officer and the Queen's grandson. Jack the Ripper is always seen in 'black tie' or 'white tie' evening dress with a top hat, long black cloak and white gloves. In *Jack's Back* (dir. Rowdy Herrington 1988) the killer copying Jack the Ripper's crimes turns out to be the senior doctor at an American 'free' clinic. Although this doctor is not presented as particularly attractive to any of the people he comes into contact with, this is because of his abrasive personality and not because of his physical appearance or lack of resources. Similarly in *Whitechapel* he is a doctor and he is charming and socially skilled, he is seen dining with the parallel victim to Mary Kelly just prior to an attempt to murder and mutilate her, and presenting her with a meal with all the social skills of a middle class educated man.

The cultural standard of the attractive male may include significant stature, both physically and socially. It is also common to represent males with a disregard for rules and standards as sexually attractive. Many attractive male attributes have been superimposed onto the image of Jack the Ripper, who in most film representations is presented as menacingly sexually appealing. Like the images of the victims he is not presented as what he might well have been; poor, physically unattractive, uneducated and socially inadequate. Lester states that victims of murderers resemble their killers in several ways and that 'typically they are the same age and the same race' (1995:5). If Jack the Ripper did resemble his victims, he would likely have been a poverty stricken, socially disadvantaged local man and this seems probable because he was able to move freely about the East End without drawing attention to himself. The possibility that he had medical knowledge, though this is not universally accepted (Odell 2006), has enabled speculation to drift from this profile to more socially advantaged suspects. Frayling (1986) cites three of the main characterizations of Jack the Ripper and questions their potential accuracy:

> What is surprising, on the face of it, is that these explanations are still accepted by self styled 'Ripperologists' and their readers, when there is so much evidence, social and psychological, to contradict them. (1986:205)

There was much speculation at the time of the murders that the killer was of foreign extraction, quite possibly a poor Jewish immigrant which reflects the racist sentiments of the time. However, when Jack the Ripper is represented as British and white, as in these modern films, he is at once clever, attractive and socially advantaged and Dyer (2002) notes that serial killers are widely perceived to be white males who kill white females:

> In the hands of serial killers it [killing] is cerebral and clean, two of the master values of whiteness. This produces one of the dominant images of the serial killer: the cold genius of death. (2002:112)

Whilst Jack the Ripper is required to be sexually attractive, of the professional or upper classes and clever, he is portrayed as white and is jealously guarded as such. Schmid (2005), for example, notes that when the American Hughes brothers were suggested as directors for the film *From Hell* there was concern that they were not the best choice to make a film about a British Victorian serial killer. However, this was not because they were American, but because they were black. Jack the Ripper, despite his brutal use of violence against women, will be fiercely defended as being a white British man whilst his crimes are perceived as methodical, skilled, heterosexual and cerebral.

The legacy of Jack the Ripper

There is a significant legacy from Jack the Ripper's crimes. Whether this legacy originated with misogynistic interpretations of the violence, or from the violence itself, is a matter for debate. It is true that sexually charged danger and threats to women have been a staple of entertainment media since the birth of the cinema. But can we compare the menacingly seductive performance of Count Dracula, or the impotent desires of King Kong as comparable to the blunt, anti-aestheticism of the actions of a woman hating butcher? To problematize the sexualizing of these crimes is not to deny that sexual excitement can be heightened by danger in many forms, or that men and women might indulge their own fantasies in this way. It is to suggest that it is only the brutal murder of *women* that is an accepted site for sexual stimulation and that this should deeply concern women. When, for example, we talk of these crimes as erotic, who is stimulated here? It is certainly not the victims despite their orgasmic death throes. The sexual symbolism and eroticism privileges the male perspective and male hetero/sexuality. In this sense male sexual fantasy represents human sexual fantasy; female sexuality is subsumed into its discursive embrace and is reconstructed to complement the sadism, as an inherent masochism. Women enjoy violation in this discourse – this means that mutilation, disembowelment and strangulation are legitimately and generically sexual.

Frayling (1986) in discussing film rapists and murderers posits that 'they are frightening but only in the way that a nightmare is frightening; everything is fine when you wake up' (1986:175) and Pinedo claims that they are a simulation of horror like a 'roller coaster ride' (1997:5). Whether these images and the loaded narratives are discarded as soon as consumption of them stops is certainly a matter for debate. It seems unlikely, for example, that both genders, outside the celluloid buffers of the East End/Ripper simulacrum, experience the hetero/sexual symbolism and misogynistic violence, similarly. The very idea that women can awake from consumption of such institutionally constructed and authorized violence as if alighting from a fairground roller coaster; full of adrenaline but otherwise free from any pernicious effects is, potentially at least, anti-intuitive. I am not suggesting that women simply identify with the female characters and men with the males, there are clearly as Clover (1992) notes, many layers of cross identification. My argument is that we are being shown over and over again who the victims are, and who they are not. It is even difficult to see how Clover's 'final girl' might subvert the 'woman as victim' constancy. Clover describes her as a victim-hero, a developed and multi-dimensional character who escapes death and appears, even if only temporarily, to triumph over the serial killer. The strong and resourceful woman is just as much a fertile ground for victimization as the stereotypically fragile and insipid; she can be chased, frightened and sexually menaced in a way which would be impossible for a male. The term victim should not be simplistically equated with weakness, fragility or passivity. What I argue is that we surely cannot separate the messages in these films from the warnings from loved ones, the police and even employers to avoid dark public spaces and to contain sexuality; or from the omnipresent narratives of sexual violence that are over-represented in press reporting; or from the potential lived experience of sexual and/or domestic abuse; or from the myriad of other sites which reinforce these messages like advertising, pornography or art and literature. It is well established that women take many precautions to avoid the dangers posed by strangers and these are written into their behavioural practices at both a sub conscious and conscious level. This is a discursive practice. When these sexual threats have such a profound effect on the psyche of women, how can we assume that reinforcing the threat, in whatever form, has no lasting effect?

Quite apart from the fear women may experience, is the conflating of rape and murder which is exemplified in Jack the Ripper films; the wider effects of this practice are discussed more fully in Chapter 7 but the skewed perception of rape, the prevalence of Rape Trauma Syndrome and the increasing sexualization of violence against women is part of the legacy of the Jack the Ripper narrative. The strap line from the film *From Hell* spoken by Jack the Ripper: 'one day men will look back and say I gave birth to the twentieth century' is menacingly prescient.

5
Violence Against Women in News Report Narratives

Introduction: journalistic culture

There have been concerns expressed by scholars of news media that journalists do not act in a socially responsible manner or with a strong code of ethics when reporting sexual violence and that journalistic culture in this respect is problematic (Carter and Weaver 2003, Greer 2003, Howe 1998, Carter 1998, Soothill and Walby 1991). Much research tells us that the news media misrepresent sexual violence against women to a significant degree (Greer 2003, Carter 1998, Howe 1998, Soothill and Walby 1991) both in the amount of coverage which is dedicated to apparently atypical events and the narrow framing of the narrative. Carter and Weaver (2003) argue that most journalists operate without a clearly defined framework of ethics when covering violence and as a result reporting may contribute to 'public misunderstandings, of the complexities of violent situations' (2003:22) and they state that:

> Cameron and Frazer (1987) argue that representations of sexual violence are endemic to Western culture, having roots deeply embedded in patriarchy. In their view, the popular press has long drawn upon a traditional (male) fascination with sexual violence symbolized by figures like Jack the Ripper in the nineteenth century and Peter Sutcliffe (The Yorkshire Ripper) in the 1980s.(Carter and Weaver 2003:36)

As has been noted in Chapter 1 it is difficult to pin down exactly what sexual violence is and Howe's (1998) argument that violence against women is 'sexed' rather than sexual may account for the disproportionate amount of 'sexual' violence reported. It seems that gendered violence and sexual violence are interchangeable concepts such is the extent to which violence against women by men is reconstructed in news reports as having a sexual aetiology rather than perhaps, what could be described as a social hetero/sexual aetiology or even an auto-telic dimension. In this sample of news reports it was found that in all the categories of violence examined the concept of sex had primacy in defining motivation. Even in reporting of cases of domestic violence, which is limited in newspapers to stories of domestic homicide, the narrative situated the motivation in a sexual frame.

Greer (2003) argues that it is event-based reporting practice that leads to a story type narrative dominating the coverage of sexual violence against women. Incidents of violence or homicide are individualized and journalism fails in this respect to uncover or discuss the social conditions which may give rise to such violence. Extreme examples of offending will naturally attract the most coverage and crimes which occur in a public place and are perpetrated by a 'psychotic stranger' form a definite event in the eyes of the press and lend themselves to sensational report-ing of a 'story'. *Guardian* Journalist Julie Bindel examined a weeklong 'snapshot' of rape reporting and found a disproportionate number of stories documenting atypical events. She cites, for example, the case of Austrian Josef Fritzl who hid his daughter in a basement to routinely abuse her over many years, and John Worboys, the taxi driver convicted of 19 charges of rape committed against female customers as he worked. Bindel found that it was the more shocking assaults that were reported at the expense of other equally serious sexual violence (Bindel 2009). The over-reporting of extreme or shocking violence can create the impression that those events reflect the commonplace characteristics of a crime of violence against a female. Young (1998) says that 'these types of rape, which should be considered aggravated rapes, tend to be seen as real, at the expense of situations in which victims and assailant know each other' (1998:146). She argues that because of this these assaults can be de-criminalized as 'non-rape', 'that is seduction gone wrong, or a lovers' quarrel, or a vengeful feminine allegation' (1998:146). This applies equally to representation of offenders, whilst they are considered to be 'evil others', issues relating to their similarities to 'ordinary' men cannot be addressed. Greer found that terms like 'beast' and 'monster' were consistently used to describe perpetrators of crimes that were sub-stantively different in terms of deviousness, dangerousness and level of harm done:

> The indiscriminate use of these stereotypical labels makes explicit a reductionist sentiment underpinning the majority of sex crime

stories. ...Predatory child sex abusers, people who steal underwear and consenting adult homosexuals who engage in sexual acts in a public place are the same – they are all 'sex beasts', 'sex fiends' and 'sickos'. (2003:140)

It is precisely the argument of many news and crime scholars that the normality of gendered violence and the ordinariness of its victims and perpetrators is hidden in the language used and the types of narratives chosen. However, it is also argued that the extreme examples routinely reported on, are part of a continuum of offending with identical precipitating social causes to less extreme examples, which are not explored. Carter illustrates this point when she tells of the case of Marc Lepine who, in 1989 entered a room in the Ecole Polytechnique in Montreal armed with a gun. He demanded that women stand on one side of the room and men on the other. He proceeded to shoot the women shouting 'feministes'. Carter states that Lepine was described in the press as a 'monster' but that this characterization of him was challenged by some who argued that there was only a 'difference of degree' (1998:219) in this spectacular newsworthy event and the mundane and droning cases of domestic violence that occur every day in their millions across the world. Cases like that of Lepine are not linked in any way to other cases of male violence but are represented as bizarre and unusual isolated incidents perpetrated by men with mental health issues.

When cases of rape are reported it is clear that the individualizing of the event using what Carter and Weaver (2003) call a 'his word against her word' framing, readily enables focus on the main 'characters' turning the report into a story drawing from durable stereotypes and popular moral standpoints. The perpetrators of the violence can be described as 'beasts' or 'perverts' and distanced from 'ordinary' men and it is easy also to create a female lead who appears blameworthy in some way which may distance her from 'ordinary' women and create a feeling of comfort and distance from the crime.

Carter and Weaver (2003) illustrate that gender stereotypes permeate crime stories when discussing the reporting of the murder of TV presenter Jill Dando in 1999. They claim that Dando's 'nice girl' image was called in to question during Barry George's trial for her murder and attracted headlines like 'Dando Suspect: Was He Driven Mad by Sexy Pose?' They discuss how the *Daily Star* speculated that George was 'enraged' by a picture of Dando in 'racy leather gear' without clarifying why he would be 'enraged'. The implications of this type of dialogue are powerful and as they note 'women are much more likely to be blamed for their own victimization, even death, if it is thought that they somehow failed to contain their sexuality within patriarchal limits' (2003:40). Benedict notes that sex crimes have a unique ability to touch upon the public's deep seated beliefs about gender roles and sums up the problems noted in much research:

> the press has a long tradition of slighting women, which, compounded by the anti female bias in our language and the myths about rape determine more than any other factor how sex crimes are portrayed by the press. (1992:9)

This chapter explores British print news reporting of violence against women, specifically rape and/or murder, through case studies. It will be argued that the murder of women is regularly sexualized and conversely that sexual assaults on women are framed within a discourse of murder. Consequently, where one aspect of the attack exists, journalists will speculate the existence of the other. Whilst it is accepted that there is ostensible diversity in print media, in this research it was discovered that there was remarkable consistency across publications in their production of narratives which represent violence against females as sexual. Six case studies are used which represent six different categories of violence which include rape and/or murder which are:

	Murder without rape	*Murder with rape*	*Rape*
Stranger assault	Margaret Muller	Hannah Foster	*Victim X*
Domestic assault	Vicky Fletcher	Louise Beech	*Spousal rape*

A seventh case study is offered which has a slightly different focus; that is the murder of Camilla Petersen by Richard Kemp in 2003. This case is used to explore the way that the offender in the case was constructed as one dimensionally 'consumed by sex' (Lacombe 2008). The analysis for the six case studies is confined to seven British news publications which represent three broad categorizations of newspaper; tabloid, middle range and broadsheet, and the newer forum of online news media. They are: the *Sun,* the *Daily Mirror,* the *Daily Express,* the *Daily Mail,* the *Guardian, The Times* and the *BBC Online News.* The *BBC Online News* was chosen specifically because of its unique coverage of regional news stories which are often lost in national reporting. In the discussion of the reporting of Camilla's murder which is separate, all British publications which reported on the story are used, both print and online.

The primacy of sex in gendering violence

Both the murders of Margaret Muller and Hannah Foster were perpetrated by individuals unknown to the victim; these were stranger assaults. Hannah was sexually assaulted, though this was not revealed to the press in the early stages of the investigation and could only be speculated, but Margaret was not. Both murders were committed in public places. Both murders also, were described in press reporting as 'random' attacks, in other words Margaret and Hannah were not selected for any particular reason and were merely in the wrong place at the wrong time. However, it is clear from the reports that 'random' actually means 'random female' and not 'random person'. This supposition serves to 'gender' the assault making explicit the assumption that both Hannah and Margaret were killed *because* they were female. By this I mean that both these murders appeared to be 'isolated' incidents in that they had not at this time been linked to any other offences; they did not form part of a series of assaults where the targeted victims were all female. However, the police and the press immediately speculated that women only should take care. They did not consider any other group to be at risk. This killer, in their opinion, targeted a female and if they were to strike again it would be another female; therefore this is considered a gendered assault in the earliest stages. This kind of immediate supposition also indicates a resistance to perceive adult males as victims of 'random killers', a resistance that is part of a discourse of sexual murder and can be identified as a discursive constraint.

On the day after Margaret's death a headline in the *BBC Online News* declared 'Joggers Warned after Park Murder'. The opening paragraph read: 'Police have advised women to take care after an American artist was stabbed to death in an East London park while she was out jogging' (*BBC Online News* 2003a). Clearly it was not joggers who were deemed to be at risk, but specifically female joggers; police specifically warned women to take care. The murder was, however, described as 'a random attack' by the *BBC*, *The Times*, the *Sun*, the *Daily Mirror* and the *Daily Express*. Hannah Foster's murder, like that of Margaret Muller was described as random and similar to warnings in reporting of Margaret's murder, it was women who were warned to be vigilant and careful:

> It looks like there is every chance that this was a random killing...we would advise women living in this area to exercise extreme caution and not to walk alone in the dark. (Bird 2003)

Student Hannah Foster found murdered after a night out was probably the victim of a random attack...there is no indication she knew her attacker. It may well be that Hannah was in the wrong place at the wrong time...and he (police officer) warned women to be vigilant. (North 2003)

The murder of Marsha McDonnell occurred less than 24 hours after the murder of Margaret Muller and the two events were often linked in reports. Marsha's murder was also described as 'random' but the *Daily Mirror* states 'Women are warned to take extra caution' (Edwards 2003). An interesting dimension in the case of Marsha McDonnell was the 18-year-old male who presented himself to the police as a possible victim of the same attacker:

A few weeks after Marsha's death an 18 yr old boy was attacked by a hooded man who lunged at him with a blunt instrument in nearby Hampton Hill – The boy escaped unhurt. (*BBC Online News* 2003b)

The *BBC Online News* followed up this aspect of the story:

An 18yr old who claimed he was the victim of an attack linked to the murder of Marsha McDonnell has been arrested for wasting police time. The man was arrested by Scotland Yard's specialist crime directorate and bailed to return on Wednesday. (*BBC Online News* 2003d).

It is curious to note the change in descriptive of this 18 year old. Whilst considered a victim of a serial killer still at large, he is described as 'a boy'. Once it is established that he is not a victim, he is described as a man. Again the scope of the discourse restricts presenting adult males as victims or potential victims of this type of 'stranger' killer. In this sample of reporting, adult heterosexual males were not considered to be victims or potential victims of 'thrill killers', 'random killers', 'serial killers' or 'stranger killers'. In a leader article in the *Daily Express* Gary Mason laments the problems police have with detecting 'stranger murders' (Mason 2003b). At no point in the report, even though the word 'random' is used five times, is an adult male victim named or referred to. The murders of Margaret Muller, Marsha McDonnell and Hannah Foster are given as examples, as well as the crimes of Peter Sutcliffe, Patrick Duffy (this actually refers to John Duffy and was an error) and Robert Black who exclusively targeted females. The report clearly links the term 'stranger murder' to murders of women and children. In a report headlined 'Killed at Random' (Riches 2003a), the *Sun* chronicles 'the grim toll' by illustrating the growing problem of random killings and cites the cases of Hannah Foster, Margaret Muller, Letisha Shakespeare, Charlene Ellis, Milly Dowler, Marsha McDonnell, Holly Wells, Jessica Chapman and Sarah Robson. All examples given are of female victims.

The infused and inescapable certainty that Margaret, Hannah and Marsha's gender was central to their victimization in the news reporting is so powerful that terms like 'random' and 'totally indiscriminate' can be used without prejudicing the assumption that these terms refer only to females. The term 'random' was used in the earliest stages but if these were truly random assaults, then warnings should be more general and aimed at 'joggers', for example, or park users in general. It appears that we can assume immediately, because the victim was female, that a female was specifically targeted and not a 'random' person and that she was targeted *because* she was female. It should be a source of more popular critical concern that we routinely accept that *women* face this kind of threat without any serious public debate as to why this should be so except to cite the analytically nebulous concept of sex.

A second attack in a London park some months after Margaret's murder and (wrongly) linked to her killing, made speculation that women were targeted in these 'random' attacks confirmed. The *Guardian* displayed the headline 'Women Warned after Second Park Stabbing' and stated:

> A knife wielding murderer who targets lone women joggers in public parks could strike again. (Bowcott 2003:4)

The Times had a substantial report about the fear women have because of the two attacks:

> Women are frightened to run in London parks. ...A terrifying killer hunts lone women in the parks of North London. (Campbell Johnston 2003a)

Margaret's murder was a particularly stark example of the gendering of stranger assaults as was the example of the murder of Marsha McDonnell. Both these women were killed by a stranger, quickly and with no further assault. Margaret was stabbed in the back and neck and Marsha was hit about the head with a blunt instrument. There would appear to be no reason to think that these women were killed because of their gender unless the narrative is telling the story of a 'sexual murder'. In assuming a crime is gendered, the relationship between victim and offender becomes pivotal in making meaning of what may have happened. Where the victim is female and the offender is speculated or known to be male, the relationship appears to be prescribed a heterosexual dynamic. It is the heterosexual dynamic that produces the gendered subjectivity. Thus the relationship between the offender and victim is indivisible from subjective constructions of gender that are culturally prescribed. The assumption that Margaret Muller was killed because she was female is illustrated further in comments made by celebrity gardener Tommy Walsh who was jogging with his wife in the park at the time of the assault. They had, at about the time Margaret was killed, become separated and both were running alone. Speaking to press on the anniversary of Margaret's death he said:

It could quite easily be the first anniversary of my wife's death but the killer was looking for a woman on her own. (*Daily Mirror* 2004)

The *Daily Express* gave this story the headline 'Star's Wife Escaped Park Killer' (*Daily Express* 2004). The *Daily Mail* stated:

(Tommy Walsh) revealed how his wife nearly fell victim to the killer of American artist Margaret Mulle.' (Taylor 2004)

No one speculates, not even Walsh himself, that *he* could have been the victim of this assailant. This precept works not only to homogenize violence against women which gives the violence a very particular meaning and emphasizes a gender dynamic, but to represent women as the natural target of stranger killers. The use of the word 'random' in this context actually indicates that a discourse of 'sexual murder' is framing the response. What is more interesting is not so much that the assumption is evident, but that it was immediate. Crucially, it seems that the discourses of gendered and sexual murder have merged, with the term 'sexual' having predominance and sidelining the social and political issues originally raised in discourses of gendered violence.

The primacy of sex in skewing perceptions

In homicide reporting there is a focus on extreme forms of killing, i.e. serial killers and stranger killers, and Lees (2002) states that this concentration leads to a perception that the typical murderer is psychopathic. In most cases of sexual assault and murders of women the offender is far more likely to be someone known to them and not typically psychopathic. For example, as noted in Chapter 1, of the 208 women killed in 2007/08 only 28, or 13 per cent, were killed by a stranger (Coleman 2009) and in 2008/09 only 23, or 11 per cent (Coleman and Osborne 2010). It is a criticism that extreme examples of violence are starting to look as if they are the standard along with the idea that most offenders are typically abnormal and psychopathic. Stranger violence is represented as a phenomenon of modern society, a real cultural issue with women represented as being in real and significant danger. A report in the *Express* by a former editor of *Police Review* describes the growing number of stranger murders as alarming and claims that police are struggling to deal with the growing numbers of rapes and murders by strangers (Mason 2003b). It is interesting to note the collocation of rapes and murders in this report; a logical pairing of the offences which makes it clear that we are talking about sexualized violence against women in particular and not addressing the much higher rate of stranger violence perpetrated between and against men (Brookman 2005, Coleman 2009). *The Times* further discusses the apparent phenomenon of 'thrill killing' in an article one year on from Margaret Muller's murder and marking the anniversary of her death, which states explicitly that this type of killing is rising. The phenomenon of stranger murder and rape that is represented as a growing menace is not linked in these discussions to social attitudes towards women and can only serve to create fear without any attempt to seriously question why there may be the rise in the type of assaults documented. The spectre of rape was the weapon described by Brownmiller in her 1975 polemic which stalked women; the spectre of the sex killer/serial killer is far more dangerous but is framed in exactly the same terms appearing to escalate the threat posed to women.

The primacy of sex as motivation

The gender female appears to be the catalyst for the normative assumption of *presence* of sexual motivation or assault in news reporting of violence against women. The assumption is instant and is not so much established in reports as *re-established* and this is an important distinction. There is little need to establish sexual motivation in the first instance; it is already established by the gender of the victim. The discourse of sexual murder very powerfully dictates that women are killed for sexual reasons therefore this is merely re-established or proved. The presumption of presence of sexual motivation prompts the reader to understand the offence in a particular way and must be disproved if the crime is to be re-assessed or re-conceptualized. There is no effort in any of the reporting to undermine the assumption and this makes it very difficult to perceive the offences in any other way than sexually moti-vated, the language does not exist to reconstruct or re-define how these offences could be understood within this discourse of sexual murder.

When Hannah Foster's body was found in undergrowth by the side of a road the state of dress of her body was the subject of much comment in the news reports, all reporting described the finding of Hannah's fully clothed body:

> 'Her fully clothed body was found in undergrowth.' (*BBC Online News* 2003c)

> '[A] walker found Hannah's fully clothed body next to Allington Lane.' (Pyatt 2003)

Hannah's body was not found, her *fully clothed* body was found and this is a critical distinction. It reveals more about the scope of the discourse than it does about the crime. By this I mean, the fact that Hannah's body was clothed does not inform the reader of anything, but its con-sistent mention does reveal that this piece of information is relevant within the discourse. The implication is that the reader would expect that her body would be unclothed, or her clothing in disarray. Coupled with this piece of information was negative reference to sexual assault. Several newspapers commented that there was no evidence to suggest that Hannah had been sexually assaulted and this was part of a state-ment from the police. These two statements, that the body was fully clothed and that there was no evidence of sexual assault would seem to delegitimize further speculation that the murder was sexually motivated. However, sexual motivation is a fundamental part of the discourse and these negative statements are built upon in further reporting:

> There were no signs that she had been sexually assaulted but police have not ruled out that the killer's motive was sexual. They have contacted known sex offenders in the area. (Bird 2003)

> A sexual motive has not been ruled out and cops have been studying sex offences in the area. (Riches 2003b)

Similarly there were no indications that Margaret Muller had been sexu-ally assaulted:

> Even though there was apparently no sexual motive behind either attack (Margaret Muller and another female jogger) experts believe

the killer might indulge in sadistic sexual fantasies. (Wright *et al.* 2003)

The *Express* speculates possible sexual assault as the motive, and then denies any sign of a sexual assault suggesting that the offender fled quite early in the assault (Chapman and Twomey 2003) implying that the motivations were not apparent because the offender fled before the motive became apparent. The *Daily Mail* quoted the officer leading the enquiry:

> There was no obvious sexual motivation for the murder...the only motive for this murder was the killer's gratification. (Reid 2003)

In stating that the sexual motivation was not *obvious,* the narrative is leading the story to less obvious sexual motivations which are indicated by use of the word 'gratification' and may include deviant sexual practices.

The use of official and professional sources and quotes in the reports adds authority and legitimate 'knowledge' to the speculations. The police provide much of the information and their 'knowledge' of these crimes provides a legitimating voice for the inclusion of sexual elements in the narrative; the police are 'experts' who are authorized to speak, they are what Hall *et al.* (1978) describe as 'primary definers', thus the truth of these crimes is being institutionally structured. Detective Chief Superintendent John Shatford is quoted as saying:

> We believe this killer is turned on by the act of stabbing. (*BBC Online News* 2003e)

Other reports include the voice of 'experts':

> Detectives are investigating a possible link between the murder of Margaret Muller and the killing 11 years ago of Rachel Nickell...and in both cases criminal profilers described the offender as a risk taker who hated attractive women. (*Daily Mail* 2003)

> Experts believe the killer might indulge in sadistic sexual fantasies. He could be singling out victims who remind him of a woman he believes mistreated him. (Wright 2003)

Though the killer may be acting out of hatred, it is suggested that this is manifested in 'sadistic sexual fantasies' and when comparing the crime to the murder of Rachel Nickell, a hatred of *attractive* women is specified. In the first quote, the superintendent uses the words 'turned on' which have clear sexual connotations. The standard assumption of sexual assault or motivation is not always established in fact but the assumption remains stubbornly and is justified by conceiving of 'sexual' in alternative ways. The suggestion that misogyny may be a motivation is evidence of a circulating counter-discourse. However, there is also an apparent resistance to participate in the wider discursive scope of this approach. Whilst it is speculated in selected quotes from criminal profiling experts that hatred of women or difficulties in relationships with women may form part of the motivation, this is under explored. Hatred of women or misogyny is spoken of as if it were in no need of further explanation with no discussion of why 'women haters' exist or why they hate so much they kill, and why there is no corresponding category of man hating killer. Ironically, it is interesting to note here that feminists are often described in the most pejorative terms as 'man haters' with plenty of discussion about why this makes them unstable and deviant. This apparent counter-discourse of misogyny, rather than sex, being the motivation is nullified by reconstructing it as sexual motivation and so eliminating its status as a challenge or alternative to the dominant sexual frame. The feminist position is subsumed into the sexual discourse and those alternative positions become another manifestation of sexual lust. Their acquired sexual conventionality then undermines them as a radical departure; misogyny becomes a kind of paraphilia in this context.

It is not only that motivations are homogenized, offence characteristics are too. In the case of rape and/or murder of women the defining characteristics of a rape and a stranger murder are almost indistinguishable. Antoni Imiela was convicted of raping women and girls who were strangers to him and an example of the confusion that often exists between rape and murder can be seen in a quote from the *Crimewatch* online web page advertising cases solved with the aid of the *Crimewatch* programme, and specifically related to Imiela's crimes:

> In October 2002, following one of the biggest hunts for a serial rapist since the Yorkshire Ripper, police appealed on *Crimewatch* for help to catch a man who became known as the M25 rapist. (*Crimewatch* 2005)

The Yorkshire Ripper was not a serial rapist, he was a murderer. The murders are not mentioned in this piece, the speculated rapes having equivalence with murders and perhaps suggesting that rape is a causal dimension in fatal violence. The following passage is taken from the Rape Crisis website and further illustrates the way in which serial murder and rape are routinely blended:

> Fact: ...The popular image of a rapist is of someone who spends all his time lurking in bushes ready to pounce on lone women. The police interviewed Peter Sutcliffe nine times before they discovered that he was the Yorkshire Ripper. He didn't fit their image of a mass rapist and murderer because he was married, had a steady job and a nice home. (*Rape Crisis* 2005)

In the London Rape Crisis Centre publication *Sexual Violence, the Reality for Women'*(Rape Crisis 1999) it is stated in the 'Myths and realities' chapter that:

> The crimes of Peter Sutcliffe, the 'Yorkshire Ripper', in 1975–80 only became truly shocking when he moved from "just raping prostitutes" to attacking "nice girls too" (1999:13)

Peter Sutcliffe is clearly being portrayed as a rapist and this is possibly a reference to the symbolism attached to his acts of violence that allows them to be seen as 'virtual rapes'. It is also interesting that during Antoni Imiela's trial for rape, the prosecution barrister referred to him mistakenly as a serial killer. Imiela was reportedly incensed:

> During his questioning of Imiela at Maidstone Crown Court, Mr. Dennis had referred to the attacks as being the work of a serial killer. Mr. Dennis said it was a "slip of the tongue" and told the jury: "There is no suggestion that Mr. Imiela has killed anyone". Imiela flanked by four guards, mouthed the word b****cks and then leaned forward and yelled: "why don't you tell them I have no sexual offences either you b*****d"' (Shaw 2004) (Omissions as original)

It is noteworthy that Imiela wished it to be known that he had no previous record for sexual offences. Whilst his reason for this may have been to distance himself from the crimes, it is common practice to search for known sex offenders when 'stranger' rapes *or* murders of women occur; there is a link between these offences and sex offenders in particular. When Imiela was first arrested his friends and family were interviewed for their reactions and his brother is quoted as saying: 'I can't believe anyone could think this of my brother. He is just not like that. He has a good sex life with his wife...' (Gysin 2002). This comment indicates that the motivation to rape was perceived to be part of a sexual *need*. An article in *The Times* describes how criminal profilers will have to re-write their books because of their failure to identify Imiela as a suspect:

> Experts trawled through thousands of criminal records and medical files for a year trying to match the Trophy Rapist but police concede that Imiela 'ticked none of the boxes'. Detective Superintendent Colin Murray, of Kent Police said 'Imiela is in a category of his own. (Smith and Tendler 2004)

Imiela had a criminal record for violence and lived near the location of the first assault, but because he wasn't a known sex offender he was discounted. Detective Superintendent Murray commented further that: 'there were other potentially more interesting subjects who had previous sexual offences who scored higher' (Smith and Tendler 2004). The relative importance of previous sexual offending in predicting serious future offending is addressed in Soothill *et al.* (2002) and is discussed in Chapter 6. The same kinds of problem existed in the Yorkshire Ripper investigation and Nicole Ward Jouve's (1988) feminist examination of the manhunt for and trial of, Peter Sutcliffe, identifies overt sexual discrimination and assumptions on the part of the police and journalists. The police failed to identify Sutcliffe over a period of six years of criminal activity. One of the reasons for this was seen to be the concentration on a (hoax) tape recording of what was thought to be the killer's voice. Ward Jouve states:

> But the whole enquiry began to go hopelessly astray when the Ripper squad received, and decided to consider as authentic, letters and a cassette tape from a man who called himself "Jack" (1988:9)

The similarities to the case of Jack the Ripper are crystal clear. Sutcliffe had already been dubbed a 'Ripper', he had apparently, at least in the early stages, appeared to single out prostitutes for victimization and he had brutally violated the bodies of the victims. The tape and letters, similar to correspondence received by the police during the investigation into Jack the Ripper's murders, may have received so much attention because of their links to the original Jack the Ripper, and the hoaxer called himself Jack; he had even copied extracts from Jack the Ripper correspondence of 1888. This for them was a series of sex killings and they must have believed that they were dealing with a set of crimes so similar to the original that their assumptions were wholly justified. However these assumptions were of little help in identifying Sutcliffe or understanding his motivations:

> There was considerable surprise at who the now self confessed killer turned out to be. He had been imagined as an unmarried social outcast, a monster'. (Ward Jouve 1988:10)

Assumptions about so-called sex killers are often inaccurate and there is always surprise when these killers are finally identified. Often they do not present as sexual deviants or as socially inept and sinister weirdos with no social or familial networks. Maninder Pal Singh Kohli who was convicted of the rape and murder of Hannah Foster did not have a record for sex offences and was identified *despite* the assumption that sex offenders should be targeted. None of the offenders identified in this sample and from the police interviews was listed as sex offenders. The standard assumption and subsequent centrality of sexual motivation and assault does not appear to aid in understanding violence against women or apprehending offenders. Gekoski (2005) states that: 'When we look at research done into the backgrounds of serial killers we see that if they have any past convictions they are hardly ever serious and usually not sexual' (2005:11). Similarly Sample (2006) found that sex offenders as a category were one of the least likely offending groups to commit a subsequent homicide (2006:240). In fact from her study Sample stated that 'robbed and killed' more accurately reflects a clustering of criminal behaviours than 'raped and killed' (2006:244).

Whilst in a murder investigation there is a standard assumption of presence of sexual assault or motivation, in reporting rape assaults there is an equivalent presumption that the rape could have ended up as a murder. In reporting rapes the sexual motivation is popularly and problematically established by the presence of sexual intercourse; there is a simultaneous stressing of a threat to the victim's life. Brownmiller observed that 'one could almost get the idea from reading the tabloids that a rape can easily wind up as a murder' (1975:197). Lisa Sample also reports that media reporting of sex offending can 'easily lead people to believe that sex offenders are murderers as well' (2006:232) and that there is a suggestion that 'rape is a precursory crime to homicide with the two offences intricately intertwined' (2006:232). Similarly in a list of published rape myths it is stated that: 'FACT Rape is potentially life-threatening. Whatever a person does to survive the assault is the appropriate action' (University of Minnesota 2009). The spectrum of rape characteristics and potential outcomes sees the threat to life as absolutely integral to the assault.

The reporting of Imiela's crimes included significant referral to threat to life of the victim and this was achieved by describing the fear of death felt by the victims and quoting Imiela's threats to kill:

> She told police officers she thought she would die during the horrific attack (Branigan 2002)

> You overwhelmed your victims with brute force. Most thought that they would die by your hands' (Smith and Tendler 2004)

> 'Afterwards he bound her feet with her bra and said 'don't move for five minutes or I'll come back and slit your throat'...She later said 'I thought I was going to die' (Bain 2004)

The reporting of the spousal rape assaults similarly included fear of death or grievous violence and in the *Express* a report tells of a man attempting to strangle his wife before raping her (Fagge 2003). A report in the *Mirror* states:

> He also subjected his wife to a violent rape and beat her senseless. (Foster 2003)

By selecting rape assaults that include overt aggravating violence and stressing an implied or real threat to kill, the criteria for what a rape is, is set. It should also be considered that threats, real or implied can be received as very real by the victim, especially in a culture where there is such a strong association between rape and murder. However, so-called acquaintance or date rapes where little violence may be necessary to complete the offence are significantly devalued irrespective of the experience of the victim and the split in opinion is exemplified by columnists like Sue Carroll who states that:

> A distinction must be made between the violent sexual attacks by the likes of the Trophy Rapist pouncing on women in secluded woodlands, and confused sexual encounters where the lines are blurred. (Carroll 2002)

Ms Carroll calls for a distinction between stranger rapes and what she describes as confused sexual encounters. Without her defining exactly what constitutes a confused sexual encounter it is difficult to clarify what she is talking about – is a confused sexual encounter rape? Are most rape allegations then from women who are confused about whether they consented or not? Who says the encounter was confused, Ms Carroll or the victim or perhaps the offender? This approach to rape, that the encounter could just all have been a misunderstanding if only the woman making the allegation could see it like that, is part of the skewed perception and includes an inability to recognize sexual violence in all but the most extreme cases; there is a correlation between belief in rape myths and an inability to identify sexual assault (Estrich 1987, Varelas and Foley 1998). Real rape is thus perceived to have occurred where extreme violence is used and maybe incorporates an explicit threat to the life of the victim. This position which *is* the rape template and part of the discourse of sexual murder seriously undermines what the offence of rape is and disregards legal definitions. This position on rape utilizes a perception of the offence that is so closely linked to perceptions of murder or attempted murder that the original definitive part of the offence is invisible. Legal rape definitions would have to be re-written to match the perception of what a rape is in this discourse.

The primacy of sex in rationalizing violent hetero/sexual relationships

Reports of Intimate Partner Homicide (IPH) are also significantly gendered using constructions of heterosexuality and stereotypes of masculine and feminine roles. The news narratives concentrate upon the heterosexual relationship of the victim and the assailant and the assault is perceived through the lens of the individual 'relationship' and not as a phenomenon of violence.

The murder of Vicky Fletcher by her estranged partner is atypical only because a gun was used, though Dawson (2003) notes that where the relationship has ended and the degree of intimacy is diminished, firearms are often the weapon of choice. The construction of this story and also the reporting of the murder of Louise Beech by her (semi-estranged) husband, relied upon a narrative identified in much previous research (Boyle 2005, Lees 2002, Websdale 1999, Carter 1998, Soothill and Walby 1991, Dobash and Dobash 1980) which is part of a discourse of Intimate Partner Violence more generally. Intimate Partner Violence has less status as a criminal event than stranger violence (Dawson 2003) and the 'knowledge' produced in the discourse of sexual murder is not insignificant in manipulating the status afforded to intimate partner assaults and homicides. Individual crimes of IPH received significantly less coverage in my sample, than stranger murders. The reporting largely focused on the emotional response of the male offender to the actions of the female victim prior to her death. In the two cases documented here, both employed a narrative of alleged female sexual infidelity. Male sexual jealousy and female rejection of male love are presented as causal, explanations which are also found in a study with a much larger sample (Monckton-Smith 2010). Vicky Fletcher was not sexually assaulted, she was shot in a pub car park whilst out with friends by her estranged partner, Thomas Shanks. Vicky was described as a 'lover' of Shanks, a descriptive which draws their previous sexual relationship to the centre of the narrative:

'A former SAS trooper and doctor machine gunned his former lover to death with a Kalashnikov automatic rifle smuggled home from the Gulf war, Leeds crown court was told yesterday. (Wainwright *et al.* 1999)

Shanks was also described as jealous of Vicky's new relationship with another man:

'He wanted a reconciliation and expressed loving sentiments, but it was clear he was not prepared to accept her relationship with another man. (Wainwright *et al.* 1999)

This report is headlined 'Jealous Doctor 'Machine-Gunned Ex-Lover'' (Wainwright 1999). Vicky's new relationship and her rejection of Shanks's love is consistently described as the cause of her death. In some publications her new relationship is even described as an 'affair' implying that she was not estranged from Shanks. Shanks himself is quoted as saying that she was messing with his emotions, speaking as if they were still a couple and she had some responsibilities towards him.

There is also mention in reports, that the new man Vicky was seeing was a former patient she had nursed. There is implication in the framing of the narrative that this type of relationship, between a professional and patient is less morally acceptable than a relationship between two professionals, especially a doctor and a nurse. When the information is presented alongside the moral superiority of a war hero, Vicky's behaviour could appear to lack integrity:

Shanks, who was mentioned in dispatches, broke down in tears while giving evidence. The attack followed his former girlfriend having a relationship with a patient she had nursed at Pontefract' (Wainwright 1999)

The centrality of Vicky's sexual behaviour not only genders, but sexualizes the account and the narrative places Shanks' behaviour as a *reaction* to Vicky's *action*. This acts to remove some of his agency as a violent individual and places sexual behaviours and acts on her part as causal in this fatal assault. It is well established in the research that women are more likely to be killed by their intimate partners or former partners than anyone else (Coleman and Osborne 2010, Coleman 2009, Brookman 2005, Websdale 1999, Polk 1994, Dobash and Dobash 1980). Wallace (1986) concluded that 'the marital relationship provides the context for some of the most violent encounters in our society' (Wallace 1986:83 cited in Polk 1994). In Polk's (1994) examination of male homicidal violence two sub patterns to this type of homicide were identified: where violence is employed as a control strategy in issues of sexual possession and in patterns of male suicidal depression (1994:28). Polk cites Wallace who observed that:

> either separation (or its threat) or jealousy were the major precipitating events of homicides where men took the lives of their spouses. This, she argued was a reflection of the ultimate attempt of males to exert "their power and control over their wives" (cited in Polk 1994:28)

Shaun Beech used this excuse to explain why he murdered his wife, Louise. He is quoted as saying in court:

> She said, "I have been seeing Stephen Walton and I'm going to stay with him" ... I put my hand around her throat to stop her screaming. I just kept my hand there until she stopped screaming. I knew she was dead. I checked her heart. (*Daily Mail* 2004)

Shaun Beech actually beat his wife around the head with a rolling pin before strangling her. The reason is explicitly explained as her sexual affair with another man causing Shaun Beech to become jealous. Beech then, after checking she was dead, had sexual intercourse with her dead body. He told police that he needed to possess her and to be the last man to have had sex with her (interview with police respondent). Websdale (1999) reports that men are encouraged via legal, religious and cultural means to believe that they have ownership of their intimate partners and that proprietarial behaviour is natural; a behaviour which can be violent and controlling whilst simultaneously represented as demonstrating love (Dobash and Dobash 1980). Similarly, Polk (1994), Websdale (1999) and Buss (2006) noted proprietarial behaviour as significantly implicated in cases of IPH. There is strong argument then that IPH against women by men is rooted in patriarchal belief systems where women in heterosexual love based pairings may be considered to some extent, property. Richards summarizes the position of many homicide offenders as an attitude of 'If I can't have you, no-one can' (2006:61). Neil Websdale's archival studies reveal that patriarchal belief systems are more than a mere 'cultural residue' in those men who killed their partners, they were in fact 'beliefs, values and norms deep in their ideological bone marrow' (1999:206).

Shaun Beech, despite the violence and nature of the post mortem assault was convicted of manslaughter not murder, and sentenced to seven years in prison. His jealousy and subsequent depression and her actions were powerful mitigation for him; the sexual violence used was not reported in the press at the time. Conversely Mark Dixie who was convicted of the murder of Sally Anne Bowman in February 2008 received a full life sentence. He stabbed Sally Anne seven times after apparently happening upon her in the driveway of her home in September 2005; he then had sexual intercourse with her dead body. There is little difference in the violent offending characteristics; both men brutally killed and defiled young women, what clearly separates the violence is the relationship with the woman; in one case there had been intimacy, in the other there had not. The disparity in sentencing however is staggering; one receives seven years, one a whole life sentence. As noted in Chapter one a move by the Government's equalities minister Harriet Harman, to stop sexual infidelity being used as a partial defence in murder charges, was defeated in the House of Lords in October 2009 and at this time it is yet to be established whether there will be future success. In fact Harman's attempt to stop men using this excuse was called 'obnoxious' by a retired Judge and Law Lord (Slack 2009).

Similar to the murder of Vicky Fletcher, military service was a focus in the court narrative in the murder of Louise Beech, but the serving reservist was Louise herself. Her service in the Gulf War is mentioned but only to frame how she met and started her extra-marital affair, not to represent her as a hero as was done with Thomas Shanks:

> Mrs. Beech flew out last autumn and on the plane she met Mr. Walton, a fellow reservist...the relationship soon flourished...Mrs. Beech and

her lover were spending time together, even having sex at her marital home in Gosport, Hampshire. (*Daily Mail* 2004)

In explaining the violence as precipitated by 'sexual jealousy' and the rejection of his love by his wife, the narrative provides the news consumer with some answers; though male sexual jealousy is neither defined nor examined, but taken to be a static and fundamental part of male sexuality with links to biological determinism. IPH is a significant social problem and on average two women are killed every week in the UK (Coleman 2009) though according to latest Home Office figures this is now about 1.9 women per week (Coleman and Osborne 2010) and similar, if not worse rates of victimization are noted across the world (see Chapter one) by their intimate partners or former partners. There are moves to try and resolve the disparity in sentencing and to address the prevalence of domestic homicide, in much the same way as there are moves to try and increase rape convictions and reduce its prevalence. It was reported by *The Times* on 28 November 2005 that 'Jealousy is no longer an excuse for murder' (Gibb 2005). In a move which reflects growing concern that men who kill their wives and intimate partners in fits of anger or jealousy are often escaping with more lenient sentences, new sentencing guidelines were announced by the Lord Chief Justice. The guidelines acknowledge that IPH is treated less seriously than stranger murder and propose that three new categories of killing are to be introduced based on the degree of provocation and other factors such as 'whether a body was dismembered or mutilated'. These categories come very close to comparing the characteristics of an IPH with a so-called sexual/serial murder. The closer an act of violence against a woman correlates to those defining characteristics of a classic sexual murder, the more sympathy the victim will have, the more press attention the crime will receive, the more status as an act of violence it will have and the more severe punitive response it will receive.

The primacy of sex in linking and comparing offending

The dominant discourse of sexual murder allows or encourages comparison and linking of offences. Any offence that could be conceived as 'stranger' sexual violence may be compared or linked to any other offence of stranger sexual violence. The established similarities between them are so powerful that the connections need only be the gender of the victim as female and the speculated gender of the offender as male and their relationship as strangers. This allows for comparison and links with any other offence fulfilling those criteria. However, the converse is true of IPH, offences are rarely, if ever (I did not find any) compared. Comparison of IPH would immediately raise social issues that would require attention for it is too common to represent the offenders as aberrant and this would raise issues that would criticize harshly, male hetero/sexuality. As Roland Barthes stated in his discussion of modern myth making 'A little confessed evil saves one from acknowledging a lot of hidden evil' (2001:122). For society to confess to the evil of male violence against women, which would be achieved in the comparison and linking of offences of IPV and IPH, would not be to confess to 'a little evil'. However, society admits to the evil of predatory stranger killers, a very small proportion of males represented as different from the ordinary male. Society gives time and resources to warn women of the dangers he presents. But as Barthes theory suggests, there could be benefit to the social elite in acknowledging his existence:

> In admitting the accidental evil of a class bound institution the better to conceal its principal evil. One immunizes the contents of the collective imagination by means of a small inoculation of acknowledged evil; one thus protects it against the risk of generalized subversion. (2001:123)

Acknowledging the existence of serial killing as a phenomenon of male violence by comparing and linking offences may protect other forms of institutionalized violence from scrutiny. Whilst the problem of male violence is limited to discussions of the predatory stranger killer who is represented as the immediate and real threat to women, IPH and the facilitating cultural and social beliefs and practices remain insufficiently challenged. Also constructing the serial killer as a sexual menace reinforces the *normality* of the sexuality being demonstrated in IPH which again protects it from negative scrutiny. It is a heterosexuality tested to its limits by the deviant sexuality of the victim.

Comparisons between stranger assaults which emphasize the similarities between offenders and offences remind us that they are not isolated incidents and that precisely because they can be compared, a real phenomenon of sexual danger exists. Offences against women where no sexual assault is established are compared or linked to offences where there *was* presence of a sexual assault making an erroneous but powerful association between the violence and sex and also the two unrelated offences. The comparisons are rarely confirmed and are not justified beyond the gender of the victim as female and her relationship to the offender as stranger. Margaret Muller's murder was compared to another stabbing, a gang rape, a rape, a bludgeoning and rape/murders. Gary Mason in the *Express* compares the rape of a woman in central park by a gang of youths with Margaret Muller's stabbing and states that the comparisons are uncomfortably clear (Mason 2003a).

The comparisons may not be as uncomfortably clear as the author suggests. If one woman is stabbed to death by a lone male stranger and one is gang raped by several males, the comparisons are not crystal clear unless there is an explicit acknowledgement that much violence against women is both motivated and encouraged through hetero/patriarchal belief systems. This is rarely adequately articulated in discussions which reference an analytically nebulous sexual explanation as causal.

Similar to comparisons, links are used in news reporting in cases of stranger violence but not IPH. Establishing links between stranger homicides could lead to discovery of a serial killer, a really dangerous psychopath which gives the story more longevity and takes events to their ultimate conclusion 'another Jack the Ripper'. Similarly offence linkage is also routine in reporting of stranger rapes as the notion of a 'serial rapist' is conflated with the serial killer. At one point the *Sun*, the *Daily Express*, the *Daily Mail* and the *Daily Mirror* referred to Margaret Muller's assailant as the 'Park Ripper' an allusion to Jack the Ripper and the Yorkshire Ripper, both of whom are considered sex murderers. This is an effective way of re-establishing the links to sexual motivation and serial killers. Hannah Foster's murder was linked to that of Milly Dowler:

'Was Strangled Girl Victim of a Serial Killer?' (Gardham and Gysin 2003)

'Has Milly's Killer Struck Again?' (Wansell 2003)

The *Daily Mail* states:

It is even possible that Canter's terrible forecast may already have come true. Southampton schoolgirl Hannah Foster, 17, was abducted and killed at the weekend and the similarities between the cases are striking. (Wansell 2003)

However, the comparisons made in news reports do not generally situate the violence in the wider social problem of hetero/patriarchal belief systems, it is the sexual element that is the link; that there are evil sexual psychopaths stalking the streets and parks in search of lone females.

The primacy of sex in constructing evil

It is a staple in news reporting of serial/sex killers and serial rapists that offenders are represented as hunters and victims as prey. This binary division reproduces a gendered subjectivity with the male hunter constructed as strong and controlling and the female victim as weak and vulnerable. This is very similar to the dynamic represented as present in male/female heterosexual relations which positions the female as the 'natural prey' of males. This representation is also reproduced in professional approaches to the investigation of sexual murder. Rossmo (2000) describes a 'hunting typology' when assessing serial murderers in geographic profiling. He describes 'search and attack' methods identified in serial killers using the terms 'Hunter, Poacher, Troller, Trapper, Raptor, Stalker and Ambusher' (2000:167). He also characterizes these techniques as 'remarkably similar to Schaller's (1972) description of certain hunting methods used by lions in the Serengeti' (2000:167). Predatory behaviours in Great White Sharks too have been used in comparisons with serial killers. A research study published in the *Journal of Zoology* documented the use of Geographical Information Systems, used in analyzing the spatial behavior of serial killers, to study hunting behaviours in Great White Sharks (Martin *et al* 2009). The research results were heralded as establishing that Great White Sharks share behavioural traits with serial killers, and that Great White Sharks are the serial killers of the seas. The enthusiastic press response to the research basked in the popularity of this close linkage between a serial killer and an efficient and notorious, emotionless predator. The comparison reinforces biological and evolutionary discourses which lionize male humans (and animals) who demonstrate these 'primal instincts'. This androcentric interpretation also reduces victims to mere pawns in the important male dominated game of 'hunting' which, in anthropological terms, is his heritage and birthright. Green (1993) states:

> Throughout accounts of serial murders run themes of adventurous risk in the stalking of human prey by stealth or deception, the excitement of the kill...The egoism of the hunter permits the degradation of potential victims to the level of wild game. The planning, excitement, and thrill of the hunt overrides all other considerations except eluding capture. (1993:166)

That a man would be described as 'hunting' for a woman is not unusual in the normalized cultural perceptions of securing a mate. Hunting for a victim is perhaps an extreme example of this behaviour but is within normally accepted male sexual behaviour patterns. Human evolution is dominated by constructions of early 'man' as a hunter (Morgan 1972), the human male has a long history where the hunting instinct is represented as normal and desirable; human women conversely, have never been represented as hunters. That women are the 'hunted' is the perceived natural state of affairs, especially in the socially constructed double standard of the heterosexual dynamic (Box 1992, Lees 1997). As documented in chapter two Tatar (1995) quotes film director Brian De Palma who states 'using women in situations where they are killed or sexually attacked is nothing more than a genre convention...like using violins when people look at each other' (1995:8). But Tatar asks 'What makes women's position as victim, either in cinema or real life, "natural"?' (1995:8) She argues that our interpretive habits prevent us from facing the full implications of what is represented. Interpreting the hunter/prey division as natural to the male/female relationship has a long cultural history and is a familiar explanatory framework for the dynamics present in a gendered murder as exemplified in these news reports:

> A nurse who dumped her doctor lover for a former patient paid with her life when he hunted her down and shot her, a court heard yesterday. (Loudon 1999)

> 'There are also similarities in the parks themselves in that both have deer enclosures, which offer an element of cover as well as providing open landscape. (Thompson 2003)

The serial killer is constructed as an 'evil' individual whose 'natural' hunting skills have been exploited to further a deviant fantasy, whereas the Intimate partner killer's natural hunting ability is perverted by psychological disturbance in response to deviant feminine behaviours. The dangerousness of the 'stranger' offender is aligned with evil sadistic sexuality and *not* a desire or even a plan to commit violence for its own sake, the sole intention is perverse coitus. Neff (2005) takes a moral stand and argues *for* the use of words like 'evil' to describe serial killers and suggests that even in the 'psych' disciplines there are signs that these types of killers could be constructed as 'not merely disturbed but evil'. This is at odds with a more traditional psychiatry because the discourses and vocabulary of evil are said to lack precision and analytical clarity perhaps indicating, as Neff points out, that evil may indicate moral, rather than clinical judgment. The term 'evil' may well be inappropriate for assessing the actions or behaviours of domestic *or* stranger offenders, but its 'essence' is an alternative to 'sexual' and in this context the term is more inappropriately applied based on victim/ offender relationship than if it was applied as a term lacking analytical clarity. I make this point to illustrate that offences of violence against women are judged to be 'evil' or not, more by referring to the relationship between offender and victim and not by the violence or depravities present in the attack. For example, Antoni Imiela, a serial rapist who killed no-one is considered evil because he targeted females he did not know, he received a life sentence. Conversely Shaun Beech, husband of Louise Beech, who killed his wife violently and raped her as she was dying or after she was dead with her body covered in blood from the beating of her head with a rolling pin was convicted of manslaughter and will serve less than eight years. It appears to be the victim/offender relationship that measures the evil or dangerousness of the offender, rather than the scale of violence or depravity of his acts. However, it is also interesting to note that domestic killers are sometimes referred to as being evil in cases where they failed to demonstrate enough love for the victim before, during or after the killing and demonstrate some of the characteristics and offending behaviours attributed to stranger killers. If the offender showed no remorse or tried to hide the killing this changed perceptions of him, but where he cried and showed trauma he was the subject of sympathy (Monckton-Smith 2010). It appears that we are assessing how deviant the sex is, the sex act perpetrated by Shaun Beech was not a deviant heterosexuality, he was overcome with grief and a need to possess *his* woman. The sex act perpetrated on Sally Anne Bowman by Mark Dixie was a deviant heterosexuality; she was not his. Bourke notes that a rapist is perceived as a man having sex with someone who does not belong to him (2007:5). This makes him evil.

In implicating the relationship and differentiating between 'stranger' assaults and 'domestic' assaults to assess dangerousness we reveal that killing female intimates is not as serious as killing strangers. When the male takes his pathological sexuality out of a domestic relationship this is considered far more dangerous, he has crossed a theoretical and moral line.

The primacy of sex in culpability and defence

In this news reporting, the reasons for rapes and murders of females are represented as sexual in origin and these reasons can easily become mitigation. In the trial of Mark Dixie for the murder of Sally Anne Bowman his defending barrister said in defence of his violence and defilement 'he allowed his lust to get the better of him' (Shaw 2008). In the case of stranger murders this 'defence' that it is uncontrollable, but biologically determined sexuality that caused the violence, actually acts to mitigate for the killer. Similarly sexual jealousy and sexual possession can defend men from charges of murder. For example, in the reporting of Vicky Fletcher's murder, her killer was defended using his military service. He was presented as a good and brave man suffering from the effects of Gulf War Syndrome. Her sexual relationship with another man was put forward as reason for him losing his rationality temporarily and killing her.

> Former SAS trooper Thomas Shanks gunned down his ex-lover during a bout of depression caused by Gulf War syndrome, a court heard yesterday. It was claimed the Glasgow-born doctor killed Nurse Vickie Fletcher, 21, after suffering a 'Jekyll and Hyde' personality change as a result of the 1991 war' (Salmon 1999)

Shanks was eventually convicted of murder, but only after a second trial, the first jury failed to reach a verdict. Defence narratives will often implicate female victims in their own deaths by presenting a story of female promiscuity, insubordination or nagging (Lees 1997). Sometimes character slurs will imply intolerable behaviour and this significantly causes the female victim to be represented as blameworthy in her own violation. In the small amount of news reporting of the murder of Louise Beech, the fact that her husband raped her is not mentioned, however Louise's sexual behaviour prior to her murder was extensively commented on, for example, in the *Daily Mail*:

> (her affair) became sexual, it became intense and Shaun Beech got to hear about it...Mrs. Beech and her lover were spending time together even having sex at the marital home... (*Daily Mail* 2004)

In this report Louise is referred to as Mrs Beech reinforcing her married status, but the first and only mention of Shaun Beech's sexual assault of his wife during the murder is not until 2005, the *Guardian*, in reference to the sexual assault states 'He stripped and had sex with her body' (Eden *et al.* 2005). It is not known why this aspect of the assault was not mentioned at the time, especially given the negative attention paid to Louise's sexual behavior. However, Shaun Beech was represented in reports as a cuckold and the post mortem rape of his wife would have undermined sympathetic constructions of him.

In cases of rape it is often put forward that the victim precipitated the attack by arousing the male and then withdrawing consent. Even in cases of stranger attacks, ways of making the victim partially culpable are discussed. In one of the police interviews discussed in Chapter 6 it was said that journalists will ask questions to assess 'whether she should have been there, whether she should have known better' and comments on whether the victim had been drinking or acting immorally at the time (or any other) will be present:

> The girls [Hannah Foster and friend] had been socializing in the Bevois Valley area of the city, but had stuck mostly to non-alcoholic drinks and remained sober, the police confirmed. (Allison 2003)

This report says the police *confirmed* that Hannah was sober, so it had been asked. The reporting of the murder of Margaret Muller also included speculation that she may not have been careful enough. The area in which she lived was the subject of much comment at the beginning of this case and the 'bohemian' nature of her lifestyle. The *Times* (Campbell Johnston 2003b) includes a report headlined 'Dangers of the Bohemian life'. The author infers that the cheap area in which Margaret lived may have contributed to her victimization and that 'it is dangerous living on the artistic edge'. A separate article is headlined 'Dangerous Dirty, Neglected...and Still the Place I'm Happy To Call Home' (Crampton 2003). The author speaks of the dangerousness of the area and that Margaret's reasons for living there were no less rational because of that, he stated:

> Her father said she knew hers was 'not a terribly desirable area' but, for the most part, she liked it and she felt safe, or safe enough. She was wrong, but that doesn't mean her decision was not rational. (Crampton 2003)

The dangerousness of the area is commented on in many publications and the fact that Margaret knew it was dangerous but still continued to live there. In one report it is said that:

> Artists who shared Ms Muller's studios told police yesterday that she usually carried a small backpack, which was not found with her body. One colleague had warned her to take care in the area. Peter

Burke, 44, said 'I told her "you want to be careful around here" because I noticed that she always seemed to have this bag with her'. (Cobain *et al.* 2003)

The comments that the victim knew the area was unsafe but still continued to live there and despite warnings, continued to carry her bag, infer that the victim was not careful enough. Female victims of rape or murder will have their behavior scrutinized in a manner which implies that they are responsible, not only for their own safety but for the offender's actions, they should protect themselves from attack and him from himself. The concept of sex especially will blame women whilst it simultaneously defends men from allegations of brutality, evil or even murder and this is discussed further in the following case study, but also in the next chapter which focuses on police narrative construction.

Case study: Camilla Petersen: the primacy of sex in knowing the sex killer

This case study has a very specific focus which is the way in which the press constructed Camilla Petersen's killer as a sexual deviant to the exclusion of any other potential characterizations. It is not only female victims who are sexualized, certain killers are sexualized also, especially stranger killers. But this sexualization appears to have less strategic or diagnostic value than implied in the reports.

Camilla was 15 years old when she was murdered whilst on a language study holiday on the Isle of Wight in July 2002; she had gone alone to a local beauty spot to sketch and was spotted by Richard Kemp (the offender) who often walked in the area. Twenty years before this murder Kemp had served eight years in Broadmoor for violent and sexual assaults on four children having been diagnosed as psychopathic. However, since his release in 1981 and a conviction for indecent exposure in 1982 (*This Is Hampshire* 2003) Kemp appears to have lived quietly in the community without drawing attention to himself. There are conflicting explanations offered in the news narratives which speculate Kemp's motivations and personality; however, all, except the victim's mother, prioritize Kemp's sexual deviancy in describing him and her perspective along with a fuller discussion of the police perspective is discussed in Chapter 6.

Kemp was an offender who admitted to the murder giving almost clinical unemotional detail, however he remained somewhat silent about his actual motivations; one of those offenders who, according to Foucault (1994), frustrate the process of justice by failing to declare 'who they are'. He claimed to the police that he 'was just in the wrong place at the wrong time' as if all crucial aspects to the offence converged in space and time in a tragic and unavoidable happenstance. Camilla's body was found by members of the language group who organized the trip from Denmark to the UK; they had gone searching for her when she had failed to attend a get-together on the evening of her death.

All the reporting that could be sourced formed the printed press sample including data gathered from Nexis UK and the *BBC online news* as well as some police news publications; the criteria for inclusion in the sample was that the report referred to the murder. Camilla's name was the search term used and this generated 140 individual reports. The data was first temporally ordered from the initial reports of the finding of Camilla's body to the post trial comment. This analysis will follow this temporal ordering to build a picture of the way Kemp was 'known' as more information about him was sought and discovered. There are three key time scales noted in the reporting of this offence which organize this section, pre-trial reports, trial reports and post trial reports.

The press narratives: pre-trial

The first reports to identify Kemp and provide any description of him were published on 19 July 2002. The information collected about him was minimal but recurring themes were organized around his social isolation and his love of rambling. *The Times* reported on this day that he was a loner and a rambler who lived in a bedsit and that he had never been seen in the company of a woman. The *Independent* also reported that he lived alone in a bedsit but added that it was in a rundown part of town. The *Evening Standard* and others described him as a bachelor. The focus on his rambling, unmarried status and social isolation was not part of a general description of Kemp, it was the whole description of him at this time. In the 62 reports that appeared after Kemp's arrest but before his prosecution the most cited characteristics were; his isolation with the words lonely, alone and loner being popular; his interest in rambling with the word rambling or rambler far more popular than walker or hiker; and his distance from females or heterosexual relationships.

There were some descriptions of Kemp gleaned from interviews with his neighbours in which he was described as ordinary, popular, quiet and polite, a man who had a close relationship with his elderly parents but no one else. Terms like 'loner' and 'bachelor' when used in conjunction with 'sexual assault' may be words that are conventions in discourses of paedophilia and headlines like 'Loner Is Held on Sex Killing' (*Sun* 2002) succinctly tie the two characteristics together. It could be that Kemp's identity was being written from durable stereotypes of paedophiles that would suggest what had happened in the absence of a structured narrative. Kitzinger addresses this very question in examining the ways in which journalists portray paedophiles. She argues that they are represented as easily identifiable misfits and othered from 'ordinary' heterosexual men (2004:127) and cites several examples of the common terminology used in their description; 'bachelor', a man who doesn't relate to women, a 'lives with his mother type', never married, living in run down accommodation and strange (2004:127–32); all this vocabulary, she argues, implies homosexuality. Certainly, Kemp was described in all these terms but is never explicitly referred to as homosexual or heterosexual; it is however implied that he is not 'normal' juxtaposing this with homosexual syntax which distances him from heterosexuality and alleged normalcy.

Press narratives: trial stage

The comment on Kemp's identity was more developed at the trial stage of reporting as more information about him was made available and legal restrictions were less pressing. The police and defence narratives were reproduced in the press describing conflicting explanations of what happened to Camilla and Kemp's motivations. The police had constructed a narrative which described a determined sexual predator interested in assaulting Camilla in a fairly conventional sexual way, looking at her or touching her and then driven to murder her to stop himself being identified. It also emerged at the trial that Kemp had links with the Salvation Army, which inspired headlines like, for example, 'Sally Army Strangler' (*Daily Mirror* 2003). There is popular linkage between religion and sex offending and particularly paedophilia after several high profile cases of child sexual abuse linked to the clergy (Rafter 2007, Flynn 2004,). It cannot be ignored that the popularly perceived relationship between clergy and paedophile/homosexual offending is particularly strong and Kemp is constructed in this sense as a man exemplifying a dominant discourse of paedophilia and sex offending.

The defence narrative was not as clearly elucidated in the reports, it was clear that Kemp was claiming diminished responsibility as a defence but all explanation was lost in Kemp's own apparent lack of clarity. He variously claimed that; Camilla was just in the wrong place at the wrong time; that he didn't know why he had killed her; that he could have let her go but didn't and that he wasn't sexually aroused. Despite Kemp's silence over motivation the majority of what is reported keeps him characterized as predominantly a sexual menace; the only comments which draw in the violence used and rationalize it as gratuitous or even autotelic (Shinckel 2004) come from the forensic psychiatrist who gave evidence in court. He explicitly linked Kemp's sexual predilections to violence saying of Kemp 'he had a major problem in relation to violence and sexuality' (Mitchell 2003a).

The reasons for the *initial attack* are clearly speculated in the narratives as having an expressive sexual aetiology, in contrast the reasons speculated for the violence are that it was instrumental; both the fatal and the non fatal violence used. The violence is described as separate to the sexual assault, with its own separate motivations which were utilitarian. Schinkel argues that most focus on violence asks the question 'what caused the violence?' (2004:13) and misses the potential for it to be an end in itself with an intrinsic attractiveness, what he describes as an autotelic violence (2004:15). This position is evident in the press and police narratives where there is a focus on presenting an external and rational cause for the violence. Firstly, it is speculated that Kemp used violence to subdue Camilla so he could rape her and her resistance to the attempted rape precipitated an escalation of violence which ended with her death; or alternatively that after a sexual assault he had to kill her to avoid detection. For example, a headline appeared, released by The Press Association on 12 May 2003, stating 'sex attacker murdered student to avoid being caught'. The report goes on to comment that the prosecution stated:

> after...indecently assaulting her, he decided to kill her to prevent his identity from being known...what was undoubtedly initially a sexually motivated assault turned into a deliberate, willful killing, a killing calculated to avoid detection. (Mitchell 2003b)

It is interesting to note that a report in the *Sun* had the headline 'Killer: girl begged not to be raped' (*Sun* 2003). This is apparently a claim made by Kemp, the reliability of which cannot be verified. It is possible that Camilla pleaded with Kemp, that will never be known, whether she would have pleaded for her life or not to be raped is a matter for conjecture. The report implies that the victim too was focused on Kemp's sexual behavior and *not* his violence, this keeping all considerations within the limits of a sexual discourse that acts to construct Kemp in a certain way. However the psychiatrist at the trial expressed concern with this construction of Kemp:

'Dr Somekh told the trial that much was done to convert Kemp's sexual desires from children to a normal heterosexual outlook but not enough was done to treat his violent nature.' (Mitchell 2003c)

Press reporting: post-trial

There was little post-trial comment after the day of the conviction and subsequent reporting has largely described the murder thus 'police found her naked body hidden in woodland. She had been sexually assaulted then strangled' (George 2003) distilling the whole case to a sexual assault, and in very few words implying that the strangulation and the sexual assault were distinct and separate offending behaviours, but with a more nuanced focus on the sexual aspects to the offending. The sexual assault in this case and many others is what creates the crucial psychological intelligibility (Foucault 1994).

6
Police Narratives

Introduction: police culture

Police narrative construction is a formal story-telling process necessary to focus investigative strategy and to form the basis of a prosecution case file. The narrative tells the story of the crime; what happened and why it happened. For the police the crime narrative must achieve a certain end, it must result in a successful prosecution and conviction, it must be plausible and believable, it must be supported by the evidence and it must convince a jury to convict. The police narrative will also be disseminated via the court proceedings, the press and often the wider media as an authoritative and privileged account of what happened and why. Innes argues that narratives constructed by police officers will be organized to meet the demands of the legal process and will 'tie people, places, objects and phenomena together in a plausible chronology' (2002:682). Interestingly he also notes that investigators will ensure that they tell 'the right kind of story' and quotes one officer as saying: 'Juries are not experts...if you can show them quite clearly how the murder happened and provide an indication of why it happened, then that is extremely effective in getting a result' (2002:684). The importance of this approach is reflected in the research of Hastie (2003) and Hastie *et al.* (1983) who report that the 'story model', or assembling evidence into a coherent narrative, is the most widely adopted approach in jury decision making (reported in Devine *et al.* 2001:625). The narrative must also satisfy the Crown Prosecution Service who will decide whether to prosecute or not, based on the likelihood of a successful outcome. The 'facts' of a case must then be made meaningful to achieve this primary aim, and in this respect the police interpretation of events will create meaning which will define the crime, the criminal and the victim.

The importance of the narratives produced by the police to explain what happened and why in any individual crime of gendered or sexual violence is often overlooked with much focus being on the nature of the practical police response and their effectiveness in achieving a successful criminal justice outcome. There has been more academic interest in the way journalists report violence against women and represent offenders and offences in their narratives. However, police narratives are very often the basis for a press story and have a significant amount of authority; they might be considered the last word on the circumstances of a crime given that they have access to all the key players and their explanations. But we need to contemplate when considering the narratives produced by any agency or individual what is informing their particular perception of events and how it links with other explanations or narratives offered. One of the criticisms often made of press reporting is the way that journalists fail to locate the violence in its social context (Greer 2003, Carter 1998), and also fail to persuade the criminal justice system and the public that offences have causes outside of the immediate and individual antecedents of any particular case. Similarly, when the police construct narratives, out of necessity they must focus only on the one single event; a man cannot after all be tried for the historical crimes of others. In the context of the case file the primary aim of the police narrative is to identify and convict an offender. The recent adoption of the problem oriented approach by police services (Leigh *et al.* 1996) does not and perhaps cannot apply to the prosecution of individual offenders or the construction of the case narrative/case summary; that is that there is no expectation that police attempt to solve or highlight social problems when they put together a file of evidence to prosecute an offender. Therefore the narrative, for example, telling the story of a domestic homicide, only needs to direct the prosecution of one man and not locate his actions within a wider social problem. A narrative then that explains that a man killed his wife because he thought she was having an affair distils the characteristics to what can appear to be one atypical, and often in the case of Intimate Partner Homicide, sad and unforeseeable or excusable event which may merely reflect dominant beliefs rather than challenge destructive social norms. Stelfox makes it clear that the process of investigation has far more within its remit than bringing offenders to justice; 'judgments about the quality of criminal investigation do not rest solely on the effectiveness with which its various objectives are met' (2009:17). He suggests that there is public concern with the *way* in which investigations are conducted, but also a concern that investigators consider the needs of witnesses, victims and the wider community. The police have an obligation to follow all lines of enquiry (Stelfox 2009) but this requirement does not stretch to considering all potential motivations of an alleged offender so that social or political dimensions to the offending are contemplated.

Five officers from the major crime team of a county police service were interviewed with the aim of exploring how they construct crime stories; how they interpret motivation, why they might target certain individuals as potential suspects and how the story of the crime is made plausible. This is achieved first, from a general discussion about the rape and/or murder of females; I then offer the police approach to the two case studies, the murders of Hannah Foster and Camilla Petersen. In the case of Hannah's murder I focus on issues of culpability and also the police/press relationship, examining the way the two institutions share information and knowledge systems which illustrate how discursive regimes operate. The focus in the case study of Camilla's murder is more on the way the police constructed the offender's identity and the way this impacted upon the narrative construction. There is an extra dimension included in the study of Camilla's case and that is the perspective of her mother, Lonni Petersen, on the police narrative.

Police culture, which has a significant impact on the way offenders and victims are perceived (Gregory and Lees 1999), has been the subject of some serious criticism with accusations that the predominantly white male heterosexual culture promotes racism and sexism. The police services were described as 'institutionally racist' after the Macpherson Report (1999) which investigated police handling of the murder of Stephen Lawrence. There has also been a significant amount of criticism with regard to police handling of sexual assault cases (Lees 2002, Gregory and Lees 1999) which began spectacularly in 1982 when the police response to an allegation of rape was broadcast in a documentary *Police* (broadcast 18.01.82) which focused on the Thames Valley force (BFI 2005). The episode was third in a series of nine entitled 'A complaint of rape'. The female victim was seen bullied and discouraged from pursuing her complaint by three male officers who were openly sceptical of her allegations, with one famously stating to the victim 'This is the biggest bollocks I've ever heard.' There was understandable outrage from the public and interest groups and the Thames Valley Police set up an all female rape investigation squad as a result (BFI 2005). The documentary placed the abysmal response from the criminal justice system to allegations of rape right at centre stage and the documented rape myths which were the framework within which these officers were working, were publicly challenged. As was noted in Chapter 1, similar criticisms were directed at the Metropolitan Police after an IPCC inquiry into the handling of the case of serial rapist John Worboys who was jailed in 2009 for a series of rapes. Again the police were admonished for poor practice and a failure to take victims seriously or believe them. Unfortunately, the police response forms just a part of a wider institutional attitude to female rape victims. The entire system of criminal justice is working within the same frame including health practitioners, solicitors, juries, judges and magistrates and this illustrates the reach of discursive formations which can, if unresisted, operate with power and impunity with their particular styling of truth authorized and accepted as legitimate. The entire apparatus for constructing truths about rape is the same apparatus which tells us who and what women are, so it is within this epistemological framework that the criminal justice system responds to women (Larcombe 2005). At the time the Police documentary was broadcast there was less resistance to dominant discursive constructions of femininity and heterosexuality within institutions, though the Second Wave of feminism was active in its challenge of these constructions and of institutional practices. It would not be fair to suggest that this institutional indifference to sexual violence against women is still universal for the police and the wider criminal justice system have responded to calls for a more sophisticated and informed approach and this has produced more sympathetic structures for dealing with sexual and domestic violence. It is noted in research that some convictions are now being achieved in cases where in the past, there would have been little hope of a successful outcome. It is also noted that 'the legacies of the 'real rape' template are most evident in the early stages of attrition where it affects police decision making [and] victims' willingness to report and/or stay in the criminal justice process' (Kelly 2007:11). However, Walklate (2008) reports that despite this there has been no corresponding improvement in the general rates of conviction, and the damning IPCC inquiry into the Worboys case reveals that institutional sexism and an inability to recognize sexual victimization are still stubbornly present in police institutions.

In her book *No Way up the Greasy Pole* (1993) Alison Halford documents her time as a serving police officer with the Metropolitan Police and the Merseyside Police over a 30-year period. She achieved the rank of Assistant Chief Constable but claimed she was repeatedly blocked from achieving further promotion; she managed to successfully claim against Merseyside Police for sexual discrimination. The sexism evident in her accounts is truly shocking and there is no doubt that things have had to change in the police service since that time. Gregory and Lees

(1999) see the changes that have occurred since the1960s and 1970s are a direct result of legislation rather than perhaps, a willingness borne out of reflexivity within the police hierarchy. They point to several studies which have shown that a strong male culture still exists in the police service and that despite official acknowledgement of the problems in responding to sexual and domestic violence, a cult of masculinity which devalues violence against women is still dominant.

These observations are concerning for many reasons, not least of all is that the police are not only charged with investigating crimes but have a lot of power in determining how offences, victims and offenders are perceived which may be reflected in their case narratives. De Lint (2003) characterizes the police as 'knowledge workers concerned with the 'social construction of meaning' (2003:686) rather than a coercive force because they have so much power over the 'facts' of cases that are 'funneled through the system' (2003:383). He suggests that they are strategically positioned to be able to patrol the facts given their almost sole access to information about any particular crime; thus enabling them to provide controlled or partial information to other agencies. Given the importance of achieving convictions and providing plausible crime stories for juries, the investigation of crimes and the construction of the crime narrative may not be a method for discovering the absolute truth about an event or crime but as Innes posits, rather 'a mechanism that produces an account sufficiently reliable to meet evidential standards of reasonable doubt' (2002:680).

In the investigation of homicides this structured process of investigation and narrative construction is described by Innes (2002) as substantively different for what he referred to as 'self solvers' (domestic) and 'whodunits' (stranger), which are broad categorizations of homicide events. 'Self solvers' which constitute the majority of police homicide investigations are those homicides where a suspect is immediately visible. Innes sees that the work of the police in this type of homicide is reflected in McConville *et al.'s* (1991) model of 'case constructionism', which entails putting together a coherent narrative. Whodunits on the other hand have a different investigative structure as a suspect is yet to be identified, but the case construction will still necessitate officers speculating a plausible sequence of events to enable a prosecution. This process will also include using that crime narrative to focus investigative strategy and to identify potential suspects prior to the final case construction. If a crime narrative, for example, tells a story of sexual assault then police may divert resources in the direction of known sex offenders. The murders of Hannah Foster and Camilla Petersen are clear examples of crimes constructed and rationalized as sexual murder, but how useful this perception was to the police in their investigations is debatable.

Rape and/or murder: a police perspective

The press conference so common on television news now, is far more than a forum for letting the press know the facts of an event. The press conference is a negotiated access for journalists and reporters to key individuals and information. The police and the press could be described as having diametrically opposed agendas in some respects, despite the parallels that may exist. The police, for example, often wish to suppress information whilst the journalist aims to publish information and this creates a relationship between the two, full of compromise and strategy; the press conference is often an example of that compromise. The police and the press are not necessarily seeking the same information and do different things with information when they get it. I have discussed in Chapter 5 the press approach to the rape and/or murder of women by men, here the discussion will focus on the police approach but these approaches are not meaningfully separate and they share certain conventions which will form part of the discussion; first I explore the officers' own sense of what is important when investigating and making meaning of such crimes.

Rape and scepticism

I asked officers, as an opening question, if the assumption that most murders of females were sexually motivated was correct in their experience, there was a general agreement that this was the case:

> This accurately reflects the case load we have, I'm trying to think of one that falls outside, no not in (force area), but nationally, yes there are others, drug and gang related very occasionally – women are not necessarily the intended victims though. (R 1)

> In my experience it's always been sexual whether domestic or because they want sex. (R 4)

From these comments it appears that murders of women are seen as predominantly sexually motivated with an assumption that when there is no obvious sexual motivation, the woman may not have been the intended victim. However, in discussing domestic assaults specifically, some respondents concurred that sexual jealousy, an aspect so important in rationalizing domestic homicide in the press, was more often used to mitigate his actions or to serve as an excuse for the violence rather than being a direct causal factor:

> The sexual affair thing is probably an excuse it's about violence, not sex. They are bullies, they get more and more aggressive, what gives them the right just because they are stronger physically, what gives them the right to do it? (R 3)

> Affairs and endings are not the most common cause but they get dragged in to the story, they will drag in an affair to mitigate what they have done. Mainly it is arguments and possibly drink fuelled, that have nothing to do with an affair and an escalation of domestic violence. (R 3)

There was clearly a lot of sympathy from the officers towards the victims of stranger homicide, but a feeling that victims of domestic homicide were in some respects contributing to their victimization by failing to see the signs that they could be murdered or passively accepting that it could be the end result. When discussing rape victims the approaches were mixed. The perception of what constitutes a 'real rape' has been discussed earlier in this book and is a running theme stressing the academic contention that cases of stranger rape or those rapes where there is aggravating violence are setting the standard for what a rape is. This may more often be attributed to a cultural, rather than a professional perception; it is concerning then that one officer said:

> I haven't dealt with many genuine rapes, most rape accusations are questionable. It's not often we get a real rape, a stranger rape, because usually they get murdered. There was this one, she had been out, she hadn't been drinking she was respectable and she got grabbed in (location of offence). She was punched and controlled, she was raped and then he let her go. That was a nasty genuine rape, the victim was distraught. (R 3)

This one statement contains every indication that this officer is employing a gendered subjectivity backed up by many of the so-called rape myths. First, that a real rape should involve a stranger or aggravating violence, secondly, that the genuine victim is 'respectable', third, that the victim should be visibly distraught and fourth; a myth that

I am proposing in this book, that real rapes are perceived to have the potential to end in murder. Kelly *et al.* (2005) found that there is an over estimation of false allegations by the police and prosecutors which feeds a culture of scepticism, and Bufkin and Eschholz (2000) state that several researchers have found that there is a relationship between a belief in rape myths and an inability to identify sexual victimization (Estrich 1987, Varelas and Foley 1998). Police officers must prepare evidence to meet the legal definition of offences, in this respect there should be no confusion for officers about legal definitions. However, when preparing case files for a prosecution there is consideration of the lay element's perceptions, as with a jury. If the lay element and the professional element have similar perceptions, the legal definition may be redundant. Legal theorist George Fletcher notes that 'witnesses may know nothing about the definition of crimes, yet they perceive a crime occurring' (1996:56). It may be that it is not only witnesses but key actors in the process of criminal justice who may rely on their perceptions rather than legal definitions. The officer distinguishes between 'genuine' rapes and 'questionable' allegations. Such discrimination is based on a perception of rape that is the 'rape template' and a fusion between that and the sexual murder template; this officer specifically states that real rape victims are usually murdered.

When discussing the offence of rape and its effects on the victim there was agreement that the effects were devastating:

> I was involved recently with a series of sexual assaults on (location of offence). The worst assault was on a (victim age and occupation) she was dragged up a hill and hit, she thought she was going to die, most rapes seem to have a common thread, what was happening they were almost oblivious to, they thought they were going to die, but at the time it is a fear of death. (R 1)

This position has been borne out in the research of Ann Wolbert Burgess and Lynda Lytle Holmstrom who identified and named Rape Trauma Syndrome (RTS) in 1974. They found that the key precipitating factor in onset of RTS was a profound fear for life prior to or during the assault. The research was carried out in the emergency department of a hospital, which could indicate that the victims were injured, however, the researchers documented both stranger and non-stranger assaults, the victims were aged between 3 and 73 and the amount of injury varied (personal communication with Anne Wolbert Burgess, 1 April 2004). The key factor that precipitated RTS was fear of death, even where the victim and offender were known to each other. This indicates that rape can be perceived as life-threatening, perhaps even where there is no real threat to life. It is possible that the powerful links between rape and murder produced in the dominant discourse of sexual murder could influence the perception in a wide variety of sexual assaults, that the victim could lose her life. In these discussions with police officers the examples given to me and perceived by the officers to be genuine, contained a real or imagined threat to the life of the victim. In this sense rape is more than simply the legally defined offence but is an aggravated rape or more importantly, a potential sexual murder; there appeared to be a belief among the officers that the threat to life was a constituent part of the offence of rape. However, in cases of incest or familial sexual assault where the victim was not adult, there appeared to be more sympathy and an assumption that the accusation may be genuine:

> Most interviews I've done have been family assaults, incest. They have a devastating effect on the victim. Unfortunately they are rarely reported at the time which makes prosecution very difficult as it's his word against theirs. It's very common, frightening really. They generally deny it, it's always someone else's fault. They are usually genuine. (R 3)

In discussing a case of spousal rape that included an attempted assault on the daughter of the victim, many interesting points are evident. These rapes did not involve physical beating but did involve the administering of drugs, a dangerous assault in itself. This method for achieving compliance in the victim is more than merely dangerous to her physical health, it indicates a recklessness and indifference to her life by the offender. I will document a significant amount of the comment on this case to illustrate these points:

> There was this one interesting case where this bloke had been drugging his wife for sex. We only found out because ten years on he was with a new partner and started drugging her so he could sexually assault her daughter. He was using temazepam to knock them out.

> Q. Didn't they know?
> A. Well his first wife suspected after a while. She couldn't understand why she was so tired and waking up so disoriented. She couldn't remember getting to bed or undressing herself. She would be naked

then she started noticing marks on her body. Anyway it got to the stage where the relationship was breaking up and they went to counseling. He actually admitted to it, to the counselor. She went to a solicitor and was advised not to prosecute because there was no evidence.

Q. How did it come to police attention?
A. Well the new partner, her daughter. He had drugged the woman's wine and she had gone to lie down. He had drugged the daughter's Sunny Delight but obviously hadn't put enough in because she struggled and ran to tell her mother. The mother went straight to the police and we got the evidence of the drugs from the drinks. We got the wine and the Sunny Delight. The woman said he must have been at it for years she had thought she was going mad. You know he could have killed them, if he had put too much in the girl's drink, it's so dangerous.

Q. Why was he drugging her, his first wife?
A. He was buggering her because she wouldn't agree to anal sex. He got nine years. There was no trial because he coughed to it in the end. His friends and family think he is innocent.

Q. Even though he admitted it they still think he's innocent?
A. Well he's fed them some story, why he had to admit it and they all think he is innocent. Even the wife said 'he's my husband he would never do that to me, he would never drug me'. We went back to his first wife to ask her if she wanted to pursue the charges and she said yes definitely. (R 3)

This case of spousal rape is on first inspection, extraordinary. Had the Temazepam not been found in the drinks this case would probably not have achieved a conviction or even a prosecution. The officer refers to the fact that the victims could have died as a result of the Temazepam, that it was because of this, a very dangerous thing to do and this potential threat to the life of the victims may have given them more credibility. Using drugs to commit rape or sexual assault has become the subject of much news reporting in recent years and young women in pubs have been targeted by various agencies with warnings to be especially vigilant when they are socializing. In December 2005 the Lucie Blackman Trust launched a campaign to warn young women in pubs of the dangers of 'rape drugs'. They offer kits that detect drugs in drinks and can be carried in a small handbag (Lucie Blackman Trust 2005). The drug Rohypnol has been cited as the drug of choice for the rapist. It would seem then, that drug-assisted rapes are not unusual or extraordinary but are represented as becoming far more common. What may be more extraordinary in this case is that the victim and assailant were married, but the attempted victimization of the daughter is what made the assaults visible. The adult victim said he had 'been at it for years' but she had not approached police before her daughter was involved. It is perhaps not entirely because she thought she would not be believed, but partly because she didn't really believe it herself. It is also stated that the family of the assailant didn't believe her either. The issue of 'believing' the victim is absolutely central. The discursive regime of sexual murder and rape dictates that women often lie about being raped so should be treated with suspicion and this has a long discursive history. Historical discourses are evident that share this 'truth' stretching back to women's apparent natural deceitfulness constructed in religious discourses (as discussed in Chapter 2). Putting drugs into the body of a woman is a physical assault in itself and an assault which carries with it, its own dangers. This extra dimension to sexual violence is motivated by more than an immediate sexual urge and necessitates planning and strategy. When this type of strategy is employed, the offender may appear at the very least more sinister and dangerous, despite the assertion by most researchers that the majority of rapes are planned (Keetley and Pettegrew 2005:143). Women who are victims of this type of assault may have to entirely reconstruct the offender as someone unrecognizable to them and clearly more dangerous than they realized.

When examining both domestic and stranger sexual assault and/or homicide it is routine that the victim is assessed for blame and these assessments would appear to seek to minimize the responsibility of the alleged perpetrator. In cases of sexual assault there are two key evidential points for the victim to establish, first, that the sexual act occurred and, secondly, that she did not consent. In the case discussed the victim was not even sure the act had occurred. The issue of believability is important here for it is not only that we treat women's allegations with scepticism, it may be very difficult to believe that an ordinary man would commit such violence, especially with apparent strategy and planning in place. Our skewed perception of what constitutes a 'rapist' is closely associated with our perceptions of a 'real rape' therefore a rapist may need to exhibit characteristics that we would associate with a monster or a potential killer. We should consider too that this perception of the offender may be forming in the mind of the victim *during* an assault, not just afterwards which may make the experience even more frightening and traumatic. The power of the symbolism of rape means that the accuser is alleging that an ordinary man is a one dimensionally deviant monster, an assessment of him that most of his friends, family and acquaintances would not recognize. It is a scepticism that pervades even the psyche of the victim for she does not recognize her attacker as this monster either. So believability is not entirely about the victim, it is also about setting a standard for what a 'rapist' is that most men could not possibly achieve. The offender will usually present *after* the offence as an ordinary and terrified innocent man, as far away from a recognizably dangerous potential killer as it is possible to get.

I interviewed a paramedic in the course of this research as they are sometimes called when an allegation of rape is made immediately after the event, especially where trauma or injury is evident. I was told that in at least one case she was told to 'find out what you can from the victim, see if she's genuine or not'. This was a request from a male colleague, *not* the police. There was scepticism even from the health professionals that the injured and apparently traumatized victim was genuine and that dealing with the possible innocence of the uninjured offender was a priority. It was even suggested to this paramedic that the injuries to this victim were self-inflicted.

It is also the case that where a previous sexual relationship had existed between victim and assailant that there is a belief that the assault could not have been traumatic and could not produce the kind of stereotypical notions of rape trauma embedded in public consciousness. The consultation document *Convicting Rapists and Protecting Victims* acknowledges that perceptions of what constitutes rape trauma are based on a single model in which victims are visibly crying and distressed. When I interviewed a judge about his perception of rape trials, he stated that in his experience the jury needed to see physical harm before they would believe an allegation of rape.

> Really there needs to be some kind of physical injury...juries they find it hard to see great harm where there has been a previous sexual relationship and no injuries are noted. Juries are not really buying the feminist argument.

> Q. Are you ever surprised when a rape prosecution fails?
> A. No. I always know why. It is down to the witnesses. Sometimes it is difficult to establish whether there was consent. For instance

I adjudicated a case where two sisters alleged rape by their brother. One sister was believed and he was convicted, they did not convict for the other sister. It rested upon whether that sister had allowed the brother to babysit for her. The jury did not believe that he had not babysat for her especially when a credible witness was produced to corroborate his story that he did. She lost her case at that point. ... Not all of society consider acquaintance rape as a serious offence. If there are no injuries some people will say 'What's the harm?' They cannot comprehend it as a serious offence, especially where consensual sex has taken place on a previous occasion. One woman lost her case even though she had bruises to her arms and shoulders because the boyfriend was able to establish that on previous occasions she had enjoyed that type of violence and had asked him to be rough.

It appears that the benefit of the doubt is with the offender both legally and culturally. In this example even where the jury had established that the offender had committed rape upon one woman, they did not believe the second victim and her credibility was more important than his. So even where the offender is a known rapist, the victim still must establish her credibility to a particular cultural standard which is weighted against her, to be believed. It is also clear from this judge's experience that there needs to be evidence of physical injury at the trial stage. He explicitly stated that evidence of harm is central, the more harm, the more believable the victim's story and this likens the offence of rape to an offence of Grievous Bodily Harm which has a wholly different evidential criteria, and more importantly for this research could even be assessed as a potential sexual murder. Interesting also is the comment that an offender was able to allege that the victim had on previous occasions enjoyed and encouraged 'rough aggressive' sex, which the jury believed and this relates to the perceived masochistic nature of women, a presumption which also inhibits rape prosecutions. So here there are three explanations for physical injury documented that act to defend the offender; first, as noted by the paramedic, that injuries could be self inflicted and, secondly, that they could be the result of consensual violence. It was the defence of Graham Coutts, the man convicted of the murder of Jane Longhurst, that she had consented to partial strangulation; thirdly, it can be argued that the violence was provoked by the victim in that, for example, the perpetrator was seduced by her manner of dress or behaviour.

Case study: Camilla Petersen – the primacy of sex to motivation

The circumstances of Camilla's murder are introduced in Chapter 5 under the sub-heading: 'Case study: Camilla Petersen: the primacy of sex in knowing the sex killer' (p. 110).

The officer's perceptions of Kemp were significantly focused on his status as a sex offender; their first impression and construction of events produce a narrative which describes a 'rape gone wrong':

> [We thought that it was]'a rape gone wrong, the rapist may have a need for power or control, there is resistance and it ends up going wrong. (R 2)

There is no suggestion in this narrative that Kemp had intended to kill Camilla from the outset, in fact it is stated that the police did not believe he had any intention to kill; he had urges that needed satisfying and the resistance of the victim precipitated her death. This is despite the officers describing a situation where there was minimal explicit sexual contact, but significant violent contact. By this I mean that the sexual assault was a small, described by the offender as a 'minute' amount of touching and there was no indication of penetration in the post-mortem report. However, the violence consisted of amongst other things, repeated punches to Camilla's face or bashing of her face into the ground and strangulation until death:

> Camilla was not raped, but he did use violence, her face must have been banged into the ground several times. The scene is consistent with his story. (R 2)

In this comment and others the violence is spoken of in terms of that which occurred prior to the violence which specifically caused her death. In these terms there was a sexual assault, there was punching and banging of her face into the ground and there was strangulation, represented as three quite separate and discrete offending character- istics; the sexual assault seen as the motivation, the interim violence seen as instrumental and the fatal violence as accidental/instrumental. This shows significant resistance to Schinkel's (2004) notion of *autotelic* violence, which is broadly that the use of violence itself is a stimulant in many cases. He says that 'We have hardly begun to understand violence *itself*. That is, we have largely ignored the intrinsic aspects violence possesses.' (2004:6). It seems that when men are violent to women that the *intrinsic* dimension to the motivation is characterized as sexual. This position significantly privileges the concept of 'sex' in knowing Kemp, placing it at the top of the hierarchy of offence characteristics. And whilst not accepting that Kemp was a determined killer or even determinedly violent, the investigating officers did accept that he was a determined paedophile; perhaps part of the understanding of sex offenders, and paedophiles especially, as incurable and single-minded (Hudson 2005).

A second narrative strand was offered, seemingly in contradiction to the argument that Camilla was killed for resisting too much, and that was that she was terrified and probably had not resisted but was killed to protect Kemp's identity:

> I was thinking that perhaps if she had been a local girl with a bit more savvy she may have put up more of a fight...she was very frightened, she was quite passive and did as she was told.' (R 1)

The two narratives conflict with, and in many respects, contradict each other. In one the victim resists so much she is beaten to death, in the second she is completely passive:

> [The assault on] Camilla was very pre meditated he was waiting for the opportunity, not necessarily to murder but to sexually assault. (R 2)

> It was sexual he said he had no intention of killing her...it was indecent assault for sexual gratification. (R 1)

Officers were resistant to the idea that Kemp may have planned or wanted to kill Camilla, or even that the violence itself was an intrinsic stimulus. In their narrative the killing was the result of Kemp experiencing overwhelming conventional sexual desire for Camilla and either accidentally killing her, or instrumentally killing her to stop her identifying him; a significant resistance to considering that the violence may have been expressive. After officers had interviewed Kemp and incorporated his version of events into the story, the police narrative suggests that Kemp watched Camilla sketching and then approached her in his underwear. He apparently made no attempt to hide his face or his appearance, and the respondents reported that he actively stopped himself from leaving any bodily fluids on Camilla; he did not kiss her or allow himself to ejaculate. He was described as 'very forensically aware' and had gone to great lengths before, during and after the assault to distance himself forensically from the scene. The fact that he made no attempt to hide his face seems careless behaviour in a man so focused and controlled in his attention to distancing himself from the crime scene; potentially because Camilla would not be able to physically identify him afterwards and he knew that.

It was the next day, after Camilla's body had been found that Kemp returned to the Isle of Wight and eventually telephoned the police to confess. The officers commented that Kemp had claimed to have attempted to commit suicide, but that the alleged attempt was not serious. The narrative tells a story of a man returning to the scene of the crime out of curiosity and to possibly distance himself further from the crime by removing any evidence left at the scene.

> We think he was coming back to see if the body had been found, if it hadn't we think he would probably have attempted to hide it better. (R 2)

It was also suggested that Kemp had cleared his residence, prior to returning to the island, of potentially incriminating pornographic materials as the flat was 'clean', 'no computer or anything' (R2). This perspective also suggests that Kemp was a significantly determined paedophile. I do not suggest here that Kemp did not 'clean' his flat of incriminating paedophilic/pornographic material, merely that the police were significantly focused on the sexual aspects to this offending to the exclusion of any other characteristics; they were in a dominant discourse of paedophile sexual murder and in Foucault's terms were constrained in what it was possible to think about Kemp.

The prosecution case file narrative which presents the formal story of the crime did focus on the idea that Kemp approached Camilla to look at her body or touch her sexually, killing her to stop her identifying him. This scenario does not construct Kemp as an inherently violent individual, or suggest that his violence was expressive, autotelic or gratuitous; his dangerousness being his inability to control his 'normal', though abnormally focused, sexual desires. Lacombe (2008) argues that the process of constructing sex offender identity is practiced within Cognitive Behavioural Therapy Treatment programmes in prisons, and the suggestion is that these offenders are encouraged to identify with particular constructions of themselves, accurate or not, in order to complete a treatment programme successfully; completing a programme successfully may be important in terms of parole or other benefits. In this respect the treatment itself is based upon a construction of the offender that may have limited accuracy, but it is a construction authorized as legitimate. Lacombe argues that the sex offender is constructed as 'a species entirely consumed by sex' (2008:56), a practice which can often lead to the assumption that the offender's sexual predilection is his biology and his destiny and that because of this the sex offender is not curable, merely controllable. It is important here to note that I do not attempt to speculate Kemp's psychology, merely to resist the dominant construction of him as 'consumed by sex'.

According to investigators things were further confused by the contradictory assessments of Kemp by the psychiatrists who examined him after his arrest:

> Well because of the diminished responsibility plea we had three psychiatrists examine him, the first believed he knew exactly what he was doing and that this was definitely a case of murder, the second one was sort of 50/50 he said that although he knew what he was doing, at the time he couldn't control his urges, the third one said that his sexual urges had laid dormant for a long time and because he wasn't on any medication to control them, it was out of his hands so it was diminished responsibility.
>
> Q. So the psychiatrists went with a sexual urge theory?
> A. Yes he had had medication from Broadmoor to control it, urges to have sex with children. He hadn't ever had a relationship with women, not ever. (R 3)

Sexual explanations for male on female homicide are perceived as particularly plausible and are disseminated widely in what Foucault describes as the 'literature of criminality' (1994:192) but also, sexual explanations have great rhetorical impact and social significance. There has been significant focus in this analysis on the ways in which Kemp was constructed as primarily a sexual deviant within the police and press narratives with his predilection for violence significantly marginalized. This aspect to Kemp's offending identity is key for it is via the concept of sex that Kemp is known. A sexual explanation for a male on female killing is as psychologically intelligible as it is utilitarian for it is not only plausible; there are frameworks in place for responding to it within the criminal justice and penal systems.

Lonni Petersen

I would first like to thank Lonni Petersen for participating in this research. Understandably Lonni has intense and powerful feelings about the violence perpetrated against her daughter and the individual responsible; the aim here is to explore how she perceives the narratives produced to explain her daughter's murder. Lonni was interviewed for this research some years after the offence and the court case and her construction of Kemp and the murder do not correspond with the police narrative. It became clear in this interview that she believed that Kemp had intended to kill her daughter from the outset:

> I've been wondering why he killed her all the time because I couldn't see the meaning. I couldn't see why. He could just have raped her and let her be but he didn't and I think that's because he didn't want to rape her, he wanted to kill her... there were so many bruises – it was so cruel. That's not in my mind a man who wants to rape. They are raping and holding people so they can do it. This man was attacking her.

It appeared that the police construction of events was not convincing to Lonni and she expressed some relief that she was able to hear Kemp's story unmediated by the police team during the trial. It was at this time that she was able to hear Kemp explaining the murder in his own words taken from extracts of police interviews with him:

> I was more focused on what Kemp was saying in interview, not the questions he was being asked. This was my chance to hear what had happened to my daughter, to hear why it had happened. In his interview I heard things for the first time.

Lonni felt that crucial information was kept from her by the police who, it must be considered, have almost sole ownership of the 'facts' of the case and significant power in constructing meaning. She could not understand why she could not be informed of the things Kemp had said and after hearing what he did say in court she was less convinced about the police narrative that this was an unintentional sex killing:

> I listened carefully in Court to what Kemp said and I remember thinking he is a clever psychopath who is saying all the right things to try and minimize his sentence.

It has been suggested that sex offenders may deliberately identify with certain constructions of themselves which fit with an institutional discourse (Lacombe 2008) and this approach may give them some sense of control over what happens to them. The legal and medical personnel may have ownership of the narrative and therefore the identity construction of the individual within the prosecutorial process, but this may not adequately reflect the ways in which other actors, including Kemp himself, perceive what has happened. Lonni felt that Kemp was defended by those structures charged with prosecuting him:

> I cannot under any circumstances understand how any police officer could have looked at all the circumstances around Camilla's death and thought it was anything other than an intended murder... I think that if police officers really thought that this was a sexual attack that 'went wrong' then they were in the wrong job.

Here Lonni is not prioritizing Kemp's sexual behaviour; she focuses on the violence, resisting the dominant discourses that inhibit thinking about paedophiles in such a way. After the trial Lonni commented that at least one member of his defence team had wished to distance themselves from their client, suggesting that they resisted any physical contact with him:

> I never understood why but (one of) Kemp's solicitors sent a message to me via the Family Liaison Officer. (They) wanted sympathy to be passed to me and wanted me to know that (they) had never even shaken Kemp's hand. I think (they) felt bad defending him and wanted to clear (their) conscience.

Paedophiles are particularly reviled in this culture at this time and it may be that this action reflects that revulsion. They may be especially represented as a reviled and homogenized group who we can immediately recognize (Kitzinger 2004) irrespective of the differences in their behaviours and the amount of danger they present to the public. Despite this and incredibly, Kemp's paedophilia appears to be defending him from the potentially more damning idea that his violence and/or killing is expressive or autotelic. From Kemp's perspective being a 'paedophile' frees him from admitting explicitly that he had an intention to kill *or* commit GBH which would undermine his defence of diminished responsibility and complete the offence of murder (English and Card 2007). In this respect there is an inherent defence in sexual motivation to charges of murder. If the intrinsic drive was reconceptualized as non-sexual the intention to commit serious injury would be established and no defences to murder would be left to exploit.

There seems little agreement on the part of any respondent as to whether Kemp intended to kill Camilla, his sexual urges clouding the issues. The sexual aspects again, appear to take precedence over the violent aspects and one police officer stated:

> The thing is he knew when he was a danger and this time he wanted the urges, he was not mentally impaired at the time, he wanted the urges this time, he had a system after Broadmoor where he could speak to someone and get help as soon as he felt the urges. He didn't do that. He knew he was a danger. (R 3)

It was even reported that the psychiatrist who examined Kemp thought that there was too much focus on Kemp's paedophilia:

> Dr Somekh told the trial that much was done to convert Kemp's sexual desires from children to a normal heterosexual outlook but not enough was done to treat his violent nature. (Mitchell 2003c)

Case study: Hannah Foster – the primacy of sex to investigative practice

When Hannah was reported missing by her parents on Sunday 16 March 2003, it could have been a standard missing person enquiry with every expectation that this bright and normal teenage girl would turn up safe and well having thoughtlessly stayed with a friend without informing her worried parents. However, having investigated the background of the missing girl the police decided that this enquiry warranted special attention as Hannah's disappearance was significantly out of character:

> We have to assess how much at risk she is and balance the stereotype with accounts from friends, with this it was clearly out of character. Concerns were raised after the background checks. The most likely scenario was that she had been abducted and raped; there is no other potential motive. If it was a Michael Stone type, her body would have been at the scene of the last sighting. (R 1)

The stereotype referred to by this officer would appear to be a stereotype of the type of a girl who might be expected to stay away from home, either because she had a history of such behaviour, or because she was sexually active; 'she could have been a seventeen year old out shagging', as one senior officer put it. It was stated that there is *no other potential motive* than abduction and rape. This immediate assumption, drawn only from a brief history of the girl and based on general stereotypes, indicates the enormous power and complete acceptance of the knowledge we have of violence against women provided by the discourse of sexual murder. By this I mean that a sexually motivated murder is immediately assumed as this is represented as *the* 'spectre' threatening all women, and possibly, teenage girls in particular. It also points to the fine parameters within which women and young girls operate; their behavioural patterns can be accurately assessed with a minimal amount of information and corroborated merely by drawing from powerful stereotypes. This indicates that their behavioural patterns are actually tightly controlled and surveilled by themselves as well as others. Mardorassian defines this as 'a new form of panopticism' (cited in Bourke 2007:434) powerfully demonstrating how rape justifies the social surveillance and control of women in the name of concerned protection.

Sexual motivation, as already noted, is an ill defined and nebulous concept which embraces any kind of intrinsic drive or energy of men directed at women. Because of this, violence against women, is often imagined through the concept of rape which is an immediate and easy point of reference and this links violence and sexual acts as well as violence and internal drives and desires:

> Q. If there was a murder of a female like that of Margaret Muller in a park with no obvious sexual motivation, do you consider the act of killing a kind of sexual motivation?
> A. We don't really understand the things that may make something like that sexual...they surmise it was sexual but it's not necessarily the case, it's sexual because of an historical link. (R 1)

This comment very clearly situates the knowledge system operating here as part of discourse of sexual murder. This officer is clear that the sexual motivation speculated is part of an enduring framework for assessing offences and offenders which has a stable history and not because there was necessarily any evidence at the crime scene for making such an assumption and this is the discourse of sexual murder in practice.

On the day that Hannah was reported missing the police received crucial information that confirmed their fears that they were dealing with abduction. A '999' call from Hannah's mobile phone had been received,

Hannah had not spoken directly to the operator but an automatic system had recorded what was believed to be a silent/malicious call for some two minutes before cutting off. The contents of that recording were subsequently recovered and made it clear that Hannah had been abducted and was threatened with rape:

> She (Hannah) said in the phone call, he said he wants to rape her and she is saying 'just take me home' and then she said she was going to call the police as soon as she got home. It's all on the tape, she rang 999 and her phone was on in her handbag but you can't trace it and if there's no talking it's treated as malicious and the thing cuts off after about 20 seconds. She was saying 'I only live here take me home to my Mum. (R 4)

For operational reasons the police did not wish to release any information about the phone call. If the information of the phone call had been released the police would probably have received much more interest from the press but it would have been impossible to then, suppress that information. At this time it was suspected, but not known, that Hannah's life was in danger. In contradiction to the kind of press interest witnessed at Soham, which was subject of an investigation by the Attorney General, Lord Goldsmith, if the 'event' being sold is not of sufficient interest, press attention can be difficult to attract. Editors and publishers have enormous power over defining what is newsworthy and what is not (Greer 2003) and at this stage of the investigation it was just a missing girl enquiry as far as the press were concerned:

> We weren't getting too many calls and the media weren't really interested, at this stage usually they just wouldn't be involved,…Also you know it was a Sunday evening, it is really difficult to sell stories on a Sunday, they all buy news in on a Sunday, Meridian and BBC News South is all magaziney at the weekend. No nationals would be interested at that stage.' (R 5)

> We had our media strategy and statement prepared. We were very cagey though, no info about the phone call we could have blown our hand – we had to believe she was still alive. We had to be careful with what we could release and could not release. (R 5)

Feist (1999) conducted research into the effective use of media by the police in serious crime investigations and found that the age and background of the victim and the location of the offence were important in determining the amount of media attention given to the crime. In cases where media attention is difficult to sustain there are clearly different challenges for the officers charged with the investigation. Feist also noted that decisions about whether or not to disclose information were seen to be crucial, especially the timing of information released to enable management of the situation and to allow the police to take the lead. It was possible that if Hannah was alive and being held, that information about the phone call could have put her life in danger. This was at least part of the police perspective. The police could not know, but Hannah was already dead by the time they received this crucial information. They went ahead with the press conference despite the lack of interest:

> We had a press conference set up for 2.30 at Hulse Road. There were about 6 press reps there, if that, hardly anyone, just as we were preparing there was a telephone call, they had found a body. The conference was postponed. Within half an hour it was confirmed it was Hannah's body. Things started to escalate with the media the next morning. There was a conference at Allington Lane (location where body was found) this side of the cordon, all the local media were there and the nationals and the TV news. (R 5)

> With Hannah they (the press) wanted the press conference at the scene (where the body was found), it manages the press snooping at the scene. They love pictures of uniformed PC's. We will do that to give them the footage. (R 1)

This comment indicates that there has already been compromise, with the press at least partially dictating their access, but the police allowing some access in their own interests. This interplay has little overt strategic significance for the police at this time, but may encourage witnesses to come forward. Once the police confirmed they were conducting a murder enquiry of a young girl, possibly by a stranger, press interest escalated dramatically, the circumstances fulfilling the definition of 'sexual murder'. A sexual murder is a high profile newsworthy event and attracted the full complement of news media both local and national. The police appointed a senior officer immediately to manage the press interest and deflect attention from the Senior Investigating Officer (SIO). The press attention in a high profile case can be overwhelming and needs specific dedicated police resources. The officers spoke of managing the press as a priority with a media strategy formulated at the outset. Police accountability is very high profile and the press can have significant influence over public and other perceptions of their competence and this is compelling reason to create a working relationship with them. The appointment of dedicated press liaison resources is testament to their power and influence. Managing perceptions is seen as a political task so apart from police 'detective' skills, new skills of information management are necessary and these are provided by the higher ranking officers:

> We deal with all murders in (force area) and as far as (a Supt's) role is concerned it's 'What is the potential damage to the organization?' It is about damage limitation...you need a Superintendent to deal with the political ramifications. (R 2)

> You can manage the press but you can't control them...we have to drip feed them information. The press will print information anyway and their story could become destructive so we use them as a strategy to identify key lines of enquiry. We have media management for critical incidents. Soham were led by the media and lessons were learned. (R 1)

The management of the press is seen from two very different perspectives in the last two statements, an operational and a political perspective. The first shows how the senior officers are concerned with 'damage limitation' of the police image, and the second officer is concerned with identifying means by which the investigation can be progressed using the press interest. A third impact of press attention is in the personal responses of the officers to the intense attention:

> They literally trailed me down the road, following me, badgering me. We closed the press office at night though, because there's nothing in it for us except to serve the media. It could have been resourced better, (officer) must have done 50 press releases you know, its quid pro quo, we want goodwill with the media and by feeding them we ensure their goodwill next time. (R 5)

The press conference held at Allington Lane was attended by the nation's media and this was at the very earliest stages of the investigation. The police prepared their statement being very careful to only impart information that would appease the press and not compromise the operational agenda.

> I was taken aback at the amount of media there, there were 50 or more journalists. Of course what you can't do at that time is 'no questions' you have to go armed with an agreement of what to release and a number of bog standard replies...they will ask everything from "how are the family coping?" to "was she promiscuous?" (R 1)

Here the relevance of the police/press nexus becomes crucial to the central argument of this book, here we begin to see that negotiations between the press and the police revolved around certain aspects of Hannah's murder which began to form the narrative and reflected the discursive conventions at play when responding to male on female violence. Feist (1999) found that although police can dictate what information is released and when, they have no control over the way the press portray that information. At this stage in the investigation into Hannah's death the police felt that they should pre-empt the questions that would be put to them by the press so that what was released could be carefully managed. The immersion in the discourse of sexual murder by both the police and the press meant that the police already knew what questions would be asked and how they would be framed, there being a shared discursive regime. Information that is managed by the police has a strong relationship to knowledge and the press are seeking information that will either corroborate their own particular perspective or create a 'sellable' perspective. De Lint states that:

> Indeed the police enjoy a pivotal position as gatekeepers of the criminal justice process: they provide information to the courts and other institutions...knowledge is actionable information that has undergone validity checking. (2003:385)

The officers knew that the press were seeking certain information and this was related to the sexual dimensions of the crime and the victim's life. The officers remarked that this was irrelevant and distasteful and there was an apparent resistance on their part to give this information:

> They wanted details on how the body was found and by whom and personal details about the victim...they ask the same question 10 or 15 different ways to get the answer though. The rep from the

Hampshire Chronicle was the worst, really salacious, wanted all the details of her sexual behaviour. (R 5)

They ask "was there a sexual motivation or a rape, was there an affair or any sexual motive?" ...they kept shouting out "was she promiscuous?" and "should she have been there, should she have known better?...and anything at all to do with sex". (R 1)

Q. 'What type of information do you release when the murder of a female occurs?
A. They want details of a sexual nature mainly, they always want a photo and some background

Q. Do they ask for specific information?
A. Yes, "Was it a sex crime?". (R 2)

These quotes indemnify much academic criticism of the nature of press reporting of the murder of females (Mason and Monckton-Smith 2008, Carter and Weaver 2003, Soothill and Walby 1991). The journalists were proactively seeking information of a sexual nature, not only with reference to the offence, but with reference to the sexual reputation of the victim, an aspect of our culture so vividly highlighted in the work of Lees (1997) and Tanenbaum (2007) and discussed in Chapter 3. The police were apparently deliberately deflecting this type of question but the journalists continued asking the same questions in several different ways determined to get the response for their own agenda which would appear to be less reporting the salient facts, than constructing a sexual narrative. This murder actually fitted the criteria for a classic sexual murder but the information sought reflects that the press were seeking to explain what had happened by scrutinizing Hannah's sexual behaviour. Even at this stage Hannah was being assessed for her potential culpability in her own murder. However, despite their criticism of this aspect of the press interest, the importance of sexual reputation was not absent in the police approach to the victim, neither was the importance of Hannah's beauty:

It's rare to hear but she was without a secret history. She was very normal, gifted and bright. Because she was so nice you wouldn't want to release that anyway. I mean she really was exceptional, she was clever and beautiful it was such a waste. (R 5)

She was very beautiful you know, a very beautiful girl. She was not promiscuous at all what you could call the perfect daughter. (R 4)

When they did the *Crimewatch* reconstruction the girl they got to be Hannah wasn't good looking at all, I would have been really upset about that if I had known her, she was a lovely looking girl, it was a shame. (R 1)

If she hadn't been so pretty she would probably be alive today. (R 5)

These comments frame female and male sexuality in hetero/sexual terms. First, a belief that Hannah may have been selected for her beauty rather than her availability is apparent which places sexual lust at the centre of the motivation for abducting her; and secondly, the importance of her sexual behaviour prior to this incident in assessing her worth. Brownmiller notes that Albert De Salvo, the Boston Strangler stated to police 'Attractiveness has nothing to do with it, she was a woman' (1975:204).

Part of the police media strategy was to prioritize local news services and keep the local news high profile. The police knew the offender was a local man and if they were going to get help with the enquiry that help would probably come from a local person and this in itself was problematic. All the journalists were looking for exclusives and if they could not get the information they needed or wanted from the police, they could seek it from alternative sources. The police felt also that alienating certain factions of the press would be detrimental to the overall investigation with information from alternative sources and bad feeling feeding a negative perception of the police efforts.

The (Southampton) Echo revealed stuff we didn't want released there was a police leak. There was an enquiry, the information could only have come from a police source. All the reporters have their sources, the big papers they have very powerful and influential sources. A lot of the time the press already have the story they just contact us to confirm facts and get more information. It's as much about what I do say as what I don't. They don't like getting no for an answer. (R 5)

An officer told me how one media source obtained information about the telephone call and that it was crucial that this information was not revealed as Hannah's assailant would have been unaware that the police had this information and a recording of his voice. The team had to negotiate with that source to suppress the information:

> We need the ability to bargain and persuade. (BBC) Radio 5 found out about the phone call, we didn't want it out, we promised them we wouldn't give the info to anyone else, we promised that when the time came we would give it to them first, in that way we managed to sit on it for a couple of days. (R 5)

This of course compromised the exclusivity promised to the local press and was potentially damaging to the ongoing police need for positive relations with the local media. The release of this new information, though stalled for a short time, was promised to Radio 5 and not the local reporters whose goodwill was so crucial. An important point is raised here in that Radio 5 already had the information about the phone call, they did not need to be given the information by the police. The officer states that they promised to *give* the information to Radio 5 first. It must be considered that in 'giving' the information to Radio 5 (who already had it anyway) that the police would be cited as the source, this would be beneficial to both organizations; the police appearing to have maintained control of the investigation and the media able to legitimize and authorize their information as true. In this context the suppression of the information and the 'giving back' of that information to the press was critical for the police and their public image and not necessarily only for operational reasons cited.

The phone call was potentially an explosive piece of information for the press, for it confirmed a sexual dimension to the offence. This was an aspect that the police had deliberately decided to downplay in the early stages. The police had confirmation that there was sexual violence, the press assumed it, but in drip feeding the press to keep the story current, this information was 'handled'. The press were told that there was 'no evidence to suggest that Hannah had been raped'. This information was potentially more attention grabbing than Hannah's death:

> There was no 'physical' evidence, had we found semen? Had she been sexually assaulted? We found a way round those questions, we didn't want them to know she'd been raped...they suspected sexual motivation from the outset, it usually is the reason, very rarely is the victim not sexually assaulted. (R 5)

This was not an issue that the press were willing to leave, despite the police clearly stating there was no evidence. Hannah's body was also found fully clothed and this was of interest to the press:

> State of dress is very important, it is unusual for the victim to be dressed in the kind of case of Hannah. The classic victim has her upper clothing pulled up and legs asplay. A high proportion of rape/ murders the victim is killed during the assault, Hannah was raped and allowed to dress afterwards. (R 1)

Despite the apparent lack of evidence or information from the police to support a sexual assault as having been central to this murder, the press inferred sexual assault. In nearly every report in every publication there was the information that Hannah's body was fully clothed when found and that the police had no evidence of sexual assault. However, comments from the police reported in the press stated that they were interviewing sex offenders in the area. Even though evidence of sexual assault was denied, the press reports implied that sexual assault was the motivation. The police did not appear to be denying sexual assault, rather leaving it open for speculation:

> Q. Was the fact that Hannah was sexually assaulted deliberately kept from the press?
> A. No. I used the words 'there is no evidence to suggest a sexual assault (Silence for some time)
>
> Q. It was said by the BBC that there was no reason to suspect a sexual motive was this suppressed information?
> A. It was not strategic. We were hoping it was rape, we were hoping she had been raped so there would be some DNA. There was no DNA in the Petersen (Camilla Petersen) murder it makes it much more difficult. (R 2)

However, the police did also state that that they would be contacting known sex offenders in the area clearly again locating Hannah's murder within a sexual framework. The police knew and speculated the sexual aspects to this case and just because these thoughts were not revealed explicitly to the press does not mean the police were any less focused on the sexual aspects. The police media strategy and the type and timing of information used to drip feed the press was not 'accident', this was an 'event' and everyone 'knew' what had happened, why it happened, how to report it, how to keep it current, how to investigate it, what suspects to look at and what needed to be known about the victim. However, the sexual dimensions in a case like this are particularly traumatic for close relatives. Sexual and salacious details published in the press serve little purpose other than to sensationalize the crime but in the middle of all this activity were Hannah's family. Police know that the press desire for footage of grieving relatives is tremendous. The trauma and devastation felt by relatives at this time makes them very vulnerable and family liaison officers are placed with the family with the aim of guiding them through the difficult early days of the investigation. These officers do not always end contact with the family even after investigations have ended and provide a continuum of support that can last sometimes, for years after the events:

> The family wanted no media contact at all so my advice was to do the conference and keep them at bay…it's a sick game really, the coverage of a murder for the press. (R 5)

> The press definitely have an agenda they want an in with the family, they will try and trick them into saying something, the nitty gritty, it adds spice to the story. (R 4)

> …because the releases were structured we kept them (press) away from the door. Some did use aggressive tactics they say stuff like 'if you don't tell us we'll have to speculate' it's a veiled threat but they are the minority. (R 1)

This indicates another political structuring of the information available to certain people, the family are excluded as are the Family Liaison Officers, just in case sensitive information is leaked out of the investigation team's control. There are obviously crucial operational, evidential and sometimes legal reasons for this. The releasing of some information into the wrong hands could prejudice the outcome of a criminal prosecution or cause the offender to abscond before capture. The press may be very keen on interviewing relatives and friends but the type of information that can usually be gleaned from them will be of a personal nature about the victim and the press are acutely aware of this. This shows again the importance of female reputation. Unguarded comments from friends and relatives who are less experienced in the ways of the press have the potential to be far more titillating and salacious than structured information from police sources.

It was decided to make an appeal on the BBC *Crimewatch* programme to try and speed up the process of identifying the offender. Police procedures had already identified several individuals who could be suspect, but this process of elimination was time consuming. The *Crimewatch* appeal raised issues for the police, again of what information to release to the press and problems of exclusivity:

> The *Crimewatch* programme put the police under tremendous pressure to provide something new like DNA evidence. It was really hard for (name)...they used every trick to get him to give them something extra. But he was really strong he didn't. First of all they sent over the girl presenter to flirt with him and try to get him to give something over, when that didn't work they sent Nick Ross over as the hard man, to get something, saying that it would produce better results etc. The trouble was if we had given an exclusive to *Crimewatch* that would have put the local press nose out of joint and they may have been less manageable. It is a very political process with the press. (R 1)

It was as a result of the *Crimewatch* programme that the offender was identified. There was clearly some irritation at this by certain officers and a feeling that *Crimewatch* had beaten them to it:

> We would have got there, we already had identified a number of suspects the media just speeded up the process, they only beat us by a couple of days. We would have had him without their involvement. (R 2)

There is clearly some professional pride at stake. Comment is often made in academic work of the differing agendas of the police and the press but Leishman and Mason (2003) note that there are also many parallels. In some cases the roles of the police and the press may converge in that both seek to 'solve' the crime. Reiner (1997) and Innes (2002) speak of press/police collusion for their mutual benefit but in this instance there appears to be an insecurity in the police investigating team, or more crucially in certain individual officers that the press might 'beat them to it'. This competitive nature in investigating teams has been highlighted in the cases of Peter Sutcliffe and Jack the Ripper, but has been seen to occur between forces or police investigating teams and not between the police and the press (Ward Jouve 1988).

There was some level of resentment from the police that the *Crimewatch* programme identified the offender and it was stressed that they (the police) were only a couple of days behind the programme in identifying Maninder Pal Singh Kohli as the prime suspect. It was unfortunate for them in this case, that Kohli was not only identified, but located and arrested as a result of media and family 'interference'. There is much at stake for the police in a high profile investigation of this nature; it is not only their image that needs protecting but their methods, knowledge and process structures. If the press appear to be ahead of the police this would threaten both procedures and knowledge.

Kohli had left the country and disappeared to his native India leaving behind his wife and children by the time he was identified. The police were not hopeful of locating him in such a vast country. This created further problematic issues for the investigating team. Hannah's parents had decided to travel to India and appeal directly to the Indian people for information about the murder of their daughter:

> (We) didn't want them to go to India, for a start (officer) was worried about exclusivity with the press you can't do that. (officer) couldn't have them going out there on their own talking to the Indian press so we had to go with them. ...(officer) was worried about the damage that could be done with the visit, but we were stuck in the middle between the Fosters and the press. (R 4)

The visit although difficult, produced the result the Foster's desired. The man suspected of killing their daughter was located in India near the border with Nepal. He had married a Nepalese woman and it was thought he was about to cross the border. He was taken into custody by the Indian police and extradition proceedings were started. There were still a myriad of problems to be faced by the investigating team, the offender had appeared in the Indian press, on the television, confessing to the crime and admitting to the rape:

> He coughed to it in India, to them. He said he meant to rape and not to kill, he raped her twice. He said to her that she mustn't tell anyone, but she said she was going straight home to tell her parents, then he strangled her. He showed no remorse, within 24 hrs he left the country and started a new life. (R 3)

> With Hannah the suspect has been on TV admitting it, he was probably an opportunist he was someone who had the potential to abduct and rape and having taken the first step, well the rest is history. (R 1)

It was five years before Kohli was successfully convicted of Hannah's murder. Even after admitting to murdering and raping Hannah on Indian TV he did not plead guilty to the charges when back in the UK. He claimed that he himself had been abducted over a gambling debt and forced to have sex with Hannah whilst he was bound and blindfolded. In contradiction to this defence, the prosecution claimed that Kohli had gone out on the night Hannah was murdered 'looking for sex' and that because he knew he was leaving the country in a matter of days he 'could rape somebody and get away with it' (Stallard 2008). The implication here is that Hannah was killed because Kohli wanted some 'sex' and that given he was leaving the country he could take that extra step and do what other men could not. There is an uncomfortable but nuanced intimation in the prosecution narrative that we would accept that rape is a more edgy or satisfying form of sexual intercourse for men; they say that Kohli went out looking for sex, but *because he could get away with it* he decided to rape *someone*. This does not suggest that rape is an abhorrent violence but an assault that perhaps many men would perpetrate if they could get away with it.

Police narratives: the primacy of sex

It appeared from the police interviews conducted that it is not only the media that privilege the concept of sex when assessing violence towards women. Even though the murders of Camilla Petersen and Hannah Foster are defined as sexual murder, this approach limited professional responses to the crimes. Police 'knowledge' of sexual murder could be argued to be produced in an atmosphere of what could be described as institutional sexism, which may limit its status as 'knowledge'. Individual police officers 'knowledge' of these crimes is partially at least, borne of a police culture of reverence for 'experience' in the field. The police approach to a gendered stranger homicide works from a standard assumption of *presence* of sexual assault or motivation rather than this being a *possible* motivation, and it could be argued that this distracts the investigation. Kohli was not apprehended via knowledge that this was a sexually motivated offence, he was arrested and identified *despite* this knowledge. The same was so in the case of Antoni Imiela and Peter Sutcliffe. Kohli, Imiela, Sutcliffe and Kemp were not on the sex offenders register or known to be sex offenders by any other means (except Kemp who had previous convictions but was not registered as a sex offender). Searching for known sex offenders on the basis of presence or speculation of, a sexual assault where there has been a homicide does not always appear to be helpful. Steve Wright, the so-called Suffolk strangler who was convicted in February 2008 of the murder of five women in Ipswich, was apprehended because his DNA had been taken in an unrelated offence of theft and was stored on the National DNA Database (NDNAD); Wright had no criminal history of sexual offending. Mark Dixie who was convicted in February 2008 of the murder of Sally Anne Bowman in Croydon had a long history of sexual offending but his DNA was on the NDNAD because of a conviction for minor assault in a bar fight which occurred *after* the murder of Sally Anne. Research by Soothill *et al* (2002) examined what criminal histories can tell us about future serious offending and in particular looked at serious sexual assault (of adult women) and homicide. The research established that 36 per cent of serious sexual offenders have no previous convictions and of those who do have previous convictions, only 7 per cent had a conviction for a sexual offence. The only offence correlated with an increased risk of murdering a female stranger was 'robbery' or 'assault with intent to rob'. It appears from this research that convictions for violent offences were more significant in predicting future serious offending (serious sexual assault and murder) than convictions for sexual assault. Research by Sample (2006) found that sex offenders do not frequently commit murder and that rates of homicide recorded against them are no higher than for other types of offenders.

However, in investigations for serious sexual assault and stranger murders of females in my sample, the sex takes precedence over the violence and it appears that a certain type of sexual offender is focused on. The investigation into the murder of Rachel Nickell in front of her two year old son on Wimbledon Common in 1992 was a fiasco. The police employed the services of criminal profiler Paul Britton, and all seemed convinced that a man called Colin Stagg was the culprit. His entire intervention in this case revolved around trapping Stagg into confessing by involving him in the fabricated sexual fantasies of an undercover police officer. The dominance of sex and sexual fantasy as a guiding strategy saw Stagg first imprisoned and then acquitted. Meanwhile Rachel's killer was free despite having been suggested as a suspect by a team of officers from another force investigating a series of rapes. This man Robert Napper went on to murder another woman, Samantha Bissett and her four year old daughter Jazmine in 1993. Robert Napper was finally convicted of Rachel's killing in December 2008. The focus on fantastical sexual fantasies was a distraction here and even in the wake of all this, respected criminal psychologist Laurence Allison, in a Dispatches documentary focusing on this case (Dispatches 22 June 2009

Channel 4 8pm) chose to talk of the sadistic sexual fantasies of Napper and described him as a modern day Jack the Ripper who, instead of focusing on prostitutes, chose young mums. This was another investigation led hopelessly astray by an obsessive concentration on sexual fantasy.

Given the focus on previous sexual offending the sex offenders register may be considered a useful tool for the police but whether the sex offenders register is useful in this context is a matter for debate. Soothill *et al* (2002) recommend that the amount of 'trigger' offences for inclusion on the register should be broadened to include more minor criminal acts. However, even if this were implemented the sex offenders register may still be a poor tool for identifying possible suspects. The criticisms leveled at the police after the crimes in Soham are testament to the problems inherent in the criminal justice system. Ian Huntley was not on the sex offenders register and not because he had never been suspected of committing sexual offences. No convictions were ever secured, and this says much about the system. Graham Coutts the man convicted of the murder of Jane Longhurst in March 2003 had no criminal record but had been acquitted of an offence involving him secretly filming a woman in swimming pool changing room (BBC R4 2004). Her family believe that Coutts may have been suspected and caught earlier had this acquittal been kept on file. If the previous allegations against Huntley and Coutts had resulted in successful prosecutions Huntley would not have been able to secure a job working with children, but that is not to say he would never have murdered anyone, and concerns about Coutts may have led to his predilections being less secret to those who trusted him, like Jane Longhurst. It is so very difficult to achieve convictions in the criminal justice system for sexual offences against women, that the sex offenders register is not representative of the individuals in society who pose a serious risk. Kohli, Imiela, Sutcliffe, Shaun Beech, the offender in the spousal drug rape case discussed earlier in Chapter 5 and Thomas Shanks, the offender in the murder of Vicky Fletcher discussed earlier also in Chapter 5, were not known sex offenders. There was shock and disbelief from their family, friends and colleagues when they were arrested and even though this sample is very small it may still indicate that the sexual aspects in these cases were distracting. In all these cases the sexual aspects were less important from an investigative and 'meaning making' perspective than was speculated; the concentration on sexual aspects creating a skewed perception of the offences, the victims and the offenders. The belief by police officers that Richard Kemp or Maninder Pal Singh Kohli didn't intend to kill, indicates that the police believed the motivation for these assaults was purely sexual in the conventional sense. The offenders had sexual urges that did not include gratification from an act of murder or extreme violence but more from looking, touching or sexual intercourse. The death of the victim was a result of the rape or sexual assault. It is not thought that the death of the victim was inevitable as a result of the violent predisposition of the offender, more that they would be prepared to kill where no other action would prevent their identification. Kemp was apparently mentally ill (police respondent) and had previously been treated at Broadmoor, Kohli was not and had lived and worked in the community supporting a wife and children. Both men were perceived to have killed out of panic after satiating a sexual urge. In this context the murders were separate from the sex, a different but related act with rational motivations. The officer's perception is that the offences are purely driven by sex, the sex the motivation, the murder the conclusion. The assumption is that a 'real' rapist would cover his tracks by any means and this assumption may have significant repercussions when assessing possible rapists.

The police know what the press want, what type of information or detail they seek to sell newspapers and will provide this information in the name of good relations and with apparent bad grace. However, in releasing this type of sexual detail, either negatively or positively the press are not only kept at bay, but the public can feel assured that this is a crime they are familiar with. Targeting sex offenders and awaiting results of post mortems to ascertain whether or not sexual assault has occurred may give the police valuable time and deflect attention from what is going on behind the scenes. This type of information was strategically used to 'drip feed' the press in the case of Hannah Foster, apparently to keep them interested and keep the investigation high profile, but it also gives the police a forum and procedure for releasing what is in fact irrelevant information. Release of this type of information confirms that the police are dealing with a certain type of offender and offence and keeps speculation within the scope of the dominant discourse, a discourse which sells newspapers and can construct plausible cases for prosecution.

7
Rape and Murder Related

Introduction

Sex is now an imperative; it has become the epithet for every intrinsic drive experienced by man in respect of woman however that is expressed, and this is fundamental to the problems identified in this book. We justify a substantial number of violent crimes against women with reference to its meanings, characteristics and qualities. But what is 'sexual' in the context of violence against women lacks both lucid definition and observable parameters; to rationalize rape or murder as 'sexual' actually tells us very little. Often, and certainly in my data, when men rape or murder women it is reasoned in the media and police narratives that there is an *intrinsic* motivation; however, the concomitant assumption that an intrinsic motivation is sexual, is a blunt tool with which to try and comprehend so-called sexual murders. It is of critical importance that we expand our commonsense notions of what drives men to be violent to women; 'sexual' as an all encompassing explanation which fails to situate that sexuality in its cultural or social context is analytically nebulous and intellectually crude. Jack the Ripper, for example, may have experienced some intrinsic drive to mutilate and kill, it may even be that he felt more comfortable or satisfied mutilating and killing women in particular; it may be an intrinsic or essential drive, but that is not unproblematically *sexual*. It is not universally accepted that human sexuality is fixed, stable and genetically encoded as heterosexual, there is a strong theoretical strand, for example, that constructs sexuality as a dynamic process vulnerable to environmental and experiential influence and if this is the case the whole concept of what provokes a sexual response becomes inextricably linked to societal and cultural practices and beliefs. In this respect, explanations which invoke sex as causal *must* situate that sex in its cultural and environmental context.

Violence against men is not rationalized with reference to sex. The bruised or injured body of the male subject is not a site for sexual objectification. In films, for example, which allow the voyeuristic gaze to rest upon violated male flesh, and this will often be in the context of war or battle, he will rarely be naked and exposed, he will not be displayed and made spectacle in this particular way. We often make social or political statements when we acknowledge such abuse of men and Tatar says that 'whilst there is a cultural willingness to face the horrors of war, there is a corresponding disavowal of the unheroic victims of random sexual violence' (1995:13). Male victims of rape are largely invisible in public discussions of sexual violence; they remain essentially unreconstructed as discursive objects and are what Graham describes as 'unusual victims' (2006:192). Historically, androcentric constructions of human sexuality have placed individuals in a hierarchy on the basis of who penetrates whom with the socially inferior being proper objects of penetration; women, boys, foreigners and slaves (Mottier 2008). Graham further suggests that Judith Butler's argument that the definition of heterosexuality produces gendered subjectivities based upon whether the subject is penetrated or not, reveal that in societies where hetero/sexuality is dominant, that penetration of the male body is difficult to comprehend; 'the masculine remains impenetrable and the feminine that penetrated' (2006:197). Graham further suggests that male rape is often represented as a 'gay' problem with both victim and perpetrator understood as homosexual or bisexual and distanced from heterosexuality. The nuance in these arguments is that rape is represented as both sexual and related to sexual preferences.

The governing logic that restricts or disallows such sexual objectification and signification of heterosexual men is that females are the natural objects of sexual desire but sexual desire itself is male, and therein lies a problem; desire is active, object is passive. In the context of violence against women it is speculated that *he* experiences the act as sex so it *is* sex but he experiences it as sex *because* she is a woman. The consequent argument is that what is done to the object of sexual desire *is* sex (Jenefsky 1999) and this goes some way to explaining how the concept of rape is embedded into narratives of violence against women. If rape is violence and sex, or even violent sex, then it evokes an intelligible link between any kind of violence and sex. We can see also how this discursive approach can reverse the feminist proposition that rape should be considered violence and not sex; instead the symbolic value of rape facilitates perceiving any violence, even fatal violence, against women by men as a sexual act and so reveals its potential to reconstruct violence as rape. So there are two powerful assumptions driving this perspective: first, in the context of violence against women by men all *intrinsic* drives can be perceived as *sexual*. Second, because the drive can be considered sexual, the violence can be understood as either sublimation for sex *or* enabling sex to occur both of which can be symbolically or definitively equated with rape. It is not what Schinkel (2004) describes as an autotelic or even an expressive violence, the offender is more inherently sexually deviant than he is inherently violent. Schinkel's argument that we have largely ignored the intrinsic seductions of violence for its own sake resonate with the idea that resorting to sexual explanations for any or all violence against women is myopic.

Sexual victimization is constructed as peculiar to women, it is an additional threat over and above that which threatens men, and consequently underwrites the cultural belief that women are inferior and weaker. The threat of rape is ever-present, but by this I do not suggest that women are in a perpetual state of fear. However, I do suggest that its scope demarcates social boundaries and is an efficient reminder of a gendered hierarchy. This is effectively illustrated in popular media. Strong female characters in fictional drama can be effectively put in their place with the threat of rape, automatically the hierarchy is re-written and she is less powerful. Sergeant Jane Penhaligon, played by Geraldine Sommerville in TV series *Cracker*, for example, is raped by a colleague and this reminds us that women may be police officers but they are as vulnerable as *any woman* and this undermines their status especially in comparison to male officers; Detective Constable Paula McIntyre, played by Emma Handy in TV series *Wire in the Blood* is abducted by a sadistic killer whilst she acts as a prostitute to trap him, reinforcing her feminine vulnerability for she was unable to effectively defend herself from being abducted by a sexual attacker; Police Community Support Officer Mary Bousefield, played by Sophie Stanton is shown in the first episode of TV drama *Whitechapel* engaged in crowd control and it was clear that given her capable demeanour that she was going to be a victim. She was killed and mutilated in the second episode by a Jack the Ripper copycat, an assault equated with sexual violence. Even superheroes it seems are vulnerable to rape if they are female. In the film *Watchmen* (Dir Zack Snyder 2009) female superhero Sally Jupiter/Silk Spectre is the subject of an attempt to rape her by another superhero. She is only saved by another *male* superhero. So even here the hierarchy is clear – females must forever live with their vulnerability to rape *and* the aftermath. It is stated in reviews of the film *Watchmen* that the attempted rape affected the psychology of the character Sally throughout the film (Big Picture 2008) and certainly the aftermath of character Jane Penhaligon's rape in *Cracker* dominated her screen presence ever afterwards.

Tanya Horeck tells of the offensive exchange which occurred when Carlin Romano, in a critique of the work of feminist lawyer and anti-pornography campaigner Catherine MacKinnon, published an imagined rape of her in *The Nation*. Romano decided that given MacKinnon's radical stance on pornography and rape, with which he disagreed, that he would conduct what he called a 'thought experiment' and publish the imagined rape of her by two of her intellectual adversaries. He begins his piece by saying 'Suppose I decide to rape Catherine MacKinnon before reviewing her book' (cited in Horeck 2004:2). He didn't say 'decide to try to rape' or 'try to imagine raping'; the infused certainty in this quote that he would only have to decide to commit rape for it to be realized reveals the sheer enormity of the gendered power relation in operation; this is *his* power to wield. Horeck then shows how this 'thought experiment' precipitated a heated exchange between Romano, MacKinnon, the two men 'used' to rape MacKinnon in the fantasy, and the editorial staff at *The Nation*. It is discomforting that the ensuing exchanges focused on drawing the line between what is real and what is imagined rape, I would suggest that this is not the most important point at issue. When Romano stated he could *decide* to rape MacKinnon, and then others were outraged at what Horeck (2004) calls his 'public rape' of her, her vulnerability was incontrovertibly confirmed. He could take her down by stating he could. This was a psychological game, but would have no power at all unless there were substantial mechanisms in place to synchronize and replicate the meaning of rape between all participants. This repulsive thought experiment absolutely vindicates MacKinnon's position on pornography, though its purpose was probably the opposite.

On 29 June 2009 it was reported that a so-called 'internet blogger' Darryn Walker was cleared of obscenity charges. He had written an imaginary 12-page fantasy piece which he posted on the internet called 'Girls (Scream) Aloud' in which he described the kidnap, rape, mutilation and murder of the members of all girl singing group 'Girls Aloud'. He was subsequently prosecuted only on the basis that young and vulnerable fans of the group could have inadvertently come across the material whilst searching for information about them on the internet and not because the material itself was inherently grossly offensive and threatening. The prosecution failed on the grounds that the fantasy was not easy enough to access. Walker said that it 'was only meant for like minded people' and not to offend members of Girls Aloud. The defence claimed that the material was of a type widely available on the internet and 'frankly no better or worse than other articles' (Armstrong 2009). In contradiction to the position of Liz Longhurst, mother of murder victim Jane Longhurst, it was also claimed that this type of material did not corrupt. There are similarities here with the Romano/MacKinnon debacle in that a man openly published details of a sexual fantasy about being incredibly violent to specific women. It is concerning that we are not more collectively horrified that this material produces a legitimized and acceptable source of pleasure for the viewer. Dworkin and MacKinnon ask of pornography more generally if it would be so acceptable if the violated or murdered group depicted were other than women. Would it be so acceptable, for example, if the sexual kick came from magazines, films or web pages devoted to mutilating and murdering children; or black people; or white men; or gay men; or disabled people or even poor people? If the violated group is woman then there is insufficient offence caused as the links to normal hetero/sexuality are so strong.

When the murder of women is sexualized we more than merely apply a sexual motivation to the killer, we operationalize a huge apparatus which situates the violence perfectly in a gendered hetero/sexual discourse which then makes it understandable, defensible and even excusable. The victim represents the omnipresent vulnerability of the feminine and in this sense can only experience the assault as woman; her entire body is woman. The mutilation is sex *because* she is woman, the motivation is sex *because* she is woman and the death is sex *because* she is woman. These explanations for violence against females are entirely dependent on the passivity of the female and her gendered position as recipient of sexual attention. The reverse is not true; things done to men by women are not sex and rationalizations for female homicide of men are generally framed around the utility of killing and *extrinsic* motivation, for example, in the context of self-defence, vengeance or gain.

One of the most significant repercussions for women of this highly sexualized discourse is the fear it generates. Again, I do not mean to suggest that women are in a perpetual state of debilitating anxiety but I do suggest that there is an underlying fear in *both* men and women that *women* are vulnerable and that this is etched onto social practices.

In Chapter 1 I made two propositions; first, that there is a relationship constructed in sexual murder discourse between the offences of rape and murder which allows them to share meaning and, secondly, that there are insidious and pervasive effects to perceptually linking rape with murder in this way which include the feminization of female death and the reversal of the feminist proposition that rape is violence. In this chapter I will discuss these propositions and also address certain social problems which I suggested were exacerbated by the relationship which exists between rape and murder, which are; the high rate of attrition in reported cases of rape (Kelly *et al.* 2005); the suggestion that intimate partner femicide is devalued in comparison to other categories of homicide (Lees 1997); the suggestion that women's reported levels of fear of crime are higher than men's and are related to fear of sexual assault (Scott 2003); and that fear of rape or sexual assault may be correlated with a fear for life.

Identified problems: fear of rape and rape trauma syndrome

Research tells us that women fear rape more than any other crime (CGAP 2007, Scott 2003, Ferraro 1996, Gordon and Riger 1989). Women are taught to fear rape from childhood (Lees 1997) and both men and women are 'prepared' for it throughout their lives (Box 1992). However, this is not just the irrational fear of sensitive, sexually fragile or anxious women. This is a fear of gender class woman. MacDonald (1991) interviewed convicted female terrorists about their experiences of incarceration. All the women interviewed had committed murder and/or were familiar with extremes of violence. It was interesting to note that even in this kind of environment the special power of the threat of rape remained:

> Of course the police use the fact that we are afraid of rape, and threaten us with it. (1991:27)

Even though this woman had experienced and witnessed brutal acts of torture and had committed brutal acts of violence herself, a significant fear for her was less the threat of generalized violence than the threat of rape. In a news report of the trial of Bradley Murdoch, the man convicted of killing backpacker Peter Falconio in the Australian outback in July 2001, Joanne Lees, Falconio's girlfriend who was also attacked by Murdoch, stated 'When I asked him if he was going to rape me, I was just so frightened. I was more scared of being raped than I was of dying and being shot by the man' (*The Times* 2005). The power that the threat of rape has over women is clearly significant; that power is reinforced daily not only in the collocating of the term with brutal and potentially fatal violence but in societal or familial responses to the victim. Across time and space different discourses of rape have prompted different responses to the victim and some of these responses cannot be separated from the trauma or fear of rape experienced by many women. For example, it is reported (*BBC Online News* 2009) that in Arizona in the USA a nine-year-old Liberian girl was raped by four Liberian immigrant boys. Her parents were so unsupportive of her that she was required to be taken away from the family by Child Protective Services. The reported repercussions of rape for this child were significant. The sheer enormity of the repository for such examples is testament to the fact that throughout history there have been severe consequences for victims of rape. Irrespective of whether these assaults can be popularly considered brutal enough to constitute a traumatic experience, the threat of the consequences alone could be sufficient to instill considerable fear. Rape has always threatened serious consequences for the victim. One thing is clear, the fear women have of rape is complex, but the fear may have a significant link with fear for life which may be overlooked in the cultural obsession with female sexual fragility. Men are not routinely terrorized in this way. In fact the general dangers to adult men of violent assault are largely unacknowledged which may give the misleading impression that there is no real and immediate threat to men in public or private spaces.

Characterizing rape trauma as at least partially borne from fear for life would align the assault more credibly with the types of trauma that men and therefore humans, might legitimately experience. Rape Trauma Syndrome is a type of Post Traumatic Stress Disorder and Wolbert Burgess and Holmstrom (1974) found that the key precipitating factor in onset of the syndrome was a profound fear for life in the victim. To fear or experience rape can be to, potentially at least, fear death, irrespective of whether that threat is real or imagined. The trauma is often considered to be sexual and not a more human response to a violent physical assault, despite the powerful links made with fatal violence. This makes a conflation of rape and murder a concept which has significant repercussions for women, for sex becomes the intelligible link not only to the offender's motivation, but the victim's feminized trauma.

The avoidance techniques routinely employed by women to protect themselves from sexual assault by strangers are more than a performance of femininity; they are a performance of the potential 'female victim' produced by discourses of sexual murder and rape. Because male heterosexual adults are not perceived as potential victims and a relationship between murder and rape is constructed, the fear produced is a female one. This is not always acknowledged in writing about sexual murder and serial killers. Women in the Victorian era were the recipients of the violence of Jack the Ripper and Walkowitz suggests that their fear was 'even more heavily overlaid by feelings of personal vulnerability' (1992:221) than that of men. Milligen (2006) also explicitly acknowledges the terror that women felt as a result of the Ripper murders. Yet in much writing men are subsumed into discussions of the fear generated in a way they are not subsumed into assumptions about who the victims are. We unproblematically accept that women (and other violable and feminized groups) are the natural targets for serial killers without explicitly articulating that acknowledgement. We use language like 'random' or 'audience' or 'the public' when really we should address the fears generated in women. Similarly, when talking of serial killers, we again use generic language; they are 'killers' or 'offenders' with no explicit acknowledgement that they are men. It seems there is no need to articulate this assumption for there is a deeply ingrained knowledge that this is the truth of this type of violence. It is disingenuous to suggest that because there may be an exception that we ignore the rule. Because, for example, Aileen Wuornos has been represented as a serial killer (which has its limitations as a characterization) this does not negate the fact that most serial killer (as serial killing is currently understood and defined) victims are not heterosexual males and most serial killers are not female.

Jenkins (1994) discusses 'manipulation of fear' but frames his discussion of serial killing in films and books around the fear generated in the 'audience'. He also states that the fear provoked in these representations is 'temporary and reversible' (1994:107). Frayling (1986) too, sees the fear as a nightmare that is awoken from. These authors and many others do not explicitly acknowledge or consider that it is women who are the 'natural' victims of serial killers or that their fear may be structurally very different from the kind of fear an adult heterosexual male may experience. It is also quite possible that this fear that is apparently suspended when the film is finished, is actually still present and evident in the discursive practices that see women employ behaviours to avoid meeting with such killers. Discourses of sexual murder and rape not only produce and prey upon human fears; they re-define those fears as female sexual vulnerability.

Identified problems: skewed perceptions and attrition

As has been noted, Kelly's Home Office research in the area of rape and the criminal justice system, has concluded that popular perceptions 'rely on powerful stereotypes which function to limit the definition of what constitutes a real rape' (2005:ix). We should also consider that if we limit what can be considered rape, we also limit who can be considered a rapist and a victim of rape. There are interventions in the judicial process which seek to deflect jurors from the rape template, for example, it is reported that Solicitor-General Vera Baird has instigated a move where judges must direct juries to ignore rape myths (Gibb 2009). There is also acknowledgement from the Office for Criminal Justice Reform that appreciable physical and psychic trauma is crucial in securing convictions and for this reason there are reforms suggested that would see videos of victim's first interviews with police shown in court to demonstrate her trauma, as well as expert testimony on the differing impacts of rape (Home Office 2006).

Rape, with no aggravating violence and committed by an acquaintance, friend, relative or intimate may be perceived as an act of sex, with no more real repercussions than a 'bad' consensual sexual act. Roiphe stated that 'everyone agrees that rape is a terrible thing, but we don't agree on what rape is. There is a gray area in which someone's rape may be another person's bad night' (1994:54). Roiphe is referring to the differing subjective assessments made of personal experiences by individual women, however when this distinction between what is a 'bad sexual experience' and what is 'rape' is being made by a jury, there are wider reaching problems. If a jury needs to use the ostensible evidence of visible psychiatric trauma from a single model to differentiate between 'bad sex' and 'rape', and what one police respondent in Chapter 6 described as 'questionable allegations' and 'genuine rapes' we are constructing a single model of rape victim with the requirement that she has an extremely adverse and negative *visible* and recognizable response to the experience: a homogenized female response.

French sociologist Emile Durkheim (1858–1917) spoke of the importance of societal collective agreement on what should or should not be defined a crime:

> We must not say that an action shocks the *conscience collective* because it is criminal, but rather that it is criminal because it shocks the *conscience collective*. We do not condemn it because it is a crime, rather it is a crime because we condemn it. (cited in Giddens 1972)

It may appear that as a culture or society we are offended by rape, there are severe penalties, a strong negative response to offenders and supportive services for victims and as Mona Livholts suggests, media reporting of rape appears to speak for a society with a 'humanitarian face' (2008:208) which condemns sexual violence; but the extent of that violence and its tacit endorsement is conspicuously unacknowledged and it only *appears* that there is a very strong *conscience collective*. The strongest support seems limited to the type of rape reflected in the real rape template and similar to the violence constructed in the dominant discourse of sexual murder, if it is not, support is more uncertain. An Amnesty International (2005) poll showed that at least 25 per cent of people think that women are partly to blame if they are raped; if they had been drinking or dressed provocatively; if they were alone or in an isolated spot at the time; or if she had had many sexual partners (Anderson and Doherty 2008:3). It is this kind of approach to rape that reveals how uncertain the *conscience collective* is. Given that there are interventions in the criminal justice system to try to circumvent the negative influence of the rape myths it appears that a rape as legally defined does not enjoy *malum in se* status, it is taking on the character-istics of a *malum prohibitum* offence. The difference between the two can be described thus: for an act to be considered *malum in se*, it must be perceived as inherently immoral or evil, whether or not this is prescribed by law, whereas a *malum prohibitum* act is prescribed 'illegal' status. So in other words certain types of rape appear to be immoral because they are illegal and not illegal because they are considered immoral, which is in contradiction to Durkheim's rule. The criminal justice system alone cannot remedy this perception of rape whilst we as a culture simultane-ously declare our disgust with rapists and the act of rape, yet fail to agree on what rape is. The proximity of the rape template to a sexual murder template and the ubiquity of female sexual death in our entertainment and news media impacts on our perceptions of what rape is. In many ways, both symbolic and physical, rape is correlated with death and murder, and murder of women is correlated with sexual motivation and rape. These disparate offences are united by what Tatar succinctly describes as 'Western notions of what drives men to murder women' (1995:7). This perspective also serves to limit what we perceive as a 'real murder' with domestic or intimate homicides devalued in comparison to the sexual murder template.

Identified problems: devaluing intimate partner homicide

When a woman is found dead in suspicious circumstances it appears from my data that there is an assumption on the part of police officers and journalists that her gender is implicated in her death and because of this, sexual aspects are immediately speculated. Even where the crime scene indicates no immediate evidence to suggest a gendered motivation, as in the cases of Margaret Muller and Marsha McDonnell, the assumption prevails. Polk (1994) states that the relationship between the offender and the victim is crucial when assessing a homicide; this relationship will be categorized as 'stranger' or 'domestic' homicide for legal, procedural, investigative and statistical reasons. Importantly, the criminal justice response in male/female violence is contingent upon the *degree* of intimacy between victim and offender. Cammiss (2006) found that cases of domestic violence were more likely to be disposed of in the Magistrates Court than the Crown Court than similar, non-domestic offences; similarly, it has been found that men charged with domestic homicide are often found guilty of a lesser charge than murder or even acquitted (Lees 1997, Websdale 1999, Sueffert 2002) or are given lenient sentences (Burton 2008). Dawson (2003) found that the *degree* of intimacy between victim and assailant is measured along a spectrum of intimacy from complete strangers to married co-habiting couple and acts of equal violence will attract different responses according to the position of the relationship on this spectrum; the more intimate distance between the victim and abuser, the less serious the criminal justice sanction for the violence; so the closer the relationship, the less severe the sanction and even mode of trial. This delineation of offences by police, criminal justice agencies and media is a direct result of assuming a gendered and hetero/sexual motivation and also indicates that it is not the violence in an assault that is being used to assess the offender. Males who, for example, brutally kill their spouses using gratuitous violence will not necessarily be assessed as dangerous by the police or courts by quantifying the amount of violence or sadism involved in the assault. They are more likely to be assessed as dangerous or not, by using the degree of intimacy between them and the victim as a frame of reference.

The Sentencing Guidelines Council aims to address minimizing this disparity between sentencing for domestic and non-domestic violence, but has caused controversy because it is suggested that non-custodial sentences may be used in cases of domestic violence where the offender shows remorse for their actions. This has been perceived by some organizations like Refuge, as a 'licence for men to batter women' (*BBC online news* 2006). Using the intimate relationship between victim and offender to assess the violence privileges the relationship in assessing motivation, culpability and risk, and marginalizes the violent actions of the offender. Remorse alone does not indicate after all that an offender will not re-offend. Lee Bowker in his study of masculinities and violence suggests that the causes of male violence are multiple and complex and that in particular, what he calls 'wife batterers' do not spontaneously reform on appreciating the effects of [their] violence on the victim (1998:1).

The closer a homicide is to the sexual murder template the more seriously it is taken. Even when, as in the case of Hannah Foster, the circumstances fit the template then the female victim will still be assessed for her contribution in her own death. Was she asking for it? Was she constraining her sexuality within patriarchal hetero/sexual boundaries? This was a consistent question to police from the press during Hannah's murder investigation.

Reversing the proposition: metaphor, analogy and axiom

The terms rape and murder routinely sit together in common parlance, they seem to occupy common territory and both exemplify extremes of human violence. Out of interest I calculated the amount of times the terms 'rape' and 'murder' appeared within five words of each other in news reports of any kind in the national British Press (Nexis UK) over a twelve-month period (15/06/08–15/06/09). There were a total of 847 collocations; that is the terms appeared within five words of each other in the narrative. Many of these reports were not documenting a rape and murder; the terms were acting in many cases to strengthen a story being told or to make a point or to describe some fictional plotline of a novel or film. A check of the previous five years produced similar results. The point here is that the terms are routinely sitting alongside each other, part of the same stories, and part of the same arguments. Have we reached a point where the terms are less meaningful without each other or that the relationship is now axiomatic?

I suggest that the term rape is misapplied in a significant number of narratives of murder; first, when it is used to symbolize mutilation or annihilation; and second when the term supplants the term murder in describing the assault. John Duffy, for example, who was convicted of the murder and rape of three women and jailed for life at the Old Bailey in February 2001, was dubbed the 'Railway Rapist' by media. This implies that the rape aspect to the offending takes precedence in public interest or understanding over the fatal violence and murder, or at the very least the term rape implies the death of the victims. It also appears that rape can be as much a 'symbolic' act as a legally defined one: the symbolic acts of mutilation, stabbing or beating having increasing validity as sublimation for rape. Veritable parades of authors and directors have employed acts of violence that are symbolically equated with acts of rape to represent the motivations of sex killers. The symbolic act is more often than not a method of killing or annihilating the female victim. Rape here is not an act of non-consensual sexual intercourse, it is a lethal paraphilia. If the violent stabbing to death of a woman can be re-constructed as rape then there is no degree of separation, the act itself has fatal consequences. Therefore within this discourse the symbolism attached to rape, and to violent acts construed as rape, has created a conflation of the offences of rape and murder. Rape is a metaphor and an analogy for extremes of hetero/sexual behavior and as suggested by Emsley, exists as a warning of what happens when the natural order of [hetero/sexual] things [are] broken' (2005:96). The story of Jack the Ripper has become exactly that, a warning from folklore; an appalling fable with an outrageous moral.

Reversing the proposition: feminizing and sexualizing female death

When Margaret Muller was killed there were stab wounds noted to her back and neck, eliminating speculation that the stabbing was directed at sexual organs, neither was there report of any conventional sexual assault. The offender at this time is yet to be identified so has not given an account of their motivations. In effect we have a victim who has been stabbed to death in a park. If the gender of this victim was male it is difficult to imagine that such a scenario would lead to speculation of a sexual motivation. Because Margaret was female and we can speculate that a male offender has committed the act, news reports speculated that the offender may be 'turned on' by the act of stabbing. Marsha McDonnell was hit on the head with a blunt instrument, again women were warned about safety in the news reports and the police were reported to be checking sex offenders in the area. Is the act of bludgeoning a sexual act or is it only sexual when committed against a female? Jenefsky (1999) considers this point in her examination of Andrea Dworkin's reconstruction of pornography. She states 'within the governing logic of 'woman as whore', anything done to women is presented *as sex* in pornography, despite the absurdity or the violence of the act' (1999:134). Murders and violent assaults of women by men are not erotica, but there does appear to be a similar governing logic that anything done to the female victim is 'sex'. There is an important distinction between the acts being experienced as sexual by an offender and the act being assumed to be sexual because the victim was a woman. It is a dangerous slide to move from interpreting the motivations of an offender via potential symbolism as sexual and perceiving anything done to women as sex. This is amply illustrated in the example of the crimes of Jack the Ripper and Peter Sutcliffe, the Yorkshire Ripper, as discussed in Chapter 4. Jack the Ripper's acts of stabbing and mutilation are explicitly described in some books on the subject, as sublimation for heterosexual sexual acts. Arguably, these two offenders are Britain's most famous serial killers; they are defined as serial killers and are part of the discourse of sexual murder. Wilson (1995) states that the dividing line between definition of what is a serial killer and what is a mass murderer, is in the question of motivation. He states that the serial killer's motivation is to rape and the mass murderer's motivation is gain (1995:106). This is a sweeping statement and although it is not empirically sound and is from the more popular end of the criminality market, it does reflect the epistemological basis for the discourse of sexual murder.

Sutcliffe's defence that he heard the word of God directing him to kill prostitutes can be undermined on many levels but this explanation absolutely situates these crimes outside of a sexual framework for he has an extrinsic motivation that is part of a moral crusade but as I have argued earlier, misogyny can be reconstructed as a paraphilia keeping the motivation within a sexual framework. Walkowitz (1992) discusses the way in which the veracity of the knowledge produced about killers like Sutcliffe by the psychiatric or medical community was also on trial during Sutcliffe's trial for murder. The differing interpretations of his motivations are a testament to the ambiguities, paradoxes and inconsistencies present in sexual/serial killer discourse.

Tatar holds that 'one could assert that any murder has a sadistic, hence erotic component to it'. (1995:20) and whilst this may be possible, similar acts of violence are perceived by the police and the press to have erotic components or not based solely on the gender of the victim and assailant. The discourse of sexual murder denies male adult heterosexuals as victims or potential victims of a sexual murder. In a documentary *Surviving – Peter Sutcliffe* aired on 5[t] May 2006 (Sky One 10pm) it was alleged that Peter Sutcliffe's first victim may have been a man. In 1967 taxi driver John Tomey was hit eight times about the head with a hammer by a man fitting Sutcliffe's description in Leeds. According to this documentary despite Tomey's name being passed to the investigating team as a possible victim they refused to link this crime with the Yorkshire Ripper attacks merely because the victim was male. It could be assumed that the act of bludgeoning an adult male to death would lead to speculation of a host of different motivations that may be represented as non-erotic, such as expressions of masculinity, revenge, anger, violent psychosis or accident and would undermine the narrative put together by the police. In this sense not all murder is considered to have an erotic component, even though as Tatar suggests, the philosophical and theoretical ground is there to interpret it this way.

When we see male on female fatal violence as sublimation for heterosexual sex we must then impose gender identities onto the victim and offender because that is what heterosexual popularly means, sex between man and woman. Victim is woman, she is feminized and sexualized. When we are talking specifically of fatal violence the victim's death becomes feminized. She does not die as a human subject, she dies as a woman, in a way only a woman can, and it is a highly sexualized death. Her corpse becomes a site for erotic fantasy, her death throes a metaphorical and perverse orgasm. The cultural obsession with sexualized female death is well documented and the images and narratives are ubiquitous. In art, literature, film, television, advertising, drama and pornography the subject of the rape and murder of women form a catalogue of Western sexual/cultural life. However, it is not only women who are sexualized in these processes and forums, men too are subjects constructed in these dominant discourses and men who are suspects in cases of sex crime can be constructed as what Lacombe (2008) describes as 'consumed by sex'.

Reversing the proposition: sexualizing offenders

The representation of offences and offenders in news reporting suggests that irrespective of the differences in offending characteristics and motivations, or even degrees of dangerousness, sex offenders are represented as a single homogenous and dangerous group (Greer 2003, Soothill and Walby 1991). Foucault, in arguing that there is ever-growing engagement with psychiatric discourse suggests that there is a concurrent individualizing of dangerous offenders, pathologizing their criminality. The knowledge we have of sexual offenders or serial killers/sex killers is reflected in the knowledge systems which have been constructed to identify and rehabilitate them; those systems that help us to know 'who they are'. One of the key aims of the modern process of justice is to effectively manage risk and this has encouraged the assessment of individual offenders and the forming of rehabilitation regimes in prisons. But far from individualizing the offenders these knowledge systems by their very design categorize and group offenders so that 'who they are' is only distilled to their particular grouping which can be as large as 'sex offender'. Penal rehabilitation programmes are often part of a regime of criminal justice responses for incarcerated sex offenders and Lacombe (2008) argues that the process of constructing their identity, that is 'who they are' is practised within Cognitive Behavioural Treatment programmes in prisons, and the suggestion is that these offenders are encouraged to identify with particular constructions of themselves, accurate or not, in order to complete a treatment programme success-fully; completing a programme successfully may be important in terms of parole or other benefits. In this respect the treatment itself is based upon a construction of the offender that may have limited accuracy, but it is a construction authorized as legitimate. Lacombe argues that the sex offender is constructed as 'a species entirely consumed by sex' (2008:56), a practice which can often lead to the assumption that the offender has a life which revolves around his sexual predilections and identity and that this is his biology and his destiny; because of this the sex offender is not curable, merely controllable and Hudson suggests that:

> In contrast to earlier more optimistic penal philosophies, where treatment programmes are undertaken they are no longer expected to 'cure' sex offenders but to help offenders control their behaviour in order to minimize the risk of them re-offending. (2005:2)

In Lacombe's study of Cognitive Behavioural Therapy programmes it was found that offenders were encouraged to publically recount the deviant sexual fantasies which were apparently enacted in their offending, even when they absolutely denied having them. If these offenders do not agree to recount their fantasies they cannot complete the programme. In this respect the psychological discourse is requiring the offender to corroborate their construction of him through a process of confes-sion. Self-reflection and confession may indicate an intrinsic desire to change which is a significant element in the treatment process. Ward *et al.* suggest that 'in current practice it is widely accepted that offender motivation constitutes an important requirement for selection into reha-bilitation programmes' (2006:326). However, bearing in mind Lacombe's observations, when the offender does recount fantasies as *required*, it may not be that he is revealing anything of his motivations, but merely failing to resist the dominant construction of himself as an object of discourse and give his crimes some psychological intelligibility.

In contemporary primary approaches to crime prevention the focus is the offence not the offender; a position which attracts some criticism from those who consider that the offender is the more important unit for analysis. It could be argued that even in the rehabilitative, tertiary approach to reducing offending, in the case of what is defined as sexual homicide or violence, we still sanction the offence rather than the offender. It seems that increasingly the offence *is* the offender. Sexual explanations for male on female homicide are perceived as particularly plausible and are disseminated widely in what Foucault describes as the 'literature of criminality' (1994:192) but also, sexual explanations have great rhetorical impact and social significance. There has been significant focus in this analysis on the ways in which Richard Kemp was constructed as primarily a sexual deviant within the police and press narratives with his predilection for violence significantly marginalized. This aspect to Kemp's offending identity is crucial for it is via the concept of sex that Kemp is known. A sexual explanation for a male on female killing is as psychologically intelligible as it is utilitarian for it is not only plausible, there are frameworks in place for responding to it within the judicial and penal systems. Despite its ambiguous heterosexual symbolism, its broad and at times inappropriate application and its lack of analytical precision the vague concept of sex appears to bring clarity to the problem of knowing those who come to be defined as sex killers; the sex defines the crime and also the criminal.

Paradoxically, and despite our apparent revulsion for rapists, it seems that in cases of sexual homicide *intention to rape* acts to defend the offender in many ways, the label re-constructs him as 'a man who went too far', distancing him from those madmen and monsters who use violence as sublimation for sex. It is understandable in this discourse, or at least plausible, that a rapist can accidentally end up killing the victim reinforcing the rape/murder relationship. For example, in this sample of case studies there is a willingness in the police respondents to believe that murders where an 'actual' rape or sexual assault occurs are committed by rapists who had no specific intention to kill. If rapist/killers are not to be considered as intending the death of the victim in their plan to assault this is powerful mitigation in any prosecution. Richard Kemp and Maninder Pal Singh Kohli, both claimed no intention to kill, just to sexually assault and to an extent they were both believed. Since the sexual acts are seen by the police as the sole motivation and the biological inability to resist the sexual urges seen as dominant, the murder of the victims can easily be seen as accidental; and because of the legal need to establish the *mens rea* in cases of murder, the presumption by the police that there was no intention to kill is powerful defence. It would not be in the killer's interests to resist this institutional construction of himself for he may simultaneously then establish the necessary *mens rea* to prove his intention, if not to kill, to commit GBH which would complete the offence of murder (English and Card 2007) and lead to mandatory life imprisonment.

Violence itself is not necessarily deviant for men, nor killing, it is the context in which the killing or the violence occurs that will designate it deviant or not. In this sense we have a framework for understanding sexual aggression, violence and even killing in men which is defensible. There is a real reluctance to accept that men would be motivated to simply beat a woman to death, or to use violence expressively as a result of an intrinsic drive. Ressler *et al.* (1992) interviewed convicted sex killers and when questioned about victim resistance, one is quoted as saying 'The victim did not have a choice. Killing was part of my fantasy.' (1992:201) As noted in Chapters 5 and 6 Richard Kemp had a history of using violence against children, but his status as a sexual deviant dominated assessments of him with the psychiatrist commenting that there was more focus on his sexual offending and not enough was done to treat his violent tendencies (Mitchell 2003c).

Maninder Pal Singh Kohli and Richard Kemp were not only willing, but did abduct young women from or in public places; they were not only willing, but did commit sexual acts upon an extremely unwilling victim who was clearly terrified; they were not only willing, but did murder their compliant victims. The amount of detail given by Kemp of the fatal violence used indicates no reticence whatever to re-live the killing of his victim.

Chene (2003) conducted research into the 'process of aggravating rape to sexual murder' which concerned the offender's intentions. It was concluded that 'there are very few sexual assaults in which the victim dies because the assailant had firmly resolved to commit murder' and 'some sex murders appear more like instances of manslaughter in which the assailant struck one blow too many'. It could be argued that the willingness to believe that sex murders are committed by rapists and that the fatal violence was accidental is due, in some part, to the belief that biologically determined and uncontrollable sexual urges are what precipitate a rape/sexual assault with murder. Brownmiller puts forward the idea that 'It is a rare rapist who intends to kill' (1975:206) and in most rapes, there is no killing so this assertion is clearly accurate. However, where a homicide does occur we should not necessarily be assessing the crime entirely as 'a rape gone wrong'. It may be problematic to label murderers who rape as 'rapists', especially if only one model of rapist is drawn upon.

In Geberth's (2003) *Sex Related Homicide and Death Investigation*, a publication intended to be a tool for American law enforcement, he states that:

> The sexual pervert can go into chat rooms and meet other perverts. Therefore, this person is able to validate perversion by discovering that there are others "just like him", and what he does is quote/ unquote perfectly normal and acceptable behavior. (2003:xiii)

It is worth discussing Geberth's book briefly for it is written by and intended for American law enforcement and represents itself as a manual for those investigating and prosecuting sexual murder; I picked up my copy from a publisher's stand at a conference for criminologists. It should be considered that American federal law enforcement are perceived to be 'experts' on the subject of serial/sex murder and according to Schmid are the pre-eminent source of expertise on the subject. Schmid also notes that 'the equation of serial murder with sexual homicide is especially common in law enforcement work on the crime' (2005:78). Hickey (1997) notes that 'although many offenders actually fall into the serial killer classification, they are excluded because they fail to meet law enforcement definitions or media generated stereotypes of brutal blood-thirsty monsters' (cited in Schmid 2005:78). Geberth's book is truly horrifying and includes documentation of crimes committed by those stereotypical 'brutal blood-thirsty monsters'. It is full of in-depth case studies and at times one wonders how the collection of photographs and material were selected. There are transcripts and documentation of murders and tortures, selected excerpts of rapist's diaries and many monochrome and colour photographs of predominantly female murder victims who have been mutilated and tortured. Arguably, there are too many close up photographs of female genitalia, especially given the books moralistic tone which is rather censuring. Geberth claims '... my personal philosophy as a murder cop is 'Remember: We Work for God' (2003:xix). Interestingly Peter Sutcliffe also claimed that he was working for God (Ward Jouve 1988).

The gratuitously sexual selection of photographs and the rapist's diaries concentrate on what could be described as the pornography of female violation and victimization. That these truly awful crimes occurred is beyond doubt, but the manner in which they are presented and represented reflects the importance of 'sex', lust and deviant paraphilia in assessing the crimes. The book is perhaps an extreme example of media's and law enforcement's obsession with sexual murder and the voyeuristic, androcentric nature of reporting, investigating and documenting it. This significantly illustrates and describes male sadistic sexual fantasy which fuses the rape, torture and murder of the female victims. It differs negligibly from more 'artistic' interpretations of the meaning of violence against women which can be found in fictional films, art and popular criminality literature. The power of discourse is in its claims to truth and producing knowledge, and Mills (2003) argument that:

> It is difficult, if not impossible, to think and express oneself outside these discursive constraints because, in doing so, one would be considered to be mad or incomprehensible by others. (2003:57)

This reflects the difficulties individuals may have in resisting popular beliefs. The content and tone of Geberth's book makes it easy to reject some of the arguments presented in this book. My own hypothesis, that the conflation of rape and murder is problematic and based on flawed and overly broad interpretations of what is sexual, may appear a little, what Mills might describe as, incomprehensible. Geberth's book, written by experienced law enforcement officers with its veritable avalanche of evidence that the offenders in these cases are experiencing and expressing a particular *sexual* violence, coupled with the myriad of photographs of genitally tortured female bodies, has both the official stamp of 'truth', as well as the documentary evidence. How could anyone present an alternative to this 'knowledge' or attempt to puncture its validity? In discourse analysis it is important that there should be a reflexive criticism of one's own position, that one should resist assuming that 'one has ever reached a position where one has discovered the final 'truth' about a subject' (Mills 2003:3). Geberth's book and the innumerable other forums and mediums I have trawled for this project, forced me to be reflexive and to consider my analytical position. However, the power of those representations in creating meaning and reflected in practice, only illustrates the dominance of that particular discourse of sexual murder and its presence in the psyche of our culture. To undermine its authority one need only give consideration to those sexual aspects. Why are acts of violence constructed as sexual expression? How do we define what is sexual? Is the term applied so liberally that it can no longer be used definitively? Is the term 'rape' used so liberally that it can no longer be used definitively? Is the term 'sexual' so multifaceted and filled with symbolic, historical, medical, scientific, legal, religious and cultural resonance, that it can never have any academic clarity and is the term 'rape' similarly confusing?

I have commented on the institutional practice of the discourse, but its practice does not begin and end with the police or the criminal justice system, or even with journalism. Schmid (2005) highlights Foucault's discussion of 'the significance of the moment when a new 'type' of individual is generated from acts that previously could potentially have been committed by anyone' (2005:68). Similar to Foucault's description of the emergence of the 'homosexual' or the 'criminal' as a 'type' (Foucault 1998), the serial killer, personified in Jack the Ripper is now a type, he is in Foucault's terms:

> a personage, a past, a case history, and a childhood, in addition to being a type of life, a life form and a morphology with an indiscreet anatomy and possibly a mysterious physiology. (1998:43)

He now exists.

It cannot be ignored that some murderers, especially those defined as 'serial killers' may identify strongly with these discursive constructions and employ practices, which are at least in part, products of these discourses. Warwick (2006) states that: 'it is [also] clear that serial killers read the [serial killer] biographies and other accounts preceding them' (2006:7) which suggests that the offenders themselves are not necessarily immune to the quixotic attractions of serial killer rhetoric. Serial killer Colin Ireland who was convicted of the murder of five gay men in 1993 said:

> I decided it might be fun to carry out something I labeled 'reinforcing the stereotype'. I had my radio with me and it would be on for most of the day and on it would be a vast collection of music – until I heard the staff approach the door. On hearing them I would leap up and change the station to a classical one. I would be on the bed before the door opened, my book or paper open, and as the door opened I would glance in a superior fashion around the edge of the reading material. 'Yes officers?' in my best Hannibal Lecter cold, distant but polite tone (cited in Warwick 2006:7)

Final comments

In a small scene from an Agatha Christie murder mystery film *The Body in the Library* (dir. Silvio Narizzano 1974) the father of a missing teenage girl is informed by a police Inspector that his daughter's body has been found and she has been murdered. The father looks to the Inspector and says 'You don't think she was...' he doesn't finish the sentence but looks away and shakes his head unable to speak the words. The police Inspector informs the father that there is no reason to suspect 'personal' motives and it seems that all could breathe a sigh of relief. Both men knew what they were speaking of though neither said the word. What could his overriding fear have been? His daughter had been murdered but he did not ask if she had suffered or if she had been beaten, but if she ostensibly, had been raped. When I was interviewing police officers about their experiences of investigating homicide, one officer said 'it's strange but [victim's name] mum almost had a kind of relief that she hadn't been raped, even though she was still murdered. She was glad that she hadn't been raped' (R1).

What is this fear that grips so when rape threatens? Clearly it is a violent and intimate assault, but it is its extraordinary potential that provokes such responses. I have read of some of the atrocities which claim the name 'rape' in researching for this book, and when reflecting on their singular inhumanity the power of rape is made clear. However, not one of those dreadful stories that came out of Nanking or South Africa or even the City of London was free of the spectre of death. Victims were described as killed before, during or after rape, or were horribly mutilated and tortured, some were killed because they were victims of rape by dishonoured family members or by their own hands, the horror does not need extensive articulation, but suffice it to say; bayoneting is not rape; murder is not rape; mutilation is not rape. I would like to see bayoneting called what it is, murder called what it is and rape called what it is. Rape is not death, it merely signifies death; corporeal death, social death, psychic death, virtual death. It is not in and of itself, death. This meaning has been conferred upon it. The crucial issue here is that a 'rape/death' is no ordinary death; only women can die in this way. It is a very particular form of oppression which is constructed in hetero/patriarchal belief systems.

If we are to accept that Jack the Ripper was a rapist, what does that say about the act of rape? The act of rape in this context is a 'symbolic' act of murder; it is both artistically, politically, socially and culturally interpreted. Acts of violence that are symbolic of rape and acts of rape, may be perceived by some to be at different points on a continuum of gendered violence, but the term itself is becoming as meaningless as it is meaningful. The term should be used with caution, if it is to be used at all, when referring only to an act of murder or any violence where a rape did not occur. Ferraro's (1996) research that shows that women perceive of rape as a crime more serious than murder, may indicate the extent to which rape has become symbolic of, or associated with, a particularly brutal death. Treating rape as equal to, or more serious than murder, only creates another forum for terrorizing women. No woman should consider death preferable to rape. Women in contemporary society are effectively required to be terrified of this assault and this terror is compounded by ubiquitous images of female death as a result of rape in art and media (Tatar 1995). But also the multiaccentual nature of rape (Schmid 2005) has facilitated its adoption by different groups and has given the subject high visibility, but that visibility has included and involved representing rape by extremes.

It must be considered as MacKinnon (2002) posits that the thrill of rape is not so much in the sexual act but in the victim reaction to the act and the power symbolically invested in the perpetrator. The lies about rape are revealed in the rape myths but most importantly in the context of this book we should consider and reveal every violence which fraudulently takes its name. Rape trauma, fear of rape and the practices of rape cannot be meaningfully separated from a threat to the life of the victim; symbolic, imagined or real. These considered revelations may begin to free women from the deceitful and fallacious idea that they have an inherent and fatal weakness.

Appendix 1: Film sample

- *The Lodger* (dir. Alfred Hitchcock 1927)
- *Jack the Ripper* (dir. Monty Berman and Robert Baker 1959)
- *A Study in Terror* (dir. James Hill 1965)
- *Doctor Jekyll and Sister Hyde* (dir. Roy Ward Baker 1971)
- *Hands of the Ripper* (dir. Peter Sasdy 1971)
- *Jack the Ripper* (dir. Jesus Franco 1976)
- *Murder by Decree* (dir. Bob Clark 1979)
- *Time After Time* (dir. Nicholas Meyer 1979)
- *New York Ripper* (dir. Lucio Fulci 1981)
- *Jack's Back* (dir. Rowdy Herrington 1988)
- *Jack the Ripper* (dir. David Wickes 1988)
- *Love Lies Bleeding* (dir. William Tannen 1998)
- *Jill the Ripper* (dir. Anthony Hickox 2000)
- *From Hell* (dir. Albert Hughes and Allen Hughes 2001)
- *Ripper: Letter From Hell* (dir. John E. Eyres 2001)
- *Whitechapel* (dir. S. J. Clarkson 2009)_

Docudrama style

- *The Whitechapel Murders* (1996 Marshall Cavendish – Murder in Mind)
- *The Diary of Jack the Ripper* (1993 Image Entertainment)
- *The Jack the Ripper Conspiracies* (2003 Delta Entertainment)
- *The Secret Identity of Jack the Ripper* (2003 Harmony Gold USA)

References

Abdullah-Khan, N. (2008) *Male Rape. The Emergence of a Social and Legal Issue* Basingstoke: Palgrave Macmillan.

ABS (1996) *Women's Safety Australia*, Catalogue No. 4128.0 Australian Bureau of Statistics, Canberra.

Allison, R. (2003) 'Model Daughter' murdered after night out with Friends', *Guardian* 17 March 2003:8.

Amnesty International (2005) *A Global Outrage: Global and UK Statistics*. http://www.amnesty.org.uk/new/press16618.shtml (accessed 21.11.05).

Anderson, I. and Doherty, K.H. (2008) *Accounting for Rape. Psychology, Feminism and Discourse Analysis in the Study of Sexual Violence* East Suss ex: Routledge.

Armstrong, J. (2009) 'How I'd Kill Girls Aloud' Blogger Cleared; HePut Fantasy Online', *Mirror* 30 June 2009:26.

Austen, J. (1983). Persuasion From: *The Complete Novels of Jane Austen*. Ch. 23 London: Penguin.

Bain, C. (2004) '"I'd Lost the Will To Live During Terror of Rape Attack", Says Woman', 52 *Daily Mail* 5 March 2004:29.

Barbee, L. (2009) Introduction to the Case on *Casebook: Jack the Ripper* accessed 28.05.09 at www.casebook.org.

Barthes, R. (2004) '(i) Operation Margerine; (ii) Myth Today' in Durham M.G. and Kellner D.M. (eds) *Media and Cultural Studies Key Works*. Ch. 6 pp. 121–8 Oxford: Blackwell Publishing.

Baumgardner, J. and Richards, A. (2000) *ManifestA: Young Women, Feminism and the Future* New York: Farrar, Straus and Giroux.

BBC Online News (2003a) 'Joggers Warned after Park Murder', 4 Feb. http://news.bbc.co.uk/1/hi/england/2724159.stm.

BBC Online News (2003b) 'New Witness in Marsha Murder', 6 Mar. http://news.bbc.co.uk/1/hi/england/2826057.stm.

BBC Online News (2003c) 'Police Hunt Girl's Killer', 17 Mar. http://news.bbc.co.uk/1/hi/england/2855125.stm.

BBC Online News (2003d) 'Police Arrest Marsha Victim', 19 Mar. http://news.bbc.co.uk/1/hi/england/2863677.stm.

BBC Online News (2003e) 'Animal Attacks Link to Muller Murder', 11 July http://news.bbc.co.uk/1/hi/england/london/3059893.stm.

BBC Online News (2006) 'Rape Sentence "Plans" Criticized', 12 Mar. http://news.bbc.co.uk/1/hi/uk/4799238.stm.

BBC Online News (2009) 'Outcry Over Disowned US Rape Girl', 25 July http://news.bbc.co.uk/1/hi/world/americas/8168480.stm.

BBC R4 (2004) *'File on 4'* Interview with Sue Barnett sister of murder victim Jane Longhurst. Broadcast Tuesday 27 July 2004 2000–2040. Transcript available at www.bbc.co.uk/radio4.

BBFC (2005) British Board of Film Classification http://www.bbfc.co.uk/website/Classified.nsf/0/E8131C368B60D89480256B4A0031156B?Open Document accessed 19.11.09.

Begley, S. (2009) 'Why Do We Rape, Kill and Sleep Around?', *Newsweek Magazine* 29 June 2009 can be accessed online at http://www.newsweek.com/id/202789/page/1.

Belloc Lowndes, M. (1927). *The Lodger* UK: Lightning Source.

Benedict, H. (1992). *Virgin or Vamp (How the Press Covers Sex Crimes)* New York: Oxford University Press.

Benson, O. and Stangroom, J. (2009) *Does God Hate Women?* London: Continuum.

Bevacqua, M. (2000) *Rape on the Public Agenda*. Massachusetts: Northeastern University Press.

BFI (2005) *British Film Institute Screenonline* [www.screenonline.org.uk/tv/id/464502] accessed 16.05.05.

Big Picture (2008) Carla Gugino talks about 'brutal' Watchmen rape scene available at: http://www.getthebigpicture.net/blog/2008/8/16/carla-gugino-talks-about-brutal-watchmen-rape-scene.html accessed 19.11.09.

Bindel, J. (2009) G2: Women: Just another week...: Nearly 50,000 rapes take place in the UK every year, but only a few are covered by the media. Julie Bindel gives a snapshot of which cases are reported and how. Comments and Features *Guardian*, 29 May 2009:14.

Bird, S. (2003) 'Abducted Teenage Girl Was Strangled', *The Times* 18 Mar. 2009:15.

Birkhead, T. (2009) 'Sex and Sensibility', *Times Higher Education*, 5 Feb. 2009.

BJS (2005) *Homicide Trends in the US* Bureau of Justice Statistics available at http://www.ojp.usdoj.gov/bjs//intimate/ipv.htm accessed 24.08.09.

Bourke, J. (2007) *Rape. A History from 1860 to the Present* Lancaster: Virago.

Bourne, J. and Derry, C. (2005) *Women and Law* London: Old Bailey Press.

Bowcott, O. (2003) 'Women Warned After Second Park Stabbing', *Guardian* final edin 8 Dec. 2003:4.

Bowker, L. (1998) *Masculinities and Violence* London: Sage.

Box, S. (1992). *Power, Crime and Mystification* London: Routledge.

Boyle, K. (2005) *Media and Violence* London: Sage Publications.

Braid, M. (2005) 'Related to the Ripper', *Daily Mail* 18 Apr. 2005:13.

Branigan, T. (2002) 'Biggest manhunt since Ripper as Serial Rapist Strikes for 10th Time: Police Join Forces To Catch Attacker Preying on Young Girls and Women', *Guardian* 31 Oct. 2002:3.

Brody, M. (1992) (ed.) Mary Wollestonecraft's *A Vindication of the Rights of Woman* UK: Penguin Books.

Bronfen, E. (1992) *Over Her Dead Body: Death, Femininity and the Aesthetic*. New York: Routledge.

Brookman. F. (2005) *Understanding Homicide* London: Sage.

Broughton, T.L. and Rogers, H. (2007) Introduction in Broughton, T.L. and Rogers, H. (eds) *Gender and Fatherhood in the Nineteenth Century* Basingstoke: Palgrave Macmillan.

Brownmiller, S. (1975) *Against Our Will. Men Women and Rape* New York: Simon and Schuster.

Brownmiller, S. (1984). *Femininity* New York: Linden Books (Simon and Schuster).

Bryson, N. (1986) 'Two Narratives of Rape in the Visual Arts' in Tomaselli, S. and Porter, R. (eds) *Rape* London: Blackwell.

Bufkin, J. and Eschholtz, S. (2000) 'Images of Sex and Rape. A Content Analysis of Popular Film', *Violence Against Women* Vol. 6 No. 12 Dec. 2000 1317–44 Sage Publications.

Burton, M. (2008) *Legal Responses to Domestic Violence* Oxford: Routledge Cavendish.

Buss D.M. (2006) *The Murderer Next Door: Why the Mind Is Designed To Kill* New York: Penguin.

Cameron, D. and Frazer, E. (1987) *The Lust to Kill: A Feminist Investigation of Sexual Murder* Cambridge: Polity Press.

Cammiss, S. (2006) 'The Management of Domestic Violence cases in Mode of Trial Hearing. Prosecutorial Control and Marginalising Victims', *British Journal of Criminology* Vol. 46, No. 4 704–18.

Campbell Johnston, R. (2003a) 'Dangers of the Bohemian Life', *The Times* 4 Dec. 2003:7.

Campbell Johnston, R. (2003b) 'My Heart Is Pounding and It's Got Nothing To Do with the Pace...', *The Times* 13 Dec. 2003:8.

Caputi, J. (1987) *The Age of Sex Crime* London: The Women's Press.

Carabine, J. (2001) 'Unmarried Motherhood 1830–1990: A Genealogical Analysis. *Discourse as Data'* in Wetherall M, Taylor S, Yates S.J. (eds) London: Sage.

Carroll, S. (2002) 'Sue Carroll Column: Rape Law Cries out for Common Sense', *Mirror* 30 Oct. 2002:17.

Carter, C. (1998) 'When the Extraordinary Becomes Ordinary' in Carter, C., Branston, G. and Allan, S. (eds) *News, Gender and Power* London and New York: Routledge.

Carter, C. and Weaver, C.K. (2003) *Violence and the Media* Buckingham: Open University press.

CGAP (2007) *Cross Government Action Plan on Sexual Violence and Abuse* available at http://www.homeoffice.gov.uk/documents/Sexual-violence-action-plan?view=Binary accessed 31/05/09.

Chapman, J. and Twomey, J. (2003) 'Battered Girls Final Journey Caught on Film; Seconds to Live', *Daily Express* 8 Feb. 2003:5.

Chene, S. (2003) *The Process of Aggravating Rape to Sexual Murder: The Aggressor's Intentions and Situational Data* Correctional Service of Canada – Regional Research Projects www.cscscc.gc.ca/text/rsrch/regional/summary0164_e. shtml.

Clover, C.J. (1992) *Men, Women and Chainsaws. Gender in the Modern Horror Film* Princeton University Press.

Cobain, I., Lister, S., Malvern, J. and Monaghan, E. (2005) 'Pop Singer Clue to Murder in the Park', *The Times* 6 Feb. 2005:7.

Coleman, K. (2009) Homicide in Povey, D. (ed) Coleman, K., Kaiza, P. And Roe, S. Homicide, Firearms and Intimate Violence 2007/08 *Home Office Statistical Bulletin 02/09* Supplementary Vol. 2 to Crime in England and Wales 2007/08 third edition available at http://www.homeoffice.gov.uk/rds/pdfs09/hosb0209. pdf accessed 31/05/09.

Coleman, K. and Osborne, S. (2010) Homicide in Smith, K. and Flatley, J. (eds) 'Homicides, Firearm Offences and Intimate Violence 2008/09', *Home Office Statistical Bulletin 01/10* Supplementary Vol. 2 to Crime in England and Wales 2008/09.

Cook, A. (2009) *Jack the Ripper* Stroud: Amberley.

Crampton, R. (2003) 'Dangerous Dirty, Neglected...and still the place I'm happy to call home', *The Times* 3 Mar. 2003:18.

Crimewatch (2005) www.bbc.co.uk/crime/crimewatch/anniversary/casessolved.shtml accessed May 7 2005.

Cuklanz, L.M. (1995) *Rape on Trial: How the Mass Media Construct Legal Reform and Social Change* Pennsylvania: University of Pennsylvania Press.

Daily Express (2004) 'Star's Wife Escaped Park Killer', 4 Feb. 2004:24.

Daily Mail (2003) 'Did the Same Man Murder Rachel and Margaret?; Police Probe Link Between Killing of Mother 11 years Ago and Stabbed Artist', 16 June 2003:25.

Daily Mail (2004) 'Rolling Pin Horror of Love Cheat Navy Wife', 16 Nov. 2004:25.

Daily Mirror (2003) 'Sally Army Strangler', 13 May 2003:21.

Daily Mirror (2004) 'Walsh in Killer Plea', 4 Feb. 2004:17.

Darwin, C. (1859). *The Origin of Species*. Vol. XI. The Harvard Classics. New York: P.F. Collier & Son, 1909–14; Bartleby.com, 2001. www.bartleby.com/11/. (Accessed 5 May 2006).

Dawkins, R. (2006) *The God Delusion* London: Transworld Publishers.

Dawson, M. (2003) 'The Cost of "Lost" Intimacy: The Effect of Relationship State on Criminal Justice Decision Making', *The British Journal of Criminology* Vol. 43, No. 4 Autumn 2003 pp. 689–709.

De Beauvoir, S. (1952) *The Second Sex* New York: Bantam.

De Lint, W. (2003) 'Keeping Open Windows: Police as Access Brokers', *The British Journal of Criminology* Vol. 43, No. 2 Spring 2003 pp. 379V97.

Dening, S. (1996) *The Mythology of Sex* London: Batsford Books.

Denton, M. (1986) *Evolution: A Theory in Crisis*. Bethesda: Woodbine House.

De Quincey, T. (1847) *The English Mail Coach and Joan of Arc* available in full online at: http://www.fullbooks.com/The-English-Mail-Coach-and-Joan-of-Arc2.html (part two).

Detmer-Goebel, E. (2001) 'The Need for Lavinia's Voice: Titus Andronicus and the Telling of Rape', *Shakespeare Studies* p. 75 (19).

Devine D., Clayton, L., Dunford, B., Seying, R. and Pryce, J. (2001) 'Jury Decision Making: 45 Years of Empirical Research on Deliberating Groups', *Psychology, Public Policy and Law* Vol. 7, No. 3, 622–727.

Diamond, M. (2003) *Victorian Sensation* London: Anthem Press.

Dobash, R.E. and Dobash, R. (1980) *Violence Against Wives: A Case Against Patriarchy* Somerset: Open Books.

DoJ (2007) US Department of Justice National Crime Victimisation Survey 2007 available at: http://www.ojp.usdoj.gov/bjs/pub/pdf/cv07.pdf.

Douglas, J. and Olshaker, M. (2000) *The Cases That Haunt Us*. UK: Scribner.

Dworkin, A. (1999) 'Pornography and Grief' in Manfred B Steiger and Nancy S Lind (eds) *Violence and it's Alternatives* Basingstoke: Palgrave Macmillan.

Dyer, R. (2002) *Matter of Images: Essays on Representation* London: Routledge.

Eden, I., Aune, K. and Ramful, K. (2005) 'Weekend: A YEAR OF KILLING: All the people featured on the following pages met their death in one year at the hands of partners or ex-partners. The overwhelming majority are women', *Guardian* 10 Dec. 2005: weekend pages: 18.

Edwards, J. (2003) 'Marsha Minutes Before Her Murder; Hammer Attack Victim Captured On Bus CCTV', *Daily Mirror* 8 Feb. 2003:7.

Ellison, L. and Munro, V.E. (2009) 'Turning Mirrors into Windows. Assessing the Impact of (Mock) Juror Education in Rape Trials', *British Journal of Criminology* 49 (3): 363–83.

Emsley, C. (2005) *Crime and Society in England 1750–1900*. UK{where???}: Pearson Education.

Emsley, C., Hitchcock, T. and Shoemaker, R. (2009) 'Historical Background', *Old Bailey Proceedings Online* www.oldbaileyonline.org (accessed 5.09.09).

English, J. and Card, R. (2007) *Police Law* 10th edn Oxford: Oxford University Press.

Estrich, S. (1987) *Real Rape*. Cambridge MA: Harvard University Press.

Fagge, N. (2003) 'Outrage Over Man Who Raped Wife, Jailed for Life...But Out in 28 Months?', *Daily Express* 19 Nov. 1987:22.

Feist, A. (1999) *The Effective Use of Media in Serious Crime Investigations*. Policing and Reducing Crime Unit Paper 120.

Ferraro, K.F. (1995) *Fear of Crime: Interpreting Victimization Risk*. Albany: State of New York University Press.

Finkelhor, D. (1984) *Child Sexual Abuse: New Theory and Research* New York: Free Press.

Fletcher, G.P. (1996) *Basic Concepts of Legal Thought*. New York: Oxford University Press.

Flynn, E. (2003) *Catholics at a Crossroads: Coverup, Crisis and Cure* New York: Paraview.

Forrester, J. (1986) 'Rape, Seduction and Psychoanalysis' in Tomaselli, S. and Porter, R. (eds) *Rape* London: Basil Blackwell.

Foster, J. (2003) 'My Husband Beat and Raped Me Until One Day I Stabbed Him...But it Makes Me So Sad My Kids Don't Have a Father', *Mirror*, 21 June 2003:28–9.

Foucault, M. (1998) *The Will to Knowledge. The History of Sexuality: 1* trans. Robert Hurley London: Penguin Books.

Foucault, M. (1994) 'About the concept of the "dangerous individual",' In Faubion, J. (ed.) *Power: Essential works of Foucault 1954–1984* London: Penguin.

Foucault, M. (1979) *Discipline and Punish* Harmondsworth: Penguin.

Foucault, M. (1972) *The Archaeology of Knowledge and the Discourse on Language* trans. A.M. Sheridan Smith New York: Pantheon.

Frayling, C. (1986). 'The House that Jack Built' in Tomaselli, S. and Porter, R. (eds) *Rape*. UK: Basil Blackwell.

Freyd, J. (2008) 'What Juries Don't Know: Dissemination of Research on Victim Response is Essential for Justice', *Trauma Psychology Newsletter* Autumn 2008:15–18.

Friedan, B. (1992/63). *The Feminine Mystique* London: Penguin.

Galdikas, B. (1996) *Reflections of Eden: My Years with the Orangutans of Borneo*. Boston: Little, Brown.

Galliano, G., Noble, L., Travis, L. and Puechl, C. (1993) 'Victim Reactions During Rape/Sexual Assault' *Journal of Interpersonal Violence* Vol. 8 No. 1 109–14.

Gardham, D. and Gysin, C. 'Was Strangled Girl Victim of a Serial Killer?', *Daily Mail* 18 Mar. 2003 headline.

Geberth, V.J. (2003) *Sex-Related Homicide and Death Investigation. Practical and Clinical Perspectives*. Boca Raton: CRC Press.

Gekoski, A. (2005) *Robert Black/Crime Library* [http://www.crimelibrary.com/serial_killers/predators/black/violence_1.html].

Gentleman, A. (2009) 'Growth in Violence Against Women Feared as Recession Hits', *Guardian* 4 Mar. 2009:18.

George, A. (2003) 'Oxford's Foreign Students in Terror of Knife Attacks', *Mail on Sunday* 17 Aug. 2003:38.

Gibb, F. (2005) 'Jealousy Is No Longer an Excuse for Murder', *The Times* 28 Nov 2005: Home News: 1.

Gibb, F. (2009) 'Beware Rape Myths Judges to Tell Jurors', *The Times Online* June 15 2009 http://www.timesonline.co.uk/tol/news/uk/crime/article6499404.ece

Giddens, A. (1972) *Emile Durkheim: Selected Writings* London: Cambridge University Press.

Gordon, M.T. and Riger, S. (1989) *The Female Fear* New York: The Free Press.

Graham, R. (2006) 'Male Rape and the Careful Construction of the Male Victim' *Social and Legal Studies* Vol. 15 (2): 187–208.

Green, E. (1993) *The Intent to Kill: Making Sense of Murder*. Baltimore MA: Clevedon.

Green, L. M. (2001) *Educating women: Cultural Conflict and Victorian Literature* Ohio University Press.

Greer, C. (2003) *Sex Crime and the Media* Cullompton: Willan.

Gregory, J. and Lees, S. (1999). *Policing Sexual Assault*. London: Routledge.

Guardian (2006) 'On Making Violent Porn Illegal: Is It a Victory for Women's Rights, or an Attack on Civil Liberties?', *Guardian* Comments and Features 1 Sept. 2006:18.

Gysin, C. (2002) 'Trophy Rapist Suspect Had Given DNA Sample', *The Times* 4 Dec. 2002:15.

Hall, S., Critcher, C., Jefferson, T., Clarke, J. & Roberts, B. (1978) *Policing the Crisis*, London: Macmillan.

Hansard (2010) House of Commons *Hansard* Debates Westminster Hall Violence Against Women 21 January 2010 Column 146WH – 180WH available at: http://www.publications.parliament.uk/pa/cm200910/cmhansrd/cm100121/halltext/100121h0001.htm#10012127000001

Harper, J. (2004) *Legacy of Blood: A Comprehensive Guide to Slasher Movies*. Manchester: Headpress.

Harris, J. and Grace, S. (1999). *A Question of Evidence? Investigating and Prosecuting Rape in the 1990's*. HORS196.

Harrison, S. (1998). *The Diary of Jack the Ripper*. London: Blake.

Harstock, N. (1999)' Masculinity, Violence and Domination' in Manfred B Steiger and Nancy S Lind (eds) *Violence and Its Alternatives* Basingstoke: Palgrave Macmillan.

Haskell, M. (1987) *From Reverence to Rape: Treatment of Women in the Movies*. London: University of Chicago Press.

Henry, A. (2004) *Not My Mother's Sister* Indiana: Indiana University Press.

Hickey, E.W. (2001) *Serial Murderers and Their Victims*. California: Wadsworth Publishing.

Hite, S. (2005) *The Hite Report* London: Seven Stories Press.

Hite, S. (2007) *Oedipus Revisited* London: Arcadia Books Ltd.

Home Office (2006) *Convicting Rapists and Protecting Victims. Justice for Victims of Rape. A Consultation Paper*. Office for Criminal Justice Reform available online at http://www.homeoffice.gov.uk/documents/cons-290306-justice-rape-victims?view=Binary.

Horeck, T. (2004) *Public Rape. Representing Violation in Fiction and Film*. London Routledge.

Howe, A. (1998) 'Introduction' in Howe 1998 (ed.) *Sexed Crime in the News* Sydney: The Federation Press.

Hudson, B. (2002) 'Restorative Justice and Gendered Violence. Diversion or Effective Justice?', *The British Journal of Criminology* Vol. 42, No. 3 Summer p. 616.

Innes, M. (2002) 'Police Homicide Investigations', *The British Journal of Criminology* Vol. 42, No. 4 Autumn 2002 pp. 669–88.

Innes, M. (2005) *Investigating Murder: Detective Work and the Police Response to Criminal Homicide*. NY: Oxford University Press.

Jalland, P. (1986) *Women, Marriage and Politics 1860–1914* Oxford: Clarendon Press.

Jeffreys, S. (1984) 'Free from all Uninvited Touch of Man: Women's Campaigns Around Sexuality, 1880–1914' in *The Sexuality Papers. Male sexuality and the Social Control of Women*. London: Hutchinson and Co.

Jenefsky, C. (1999) 'Andrea Dworkin's Reconstruction of Pornography as a Discriminatory Social Practice' in Manfred B Steger and Nancy S Lind (eds) *Violence and Its Alternatives*. Basingstoke: Palgrave Macmillan.

Jenkins, P. (1994) *Using Murder: The Social Construction of Serial Homicide* New York: Aldine de Gruyter.

Jervis, J. (1998) *Exploring the Modern* Oxford: Blackwell.

Keetley, D. and Pettegrew, J. (2005) *Public Women, Public Words. A Documented History of American Feminism* Oxford: Rowman and Littlefield.

Kelly, L. (2007) *Rape in the 21st Century: Old Behaviours, New Contexts and Emerging Patterns* ESRC End of Award Report RES-000-22-1679 Swindon: ESRC.

Kelly, L., Lovett, J. and Regan, L. (2005) *A Gap or a Chasm? Attrition in Reported Rape Cases*. Home Office Research Study 293.

Kelly, L. and Regan, L. (2001) *Rape: The Forgotten Issue* Child and Woman Abuse Studies Project JA1 1999/DAP/161/WP.

Kelly, A. and Sharp, D. (1995) *Jack the Ripper: Bibliography and Review of the Literature* London: Association of Assistant Librarians.

King, J. (2005) *The Victorian Woman Question in Contemporary Feminist Fiction* Basingstoke: Palgrave Macmillan.

Kinsey, A., Pomeroy, W. and Martin, C. (1975) *Sexual Behaviour in the Human Male* Bloomington: Indiana University Press.

Kitzinger, J. (2004) *Framing Abuse* London: Pluto Press.

Klein, J. (2006) 'An Invisible Problem: Everyday Violence Against Girls in Schools', *Theoretical Criminology* 2006 10 147.

Koss, M. (1985) 'Sexual Violence Survey commissioned by *Ms* magazine', *Journal of Consulting and Clinical Psychology* Vol. 55 No. 2 1987. Basis of book I Never Called It Rape by Robin Warshaw 1994.

Lacombe. D. (2008) 'Consumed with Sex: The Treatment of Sex Offenders in Risk Society', *British Journal of Criminology* Vol. 48 No. 1 January 2008 pp. 55–74.

Larcombe, W. (2005) *Compelling Engagements: Feminism, Rape Law and Romance Fiction* Sydney: The Federation Press.

Laville, S. (2010) 'Met Chief Asks IPCC To Be Sure of Findings in Worboys Case'm *Guardian.co.uk* 20 January 2010 http://www.guardian.co.uk/uk/2010/jan/20/worboys-ipcc-report-metroplitan-commissioner.

Lees, S. (1997) *Ruling Passions. Sexual Violence, Reputation and the Law*. Buckingham: Open University Press.

Lees, S. (2002). *Carnal Knowledge, Rape on Trial, rev. edn* London: The Women's Press.

Leigh, A., Read, T. and Tilley, N. (1996) *Problem – Oriented Policing. Brit Pop.* Crime Detection and Prevention Series Paper 75 Home Office Police Research Group.

Leishman. F. and Mason, P. (2003) (eds) *Policing and Media: Facts, Fictions and Factions* Collumpton: Willan.

Lester, D. (1995) *Serial Killers: The Insatiable Passion*. Philadelphia: The Charles Press Publishers.

Livholts, M. (2008) 'The Loathsome, the Rough Type and the Monster: The Violence and Wounding of Media Texts on Rape' in Hearn, J. and Burr, V. (eds) *Sex, Violence and the Body. The Erotics of Wounding* Basingstoke: Palgrave Macmillan.

Loudon, A. (1999) 'Kalashnikov revenge of SAS doctor jilted by nurse; Former Fiancee Was Gunned Down Outside Pub Using Smugled Weapon', *Daily Mail* 17 Apr. 1999:11.

Lucie Blackman Trust (2005) www.lucieblackmantrust.org.

MacDonald, E. (1991) *Shoot the Women First* London: Fourth Estate.

MacKinnon, C. (2002). 'Pleasure Under Patriarchy' in Christine L. Williams and Arlene Stein (eds) *Sexuality and Gender*. Oxford: Blackwell Publishers.

Macpherson Report (1999) *The Stephen Lawrence Inquiry*. Report of an Inquiry by Sir William Macpherson of Cluny. Available online at www.archive.official-documents.co.uk/document/cm42/4262/4262.htm.

Marriner, B. (1992) *A Century of Sex Killers* London: True Crime Library.

Martin, J. (1994) An interview with Camille Paglia *America*. 12 Nov. 1994 Vol. 171 No. 15.

Martin, R.A., Rossmo, D.K. and Hammerschlag, N. (2009) 'Hunting Patterns and Geographic Profiling of White Shark Predation', *Journal of Zoology*, 22 June 2009.

Mason, G. (2003a) 'As a Jogger's Murder Highlights Our Rising Crime Rates...Is It Safer To Live in America than Britain?', *Daily Express* 6 Feb. 2003:13.

Mason, G. (2003b) 'Stranger Murders Give the Police Their Toughest Detection Problem, Leaving Us Haunted by the Beasts Who Kill for the Thrill', *Daily Express* 20 Mar. 2003:13.

Mason, P. and Monckton-Smith, J. (2008) 'Conflation, Collocation and Confusion': British Press Coverage of the Sexual Murder of Women', *Journalism: Theory, Practice and Criticism* Vol. 9 (6): 69–710.

Matthews, S., Abrahams, N., Martin, L., Vetten, L., Van der Merwe, L. and Jewkes, R. (2004) 'Every Six Hours a Woman Is Killed by Her Intimate Partner', A national study of female homicide in South Africa. Medical Research Council (SA) Policy Brief No. 5 June 2004.

May, L. (2005) *Crimes Against Humanity* Cambridge: Cambridge University Press.

McCarty, J. (1993) *Movie Psychos and Madmen – Film Psychopaths from Jeckyll and Hyde to Hannibal Lecter*. New York: Carol Publishing.

McConville, M., Sanders, A. and Leng, R. (1991) *The Case for the Prosecution*. London: Routledge.

Meikle, D. (2003) *Jack the Ripper, The Murders and the Movies*. London: Reynolds and Hearn Ltd.

Milligen, S. (2006) *Better To Reign in Hell. Serial Killers, Media Panics and the FBI*. London: Headpress.

Mills, S. (2003) *Michel Foucault*. London: Routledge.

Mitchell, B. (2003a) 'Student's Killer Sexually Abused as Child, Court Told', *Press Association News* 14 May 2003: section: home news.

Mitchell, B. (2003b) 'Sex Attacker Murdered Student To Avoid Being Caught', *Press Association News* 12 May 2003: section: home news.

Mitchell, B. (2003c) 'Violent Paedophile Had Long History of Convictions', *Press Association* 16 May 2003: home news.

Monckton-Smith, J. (2010) *Murder, Gender and the Media: Love and domestic homicide* Forthcoming Basingstoke: Palgrave Macmillan.

Mottier, V. (2008) *Sexuality. A Very Short Introduction* Oxford: Oxford University Press.

Morgan, E. (1972) *The Descent of Woman. The Classic Study of Evolution*. London: Souvenir Press.

Myhill, A. and Allen, J. (2002). *Rape and Sexual Assault of Women: The Extent and Nature of the Problem*. Home Office Research Study 237 Home Office London.

National Gallery (2003) [www.nationalgallery.org.uk] accessed 24.06.03.

Neff, D. (2005) 'Naming the Horror: Why We Must Resurrect the Language of Evil', *Christianity Today* Apr. 2005 Vol. 49:i4 p. (74)3.

Norris, G. (2005) 'Criminal Profiling: A Continuing History' in Petherick, W. (ed.) *Serial Crime: Theoretical and Practical Issues in Behavioural Profiling* London: Elsevier.

North, N. (2003) 'Random Killer; Hannah, 17, Did Not Know Her Abductor, Say Police', *Daily Mirror* 18 March 2003:18.

Odell, R. (2006) *Ripperology* Kent Ohio: The Kent State University Press.

Paglia, C. (1990) *Sexual Personae* Yale University Press.

Peelo, M., Francis, B., Soothill K., Pearson, J. and Ackerley, E. (2004) 'Newspaper Reporting and the Public Construction of Homicide', *British Journal of Criminology* 44 (2): 256–75.

Peelo, M. and Soothill, K. (in press) 'Questioning Homicide and the Media: Analysis of Content or Content Analysis?' in Gadd, D. *et al*. (eds.) *Sage Handbook of Criminological Research Methods*.

Petherick, W. (2005) *Serial Crime: Theoretical and Practical Issues in Behavioural Profiling* London: Elsevier.

Phillips, J. (2005) *The Marquis de Sade: A Very Short Introduction*. Oxford: Oxford University Press.

Phoca, S. (1999) *Introducing Postfeminism* Cambridge: Icon.

Pinedo, I.C. (1997) *Recreational Terror. Women and the Pleasures of Horror Film Viewing*. New York: State University of New York Press.

Polaschek, D.L.L and Ward, T. (2002) 'The Implicit Theories of Potential Rapists: What Our Questionnaires Tell Us', *Aggression and Violent Behaviour*, 7, 385–406.

Polk, K. (1994) *When Men Kill. Scenarios of Masculine Violence*. Melbourne: Cambridge University Press.

Porter, R. (1986) 'Rape – DoesIit Have Historical Meaning?', in Sylvana Tomaselli and Roy Porter (eds) *Rape* Oxford: Blackwell.

Potts, M. and Short. R. (1999). *Ever Since Adam and Eve. The Evolution of Human Sexuality.* Cambridge: Cambridge University Press.

Purcell C.E. and Arrigo, B.A. (2006) *The Psychology of Lust Murder. Paraphilia, Sexual Killing and Serial Homicide* London: Elsevier.

Pyatt, J. (2003) 'Hannah Murdered On 5min Walk Home', *Sun* 17 Mar. 2003: page u/k????.

Rafter, N. (2007) 'Crime, Film and Criminology. Recent Sex Crime Movies', *Theoretical Criminology* Vol. 11(3): 403–420; 1362–4806.

Rape Crisis (1999). *Sexual Violence – The reality for women* 3rd edn. London: The Women's Press.

Rape Crisis (2005) *Rape and Sexual Assault: Myths and Truths* [www.rapecrisis.org.uk] accessed 26.07.05.

Reid, S. (2003) 'Inside the Mind of the Assassin in the Park; Special Report: With Their Offender Profile Complete, Police Stage Murder Reconstruction', *Daily Mail* 3 Mar. 2003:27.

Reiner, R. (1997) 'Media Made Criminality' in Maguire, M., Morgan, M. and Reiner, R. (eds) *Oxford Handbook of Criminology* Oxford: Oxford University Press.

Renzetti, C. (1999) 'Violence in Lesbian and Gay Relationships' in Steger, M. and Lind, N. (eds) *Violence and Its Alternatives* Basingstoke: Palgrave Macmillan.

Ressler, R., Burgess, A.W. and Douglas, J.E (1992) *Sexual Homicide, Patterns and Motives.* New York: The Free Press.

Richards, L. (2006) 'Homicide Prevention: The Findings from the Multi-agency Domestic Homicide Reviews' *Journal of Homicide and Major Incident Investigation* Vol. 2:i2 Autumn 2006.

Riches, C. (2003a) 'Killed at Random', *Sun* 18 Mar. 2003: page u/k ????.

Riches, C. (2003b) 'Hannah Called 999', *Sun* 20 Mar. 2003: section:' Murder that Shocked Britain'.

Roiphe, K. (1994) *The Morning After: Sex Fear and Feminism* Great Britain: Hamish Hamilton Ltd.

Rose, H. (2000) 'Colonizing the social sciences?' in H. Rose and S. Rose (eds) *Alas Poor Darwin: Arguments Against Evolutionary Psychology* (pp. 127–53). New York: Harmony Books.

Rossmo, D.K. (2000) 'Geographic Profiling' in Jackson J.L. and Bekerian D. A. (eds) *Offender Profiling. Theory Research and Practice* Ch. 6 pp. 159–75. Chichester: John Wiley and Sons.

Rowe-Finkbeiner, K. (2004) *The F-Word: Feminism in Jeopardy.* Emeryville, CA: Seal Press.

Russell, D. (1993) *Making Violence Sexy. Feminist Views on Pornography* Buckingham: Open University Press.

Salmon, L. (1999) 'SAS Killer "War Sick",' *Mirror* 29 Apr. p. 24.

Sample, L. (2006) 'An Examination of the Degree to Which Sex Offenders Kil', l *Criminal Justice Review* Vol. 31 No. 3 pp. 230–50.

SAPS (2005) *South African Police Service Crime Information Analysis Centre*: Rape statistics: http://www.saps.gov.za/statistics/reports/crimestats/2005/_pdf/crimes/rape.pdf accessed 23.06.09.

Schaller, G.B. (1972) *The Serengeti Lion: A Study of Predator-Prey Relations.* Chicago: University of Chicago Press.

Schinkel, W. (2004) 'The Will to Violence' *Theoretical Criminology* Vol. 8(1): 5–31; 1362–4806.

Schlesinger, L. (2003) *Sexual Murder: Catathymic and Compulsive Homicides*. Boca Raton Florida: CRC Press.

Schmid, D. (2005) *Natural Born Celebrities. Serial Killers in American Culture*. Chicago and London: University of Chicago Press.

Schoell, W. (1985) *Stay Out of the Shower: Twenty Five Years of Shocker Films Beginning with* Psycho New York: Dembner.

Scott, H. (2003) 'Stranger Danger: Explaining Women's Fear of Crime', *Western Criminology Review* 4 (3) http://wcr.sonoma.edu/v4n3/scott.html .

Seifert, R. (1999) 'The Second Front: The Logic of Sexual Violence in Wars' in Steger, M. and Lind, N. (eds) *Violence and Its Alternatives* Basingstoke: Palgrave Macmillan.

Seidman, S. (2007) 'Theoretical Perspectives' in Seidman, S., Fischer, N. and Meeks, C. (eds) *Introducing the New Sexuality Studies. Original Essays and Interviews* Abingdon: Routledge.

Seuffert, N. (2002) 'Domestic Violence, Discourses of Romantic Love, and Complex Personhood in the Law' in Thornton, M. (ed.) *Romancing the Tomes: Popular Culture, Law and Feminism* London: Cavendish pp. 8–112.

Shanahan, E.C. (1999) 'Stranger and Non Stranger Rape: One crime, One Penalty', *American Criminal Law Review* Autumn Vol. 36:i4 p. 1371.

Shaw, A. (2004) 'Outburst By Rape Suspect', *Mirror*, 26 Feb. 2004:28.

Shaw, A. (2008) 'Revealed Mark Dixie: The Man Accused of Killing Sally Anne Bowman', *Mirror.co.uk* 19 Feb. available at http://www.mirror.co.uk/news/top-stories/2008/02/19/revealed-mark-dixie-the-man-accused-of-killing-sally-anne-bowman-115875-20324089/.

Shlain, L. (1999) *The Alphabet Versus the Goddess* Allen Lane: Penguin.

Simpson, P.L. (2000) *Psycho Paths: Tracking the Serial Killer through Contemporary American Film and Fiction* Southern Illinois University Press.

Slack, J. (2009) 'Judges Sink Harriet Harman's "Obnoxious" Plan to Strip Men of Infidelity Defence', *Daily Mail* 28 Oct. 2009.

Smith, L. and Tendler, S. (2004) 'Trophy Rapist Victims "Feared Murder"', *The Times* 5 Mar. 2004:4.

Sommers, C.H. (1995) *Who Stole Feminism* New York: Touchstone books.

Soothill, K. (1993) 'The Serial Killer Industry', *Journal of Forensic Psychiatry* 4(2): 341–54.

Soothill K. (1991) 'The Changing Face of Rape', *British Journal of Criminology*, Vol. 31, No. 4, 383–92 (Reprinted in Temkin, J. (ed.) (1995) *Rape and the Criminal Justice System*. Aldershot: Dartmouth Publishing, 165–74).

Soothill, K., Francis, B., Ackerley, E. and Collett, S. (1999) *Homicide in Britain: A Comparative Study of Rates in Scotland and England & Wales*. Edinburgh: Scottish Executive.

Soothill, K., Christoffersen, M., Azhar Hussain, M. and Francis, B. (2009) 'Exploring Paradigms of Crime Reduction: An Empirical Longitudinal Study', *The British Journal of Criminology* 2009 advanced online accessed 3 Jan. 2010 http://bjc.oxfordjournals.org/cgi/content/full/azp076v1.

Soothill, K., Francis, B., Ackerley, E. and Fligelstone, R. (2002) *Murder and Serious Sexual Assault: wWat Criminal Histories Can Reveal About Future Serious Offending*. Police Research Series Paper 144.

Soothill, K. and Walby, S. (1991) *Sex Crime in the News* London: Routledge.
Soul City (1999) *Violence Against Women in South Africa. A Resource for Journalists* Soul City Institute for Health and Development Communication http://www. womensnet.org.za/files/conferences/resources/Violence_Against_Women_In_ South_Africa_-_A_Resource_For_Journalists.pdf.
Speare, D. (2003) *Jack the Ripper: Crime Scene Investigation* Xlibris Corporation.
Stallard, K. (2008) 'Hannah killed to keep her quiet', 17 Nov. 2008 Sky News online available at http://news.sky.com/skynews/Home/UK-News accessed 18.11.08.
Stanko, E. (1996) 'The Commercialism of Women's Fear of Crime. International Victimology', 8th international symposium *Australian Institute of Criminology* edited by Chris Sumner, Mark Israel, Michael O'Connell and Rick Sarre.
Stead, W.T. (1885) 'The Maiden Tribute of Modern Babylon', *Pall Mall Gazette* July 1885.
Stelfox, P. (2009) *Criminal Investigation. An Introduction to Principles and Practice* Cullompton: Willan.
Stern (2000). *The Stern Review*. A report by baroness Vivien stern CBE of an independent review into how rape complaints are handled by public authorities in England and Wales Government Equalities Office available at: http://www. equalities.gov.uk/PDF/Stern_Review_acc_FINAL.pdf.
Sturken, M. (1997) *Tangled Memories* London: University of California Press.
Tanenbaum, Leora (2007) *Slut! Growing up Female with a Bad Reputation* New York: Seven Stories Press.
Tatar, M. (1995) *Lustmord. Sexual Murder in Weimar Germany* New Jersey: Princeton University press.
Taylor, B. (2004) 'Brush with a Killer', *Daily Mail* 4 Feb. 2004:45.
The Sun (2002) 'Loner is held on sex killing', 19 July 2002: page u/k???.
The Sun (2003) 'Killer: Girl Begged Not To Be Raped', 14 May 2003: page u/k???.
This is Hampshire (2003) 'Camilla'skiller Told He Will Die in Prison' UK Newsquest regional Press *This is Hampshire* 23 May (no page number available).
Times (1888) *The Murder in Whitechapel* 10 Aug. 1888 available at http://www. casebook.org/press_reports/times/18880810.html.
Times (2005) '"I'm looking at killer" says Outback victim', 19 Oct. 2005:17.
Thompson, T. (2003)' Warning to Joggers After New Park Knife Attack', *Guardian* final edin 7 Dec 2003:1.
Thornhill, R. and Palmer, C.T. (2000) *A Natural History of Rape – Biological Bases of Sexual Coercion* Cambridge, Mass: MIT Press.
University of Minnesota (2009) 'List of Rape Myths', *Sociology of Rape*. University of Minnesota Duluth available at http://www.d.umn.edu/cla/faculty/jhamlin/ 3925/myths.html accessed 7 July 2009.
Varelas, N. and Foley, L. (1998) 'Blacks' and Whites' perceptions of interracial and intraracial date rape', *Journal of Social Psychology*, 138 392–400.
Vitz, E.B. (1997) 'Rereading Rape in Medieval Literature: Literary, Historical and Theoretical Reflections', *The Romanic review* Vol. 88, No. 1 p. 1 (26).
Vronsky, P. (2004) *Serial Killers. The Method and Madness of Monsters*. New York: Berkley Publishing Group Penguin.
Wainwright, M. and Khan, M. (1999) 'Jealous Doctor "Machine-gunned Ex-lover"; Court Told that Former SAS Trooper Smuggled Weapon as Trophy of Gulf war. Accused "Drove Calmly from Scene" After Nurse Died in Hail of Bullets', *Guardian* 17 Apr. 1999:7.

Wainwright, M. (1999) 'Former SAS Doctor To Face Retrial', *Guardian* 29 May 1999:12.

Walby, S. and Allen, J. (2004) *Domestic Violence, Sexual assault and Stalking: Findings from the British Crime Survey.* Home Office research study 276. London Home Office Wake up to Rape Survey (2010) *The Haven's Sexual Assault Referral Centre's Wake up to Rape Research Summary Report* available at http://www.thehavens.co.uk/docs/Havens_Wake_Up_To_Rape_Report_Summary.pdf.

Walklate, S. (2008) 'What is to be done about violence against women?', *British Journal of Criminology* Vol. 48 No. 1 39–54.

Walkowitz, J.R. (1992) *City of Dreadful Delight: Narratives of Sexual Danger in Late-Victorian London.* London: Virago Press.

Walkowitz, J.R. (1980) *Prostitution and Victorian Society* Cambridge: Cambridge University Press.

Wallace, A. (1986) *Homicide: The Social Reality.* Sydney: New South Wales Bureau of Crime Statistics and Research.

Wansell, G. (2003) 'Has Milly's Killer Struck Again? Six Thousand Calls, 3,000 Statements and 2,000 Vehicles Checked. Even a DNA Match. Yet Still, a Year After Milly Dowler Was Killed, the Police Have No Real Clues. And Now They're Facing a Terrible New Fear,' *Daily Mail* 20 Mar. 2003:48.

Ward, T., Polascheck, D.L.L. and Beech, A.R. (2006) *Theories of Sexual Offending* Chichester: John Wiley and Sons Ltd.

Ward Jouve, N. (1988) *'The Street-Cleaner'. The Yorkshire Ripper Case on Trial.* London: Marion Boyers Publications.

Warr, M. (1984) 'Fear of rape among urban women', *Social Problems* Vol. 32 No. 3 pp. 238–50.

Warwick, A. (2006) The Scene of the Crime: Inventing the Serial Killer *Social & Legal Studies* 15 (4). pp. 552–569. December 2006 this version from http://westminsterresearch.wmin.ac.uk/3478/1/Warwick_2006_final.pdf.

Websdale, N. (1999) *Understanding Domestic Homicide* Boston: Northeastern University Press.

Wilkinson, R. (2005) *From Enlightenment to Romanticism. Conceptions of Art* Milton Keynes: Open University.

Williams, T. and Price, H. (2005) *Uncle Jack.* Orion Mass Market Paperback.

Wilson, C. (1984). *A Criminal History of Mankind.* London: Granada Books.

Wilson, C. (1995). *A Plague of Murder.* London: Robinson.

Wolbert Burgess, A. and Holmstrom. L. (1974). Rape Trauma Syndrome 131 *American Journal Psychiatry* 981.

Wolfthal, D. (1999). *Images of rape: The heroic tradition and its alternatives.* New York: Cambridge University Press.

Wrangham, R. and Peterson, D. (1996) *Demonic Males: Apes and the Origins of Human Violence.* New York: Houghton Mifflin.

Wright, S., Clark, L. and McIntyre, S. (2003) Kill-for-kicks knife maniac stabs another woman jogger in the park *Daily Mail* 8 Dec 2003:5.

Yost, D. (2009) Did Kelly Have a Heart? *Casebook: Jack the Ripper* accessed 28/05/09 www.casebook.org.

Young, A. (1998) Violence as Seduction: Enduring Genres of Rape. *Sexed Crime in the News.* Howe, A. (ed) Sydney: The Federation Press.

Index